THE AMERICAN LEAGUE

THE AMERICAN LEAGUE

JOHN S BOWMAN
JOEL ZOSS

GREAT POND PUBLISHING

This edition published in 1992 by NDM Publications, Inc.
Great Pond Publishing, Ltd. is an imprint of
NDM Publications, Inc.
30 Inwood Road
Rocky Hill, CT 06067

Produced by Brompton Books Corp.
15 Sherwood Place
Greenwich, CT 06830

ISBN 1-56657-002-6

Printed in Hong Kong

Page 1: Reggie Jackson, ready at bat in an Angels uniform. Jackson
moved to the California Angels in 1983 after playing seven spectacular
years for the New York Yankees.
Pages 2-3: Detroit Tiger catcher Lance Parrish tags out San Diego
Padre Alan Wiggins at home in a close play during the 1984 World
Series.
This page: Ty Cobb, with a reputation for his lethal spikes, slides into
third base.

CONTENTS

Chapter One: The Beginnings of
    the American League   6
Chapter Two: The House that Ruth Built   28
Chapter Three: Heroes of the Depression   50
Chapter Four: The Fighting Forties   68
Chapter Five: The Fabled Fifties   86
Chapter Six: The Sensational Sixties   112
Chapter Seven: The Seditious Seventies   136
Chapter Eight: The Unsettled Eighties and
    Into the Nineties   162

The first recorded match between formal ball clubs took place on 19 July 1846, at the Elysian Fields in Hoboken, New Jersey.

CHAPTER ONE

The Beginnings of the American League

"Never get Mr. Cobb angry."

– Connie Mack's advice to his team

While the history of baseball reaches well back into the nineteenth century, and the National League takes the honors as the older of the two leagues, professional baseball as we know it today began with the formation of the American League in 1901. It was then that two competing leagues were solidly in place for the first time, and that grand American institution, the World Series, became as much the mark of autumn as the turning of the leaves.

There had been a number of attempts in the nineteenth century to create a second baseball league, but the National League succeeded in fighting them off and maintaining its monopoly over what was rapidly becoming the country's most popular sport. It was the drive and the dreams of two men, player-turned-sportswriter Byron Banford Johnson and first baseman-manager Charles Albert Comiskey, that brought the American League into existence. They were the ones who built the new league into a powerhouse that not only broke the National League's grip on baseball but also dominated the game for decades to come.

'Ban' Johnson, a native of Norwalk, Ohio, had played ball at Marietta and Oberlin Colleges. An injury kept him from making a career as a player, so instead he became a sportswriter for the Cincinnati *Commercial-Gazette*. Comiskey came from Chicago. Like Johnson, he played ball in college – at St Mary's in Kansas, where he was captain of the freshman baseball team. Before long, he was playing professionally for St Louis, but when owner Chris van der Ahe sold off the best of the roster, Comiskey moved to the Cincinnati Reds team. There he became Ban Johnson's drinking and cardplaying partner, and in 1892 the two began to put together the dream of a second major league.

By the time Comiskey and Johnson joined forces, success and monopoly had already begun to soften the powerful National League. Grown to an unwieldy 12 teams, it had antagonized its players with rough treatment in the Brotherhood strike of 1890. While it had weathered a series of gambling scandals and the threat of competition from such attempts at second leagues as the American Association, the Union Association and the Players League, it had not done much to clean up the game itself.

In those days baseball had a reputation as a rough-and-ready sport. Players baited the umpires as well as opposing players, and foul language was commonplace. Fistfights often broke out, and intentional spiking was not unheard of. It was not exactly an environment thought to be fit for ladies of the Victorian era. Johnson and Comiskey agreed on the need to end the rowdiness, to discourage the sale of liquor in ball parks, to stop the use of profanity, to instill respect for umpires and to encourage women's attendance. Part of their dream was a new image for the game.

Below: Byron Bancroft Johnson, the founder of the American League, poses with Albert Reach. As president of the Western League, Ban Johnson had worked to clean up the reputation of America's pastime, and he used the same determination in his fight for a second major league.

Right (inset): 'The Old Roman' Charles Comiskey, former player and manager, worked with Ban Johnson to establish the American League, becoming owner of the Chicago franchise and building Comiskey Park, the oldest baseball park still being played in.

While Johnson and Comiskey may have been fast friends in the early days, Ban had developed a strong dislike for Comiskey's boss, clothing manufacturer John Brush, the owner of the Cincinnati Reds. Ban raked Brush over the coals regularly in his columns, accusing him of stinginess, among other things. In a stroke of inspiration, Comiskey persuaded team owners in the new, minor Western League, who were eager for reform, to tap his drinking buddy Ban as their new leader. Comiskey may even have enlisted Brush's help by suggesting that getting Ban out of Cincinnati would make life a lot more pleasant for the Reds' owner. In any event, Johnson came back from the Western League's convention in 1894 as the league's new President.

Comiskey himself left Cincinnati for Sioux City, Iowa, at the end of the 1894 season, and then moved that club to St Paul. Johnson started work immediately to upgrade the Western League, which was made up of Indianapolis, Kansas City, Milwaukee, Minneapolis, Toledo, Grand Rapids, Detroit and Sioux City. Within two years, he had built its reputation as the strongest of the minor leagues. Although he was already predicting that the Western League would make it on its own, Johnson recognized that he would have to expand eastward if he were to lose the label of a regional organization. He wanted a Chicago base for his friend Comiskey, but the Chicago National League team's manager Jim Hart was dead set against competition, so Ban bided his time.

Although he might later come to be called one of the greatest organizers and executives in the history of the game, Ban Johnson was hardly the first or only one to see that the time was ripe to get a second major league going. While Johnson maneuvered to make his league strong enough to qualify as a major league, attempts were afoot to revive the old American Association, and the still monopolistic National League initially worried more about that effort. Started in 1882 as a counter to the 'rich man's league,' the American Association had lasted only until 1890, when competition with the Players League during the Brotherhood War did it in. Then in 1899 a group of those associated with the defunct American Association, including Chris van der Ahe and Taylor Spink, met in Chicago. Intent on resurrecting the American

Association, they elected former Chicago White Stockings (now the Cubs) Manager Cap Anson as their president and set about the business of trying to find financial backing, players and ball parks. Johnson was offered the chance to join forces, but turned it down, opting to stay on his own.

Struggling to keep its monopoly going, the National League pared itself down to eight clubs in 1900. The teams in Louisville, Cleveland, Washington and Baltimore were sold to the league and their franchises were allowed to be abandoned. Ban struck while the iron was hot. In October of 1899, the Western League officially had changed its name to the American League in order to develop a more national image. With financial backing from coal magnate Charles Somers, Johnson now moved his Grand Rapids franchise to Cleveland. The next step, a crucial one, was Chicago.

The American Association's Cap Anson had already come up empty-handed there, but Ban's steamroller tactics prevailed. He promised Chicago National League's general manager Jim Hart that he would abide by the National Agreement, which tied players to their current club through options, and agreed to pay for improvements already made by the National League's Cleveland club before its demise. He was also said to have given Hart options on some of the new American League's players. In return, Hart allowed Johnson to set up a ball club on Chicago's South Side, figuring that the smell of the stockyards would keep fans from patronizing it. In 1900 Chicago native Comiskey gladly packed up his team in St Paul and moved back to the Windy City.

Above: As president of the American League until 1927, Ban Johnson ruled both capably and shrewdly, contributing to baseball's growing popularity during that time.

Left: Clark Calvin 'The Old Fox' Griffith, when he was a pitcher for the Chicago National League team. Elected to the Hall of Fame in 1946, Clark Griffith pitched for both leagues and several teams from 1891 to 1914, and managed from 1901 to 1920. As a pitcher he had a winning percentage of .649 and a 3.31 ERA.

Although Hart had stipulated in the agreement that the American League team was not to identify itself as a Chicago club, the canny Comiskey named his team the White Sox – clearly evoking the earlier Chicago National League team, the White Stockings. The White Sox soon established themselves with the Chicago fans and not too many years later – 1910, to be exact – when the team acquired a magnificent new playing field, Comiskey Park, replete with steel and concrete grandstands faced with brick, it could boast probably the grandest baseball stadium of its day.

In the meantime, the first year of the new century, 1900, saw players in the National League less than happy and ready to organize. Because of this, they were to help move Ban that much closer to establishing his dream of a major league. In June, the National League players met in New York and formed the Protective Association of Professional Baseball players. They presented a list of demands to the National League management and got a cold shoulder. Johnson, however, was quick to see an opportunity presenting itself, and agreed to everything the players asked. Then when the National Agreement expired, Ban purposely did not renew. The explanation he gave National League President Nick Young was that attempts to revive the old American Association were causing a threat to organized baseball and that he had already made clear his intention to establish clubs in the East. Under such circumstances, it was no longer appropriate to honor draft protection arrangements.

Johnson even agreed to confer with representatives from the National League over his moves into eastern territories, but the National League, instead of supporting Ban, chose to ignore the offer of compromise. The battle lines were drawn. The Nationals then let it be known that they would look favorably on American Association efforts to establish eastern clubs, and awarded Kansas City and Minneapolis to a new minor Western League in an attempt to create direct competition with American League teams.

Right: Al Reach, who played both infield and outfield for the original Philadelphia Athletics, became the Philadelphia National League club president, but viewed the establishment of a second major league in a positive light.
Below: Pitcher Rube Waddell's glove, photographed in 1902. Hall of Famer George Edward Waddell began his pitching career in 1897 and played his finest years for the Philadelphia Athletics (1902-1907), ending his fabulous career in 1910. His 2.16 ERA ranks sixth in the all-time records, and he led the American League in strikeouts for six consecutive seasons. A colorful personality with a passion for fishing, drinking and chasing firetrucks, this awe-inspiring lefthander died of tuberculosis at the age of 37.

A key figure in the jockeying for power between the National and American Leagues was Albert J Reach, one-time player and business partner to influential National League owner and sporting goods manufacturer Albert G Spalding. Reach was President of the Philadelphia National League club, but he was also sympathetic to establishment of a successful second major league, viewing it as something that would benefit the game as a whole. In the battle for an American League Chicago club, it was Reach who acted as mediator. He didn't resist when Johnson moved onto his turf in Philadelphia, and in fact was to shop with what had been the Kansas City team. The next stop was Philadelphia where Johnson established a team with financial support from Ben Shibe, who was another of Philadelphia National League owner Al Reach's business partners.

Chicago Cubs pitcher Clark Griffith, despite his National League affiliation, was yet another behind-the-scenes supporter of the move to establish the American League as a major. He served as Vice President of the ballplayers' Protective Association, and when the National League turned down the players' list of demands, which included raising the salary maximum to $3000, he had the players solidly behind him.

Some 30 National League players joined American League teams before the start of the 1901 season. They deserted National League teams in droves, lured by higher salaries and the promise of better treatment. In addition to John McGraw came pitchers Cy Young and Joe McGinnity, and Napoleon Lajoie and Jimmy Collins. By the time the dust settled, 111 of the American League's 182 players came from their arch-rivals. The only National League club that remained intact in the face of American League raids was Pittsburgh. Johnson had steered clear of stealing players from Barney Dreyfuss's team because he was hoping to persuade him to join the American League.

The historic decision by American League owners to give their clubs major league status came at a

Left: Jimmy Collins, one of four players from Boston's National League team to cross over to Boston's American League team in 1901, played and managed the team to greatness, winning the first World Series in 1903. Holding the fourth-place all-time record for single-season put-outs, Collins was elected to the Hall of Fame in 1945. **Above:** Hall of Famer Nap Lajoie in a Philadelphia Athletics uniform, up at bat in the Polo Grounds. Second baseman Lajoie, who crossed over to the American League in 1901, played for the A's until the middle of 1902, then played for Cleveland from 1903 to 1914. He ended his career back with the A's in 1916, with a .339 batting average and four batting titles under his belt.

provide the official baseball for the American League, as his partner Spalding had done for the National League. Johnson's response to the National League's assignment of the Kansas City and Minneapolis franchises to minor league clubs was to pull his teams out of those towns and head East.

He moved into Baltimore and Washington first. Feisty John G McGraw, who had been with the National League in Baltimore and then cast his lot with the attempt to revive the American Association, was hired to head the new American League's Baltimore team. In Washington, Jimmy Manning set up

Rube Waddell warms up before a game.

meeting in Chicago in January of 1901. The first game took place on 24 April 1901, at Comiskey Park in Chicago between the White Sox and the Cleveland Bronchos (subsequently known as the Blues, Naps, Molly McGuires and Indians). The Sox beat Cleveland 8 to 2. While the birthing had been accomplished, the battles between the new major league and the Nationals were far from over.

Still building up the strength of his new major league, Ban was ready to move into Boston next. He preempted an attempt on the part of the not-yet-dead American Association to field a team there by sending Connie Mack north to find property, using Somer's money, after Mack had organized the Philadelphia club, and moving the league's Buffalo team there. Now the American League lineup was almost complete: in the West were Cleveland, Chicago, Milwaukee and Detroit; in the East were Baltimore, Washington, Philadelphia and Boston. With two changes over the next two years, the league would crystallize into the form it was to keep for the next 50 years.

With clubs in three National League cities, Chicago, Philadelphia and Boston, the American League now posed a serious threat to the Nationals. The National League decided to take legal action in an attempt to stop the Johnson juggernaut. Lawyers for the owners of the Philadelphia Phillies argued that celebrated former Phillies second baseman Napoleon Lajoie, who had signed with the Athletics, should not be allowed to play ball for that American League Philadelphia team. The legality of the reserve option was upheld by Pennsylvania's Supreme Court, which ordered Lajoie back to the Phillies. Connie Mack's answer was to sell Nap Lajoie and three other ex-Phillies players to Cleveland, where they were outside the Pennsylvania court's jurisdiction. When Cleveland played Philadelphia, Nap and the other ex-Phillies stayed home.

Comiskey's White Sox won the pennant that year, behind a 24-7 season by right-hander/manager Clark Griffith, who had crossed over from the Cubs. The stench of the stockyards was obviously not strong enough to keep the Sox from outdrawing their arch-rivals that year. Nap was the top hitter for the season. The Rhode Island-born athlete had been offered almost $6000 by Connie Mack to switch from the Phillies to the Athletics, and he took the Triple Crown with 14 home runs, 125 runs batted in and a .422 batting average.

Another of the all-time greats, Denton True Young, playing for the Boston American League club, was the top pitcher. Nicknamed 'Cy,' an abbreviation for Cyclone in honor of his fastball, he gave the Boston Somersets (known as such until 1905, when they became the Puritans for a brief two years and the Red Sox ever after) a 33-10 record. He pitched five shutouts, had a 1.62 ERA, and walked only 37 batters in 371 innings – a one in ten average. Yet Boston still finished four games behind the Chicago White Sox. At 34, Young already had 285 out of the 511 wins he would take before he retired in 1911.

By 1902, the National League saw that its strategy was falling flat. They decided to scrap the National Agreement themselves, and try to fight fire with fire by raiding American League teams. Their most notable success was in Baltimore, where manager John McGraw was on the ropes with Johnson over umpire baiting. In July of 1902 Ban suspended McGraw indefinitely. McGraw, in cahoots with Johnson's arch-enemy from his sportswriting days, John Brush, got hold of the majority of stock in the Orioles and sold it to New York Giants owner Andrew Freedman. McGraw took four Baltimore players with him to the Giants, for whom he became manager, and sent two others to Cincinnati. McGraw always claimed that he had been released from the American League team in exchange for $7000 in advances to players for which he had never been reimbursed, but charges and countercharges flew back and forth.

Johnson put Wilbert Robinson in charge of his Baltimore teammates and patched together a club with players from other American League teams and the minors. Baltimore finished last that year, but at least the team scraped by. At the end of the season, Johnson got ready to move it to New York. Milwaukee got shifted to St Louis in 1902 because it was the largest midwestern city outside of Chicago which didn't ban Sunday baseball, and the American League lineup was set for half a century.

One measure of the American League's success in 1902 was the fact that it outdrew the Nationals in Boston, Chicago, Philadelphia and St Louis for a total of 2.2 million fans, compared to the Nationals' 1.7 million. Six American League teams showed a profit that year. Connie Mack took the first of his nine pennants when the Philadelphia Athletics, aided by leftie Rube Waddell, topped the St Louis Browns by five games. (Stone-faced Eddie Plank was the other leftie who helped pitch the Philadelphia Athletics to 83 wins to take the 1902 pennant.) What made the American League such a hit? It was, no doubt, Ban Johnson's call for 'clean baseball and more 25-cent seats.'

By winter, the National League, beset by internal as well as external problems, sent up the white flag. The ensuing peace talks, held at the St Nicholas Hotel in Cincinnati in January 1903, were a clear victory for the American League. The Nationals asked for a merger, but settled for recognition of the American League as a major league, respect for reserve clauses by both leagues, permission for the American League to keep most of its pirated players and the green light for an American League team in New York, as long as no attempt was made to move into Pittsburgh. A three-member National Baseball Commission, comprised of the presidents of the two major leagues and a third member chosen by them, was set up to act as arbiter between clubs and between clubs and players. August Hermann, the new owner of the Reds, was tapped, along with Johnson and Harry Pulliam, who had served as Secretary of the Pittsburgh Club before being elected to lead the National League. The Commission stayed in place until the appointment of a Baseball Commissioner in 1920 after the Black Sox scandal.

Despite the National League's peace talk concessions in allowing the American League to place a team in New York in 1903 – the Highlanders – establishment of a team there was hardly a piece of cake. New York was part of the turf for Johnson's nemesis John Brush, and Brush was determined to make life difficult for Ban by pulling strings to see that any site he picked for a ball field in New York had streets run through it or was declared a public park. Whenever Johnson began to close in on a likely spot, Brush got wind of it and got in touch with Andrew Freedman, who put the word out to his Tammany Hall cronies. Finally the Highlanders found a vacant field in upper Manhattan (where Columbia Presbyterian Hospital now stands) and managed to put a fence around it before anyone could interfere. Because of this unorthodox approach, it is alleged, among the team's

Hall of Famer Eddie Plank pitched for the Philadelphia A's from 1901 to 1914, finishing with a career ERA of 2.34 and a .630 winning percentage.

Above: An overflowing crowd of Boston Somersets (later Red Sox) fans cheer their team to victory in the 1903 World Series. This first of the modern World Series championships between the two major leagues was played at Old Huntington Avenue Grounds against the Pittsburgh Pirates. Boston won five games to three.
Right: William Henry 'Big Bill' Dinneen won three out of the four games he pitched for Boston in the 1903 World Series, including two shutouts. Dinneen had four 20-plus game-winning years, ended his 12-year career with a 3.01 ERA and later became a famous umpire.

early nicknames were 'The Porchclimbers' and 'The Burglars.'

The St Nicholas peace pact had left the establishment of a World Series up to the individual clubs, and the 1903 season saw the first World Series between the two majors. In the National League, Barney Dreyfuss's Pittsburgh Pirates took their third pennant in a row and challenged the American League Boston team, managed by third baseman Jimmy Collins. With Cy Young still heading up his pitching staff, Collins felt confident that the American League was the stronger of the two majors, and that Boston could beat Pittsburgh. The series came close to being aborted when the Boston team, under contract to play only up to 30 September, threatened to strike if they didn't get all the Boston gate receipts. Owner Henry J Killilea nipped the rebellion in the bud by offering the players extra money for playing.

Pittsburgh owner Dreyfuss and Boston owner Killilea agreed that their teams should play up to nine games in the World Series. The winner had to take five, with the first three to be played in Boston, four in Pittsburgh, and then two more, if necessary, in Boston. New players, those who signed after 31 August, could not play. Hampered by injuries and other problems, Pittsburgh still managed to take the first game, 7-3. Boston took the next one, but dropped a second on its home turf before moving to Pittsburgh and losing a third. Then Boston broke through for good, winning 11-2 in the fifth game and following that with three more wins – two of them shutouts – to clinch the first World Series. Killilea's stinginess, however, resulted in the Pittsburgh players making more from the Series than the winners in Boston, and he was forced out the next season.

There would be no World Series in 1904, thanks to National League owner John Brush and manager John McGraw, who refused to give their archenemy Ban Johnson the satisfaction of matching the pennant-winning New York Giants against the American League entry. At the time Brush and McGraw made the decision, it looked as if the American League winner was going to be the New York Highlanders, a team Brush particularly despised and derisively called the Invaders. The American League pennant race for 1904 had the Boston Somersets and the New York Highlanders – not to become the Yankees until 1913 – neck and neck for much of the season. Their five-game closing series was the decisive factor, and after an initial win by New York, Boston took the next three, with Cy Young posting a 26-16 pitching record, backed up by Bill Dineen's 23-14 and Jesse Tannehill's 21-11.

college graduates, a less-than-usual occurrence in those early days of the game. Mathewson s pitching for the Giants flattened the Athletics, 9-0, in the third game of the Series, and they took the next two, 1-0 and 2-0. It was a World Series without home runs. The Giants batted .209 and the Athletics .161. A gong had even been installed next to Broad Street Station in Philadelphia, which was to ring out doubles, triples and home runs. It was rung a total of only five times. The National League was riding high again, but only temporarily.

That year was the debut for an 18-year-old Georgia rookie named Tyrus Raymond Cobb. Playing in his first season as an outfielder for the Detroit Tigers, he batted a modest .240. But in the next 23 years, Ty Cobb almost never batted under .300 and finished with a lifetime average of .367. Not any easy man to get long with, Cobb was thought to carry the psychic wounds caused by his father's death at the hands of Ty's mother. Rumor had it that the senior Cobb, suspecting his wife of infidelity, had announced that he would be gone overnight, but then had tried to sneak into the house under cover of night to confront her and her lover. Mrs Cobb, mistaking him for an intruder, allegedly shot her husband dead. Whatever

Left: Hall of Famer Joseph John 'Little Napoleon' McGraw played baseball for 16 years (1891-1906) – only one and a half years of which were spent in the American League. Primarily a third baseman, McGraw was also a talented but tough-minded manager. After a short stint as the Baltimore Orioles' manager, McGraw became a thorn in Ban Johnson's side, moving back to the National League and refusing as New York Giants manager to participate in the 1904 World Series.

Below: Elected to the Hall of Fame in 1953, pitcher Chief Bender was crucial to the success of Connie Mack's Philadelphia A's, with his .621 winning percentage and his 2.45 career ERA.

Although Johnson had protested McGraw and Brush's rejection of a World Series, saying that the 'refusal to play would be a violation of our agreement and a sign of weakness in the National League,' in fact the St Nicholas peace pact did not stipulate that there must be a World Series. Recanting after the Boston team ended up winning the American League pennant, Brush announced he would be willing to meet an American League team in 1905. It was Brush, in fact, who established the rules governing World Series play, rules which are in force to this day. The nine-game series was scrapped for a four-out-of-seven format and mandatory participation. Receipts for the first four games were to go to the players, 10 percent to the National Commission, and the rest to the managements of the two competing clubs.

Brush got his chance to play the American League, since the Giants did win the National League pennant in 1905. Connie Mack's Philadelphia Athletics had taken the American League title, led by pitchers George 'Rube' Waddell with 26 wins, Eddie Plank and Albert 'Chief' Bender, a Chippewa Indian.

The World Series that year was a pitcher's dream, with all five games shutouts. Unlike today's power baseball, the emphasis then was on pitching discipline and place hitting. Christy Mathewson won for the Giants their first game, allowing just four hits. Waddell, ever the prankster, had injured his arm supposedly chasing after a teammate wearing an out-of-season straw hat, and was out of the running for Philadelphia. Chief Bender evened the score for Philadelphia with a second 3-0 game, again allowing four hits. A crowd of nearly 25,000 then filled New York's Polo Grounds to watch the next battle of the pitchers. Both Mathewson and Eddie Plank were

Right: Lefthander Guy Harris 'Doc' White moved to the American League in 1903 and pitched for the Chicago White Sox from 1903 to 1913. Turning in a 1.52 ERA in 1906, he formed part of Comiskey's tough pitching core, who beat their Chicago National League counterparts in the World Series that year, four games to two.

Below: Hall of Famer Edward Augustine 'Big Ed' Walsh pitched for the Chicago White Sox from 1904 to 1916, Walsh pitched ten shutouts in 1906, and ended his magnificent career with an all-time record 1.82 ERA and a .607 winning percentage.

Ty Cobb, a legend in his own time, played outfield for the Detroit Tigers for 22 years during his 24-year career. His .367 batting average, 4191 career hits and 2244 runs speak for themselves.

the reasons, Ty Cobb was a cold and arrogant man who used his spikes like lethal weapons on his way around the bases. His speed, along with his bunting and place hitting talents, made him, however, one of baseball's greatest and most revered players.

In 1906 Chicago's two teams faced each other in the World Series. Comiskey's White Sox, who had been dubbed the hitless wonders with a .228 average – the lowest in the league – stole the American League pennant from New York and Cleveland, and all odds were on the Cubs to take the Series. Instead, the White Sox won four games out of six behind the pitching of spitball specialist Ed Walsh. Much of the credit went to the substitute shortstop George Rohe, who over-reached himself, giving the Sox winning triples in the first and third games, then adding five hits in the last two games and leading the White Sox to victory.

The 1907 season brought three more baseball greats to the American League and helped keep the newer league on top for decades to come. From Humboldt, Kansas, came right-handed pitcher Walter Perry Johnson. The story of Johnson's rise to baseball fame has it that Johnson never served any apprenticeship in the minors. He was supposedly discovered when he was pitching semi-pro baseball in Idaho by a traveling salesman who contacted the Washington Senators. When a Washington scout saw his fastball, he signed Johnson on the spot. Good-natured and easygoing, Johnson couldn't have been more different than Ty Cobb, who once said of him, 'That busher throws the fastest pitch I've ever seen.' Fearful of maiming players with the deadly speed of his pitches,

he refused to throw at batters and Cobb exploited Johnson's gentleness by often crowding the plate when he came up to bat. Unfortunately for Johnson, who was known as 'The Big Train,' the Senators spent most of their time at the bottom of the League, and the pitcher who many have called the fastest in the game didn't get a chance to perform in the World Series until 1924.

Another one of the American League greats who began his career in 1907 was second baseman Eddie Collins. Columbia University educated, Collins racked up a .333 lifetime batting average as a left-handed hitter for the Athletics. During the 25 years he played, Collins took the honors as the top fielder nine times, stole 743 bases, and had 3311 hits. He surpassed even Nap Lajoie in infield skills.

The third great American League player to enter the game in 1907 was a 19-year-old Texan, Tristram Speaker, who played center field for Boston. 'Tris' was known for his seemingly shallow outfield positioning which allowed him to make a record-breaking four unassisted double plays during his career. Nicknamed 'Spoke' and 'The Gray Eagle' (because of his prematurely gray hair), Speaker stayed in Boston until 1916, when he was traded to the Cleveland Indians. His lifetime hitting total of 3515 included a record 793 doubles, and his lifetime batting average was .344.

With the rising star of Ty Cobb to guide them, the Detroit Tigers dominated the American League for three seasons, from 1907 to 1909. Hitting .350, Ty took

Above: Tris Speaker hits a line drive up the middle. Hall of Famer Tristram E Speaker turned in nine dazzling years as a Boston outfielder, then played for Cleveland from 1916 to 1926. Speaker's outstanding speed, throwing arm and batting achievements made him one of the best all-around players of all time. His record of 793 doubles still stands today.

Left: Walter Perry 'The Big Train' Johnson pitched for the Washington Senators from 1907 to 1927. A big man with incredible talent and a placid temperament, Johnson won 416 games with 3508 strikeouts and a career ERA of 2.17. He was elected to the Hall of Fame in 1936.

Hall of Famer Addie Joss pitched for Cleveland for nine years (1902-10), achieving a 1.88 career ERA. In 1908, when Cleveland and the White Sox were embroiled in a pennant race, he pitched a perfect game, turning in a league-leading 1.16 ERA that year.

darkness. Then Detroit became the first team not to win a single World Series game after the Cubs took four straight, 3-1, 5-1, 6-1 and 2-0. Cobb hit an anemic .200, but the Tigers' real Achilles heel was the catching of Charlie 'Boss' Schmidt.

One of the quirks of the 1907 World Series was the fact that Tiger player representative Herman 'Germany' Schaefer asked the Baseball Commission in a pre-series meeting what its policy would be on sharing gate receipts if one of the first four games were to be a tie. The Commission deliberated and ruled that in the event of a tie, the players would have a share in the first five games. Then the first game ended in a 3-3 tie, and many cynics wondered if the game had been rigged. The Commission ordered an investigation, but no skullduggery was uncovered. In the meantime, the Commission rescinded its five-game decision and proclaimed that from then on, players would share in the receipts from only the first four games.

In 1908 the American League pennant race was a cliff-hanger. It was almost a three-way tie among the Tigers, the Indians and the White Sox, with Cleveland just a half game behind at the season's end, and Chicago one and a half games back. Although the Tigers ended up with the pennant, a battle between the Indians and the White Sox early in October became a well-remembered pitching duel. Chicago's pitcher Ed Walsh, with 40 wins under his belt and a 1.42 ERA, was matched against Cleveland's Addie Joss, who would probably have become one of the finest pitchers in baseball if he hadn't died at age 30 from meningitis. Joss's pitching was perfect in that game; he retired 27 batters in order, winning the historic game for Cleveland.

The Tigers faced the Cubs again for the World Series. With Manager Frank Chance, 'The Peerless Leader,' at first base, Johnny Evers on second, and Joe Tinker playing shortstop, the Cubs proved unbeatable. Newspaper columnist Franklin P Adams had put it into verse:

These are the saddest of possible words –
Tinker to Evers to Chance.
Trio of Bear Cubs and fleeter than birds –
Tinker to Evers to Chance.

Thoughtlessly pricking our gonfalon bubble,
Making a Giant hit into a double,
Words that are weighty with nothing but trouble,
Tinker to Evers to Chance.

Even with a .368 batting average, Ty Cobb couldn't outplay the Cubs. He got seven hits and stole two bases, but the Tigers won only one game and were shut out in the last two.

Some said the World Series that year was an anti-climax after an incident in a Cubs-Giants game that would long be known as 'Merkle's boner.' The Giants' Fred Merkle came up in the bottom of the ninth, with the scored tied at 1-1, two men out and a Giant on first. Merkle's single moved his teammate to third; then another Giant singled and as Merkle moved toward second, he saw his man from third cross the plate with the apparent winning run. As many would later insist was an accepted custom, Merkle didn't bother touching second but ran for the clubhouse. Cub second baseman Johnny Evers called for the ball, but it was alleged that the Giants' Joe McGinnity saw what was about to happen so he intercepted it and threw it into the stands. Evers, however, got another ball,

the first three of his nine batting titles, leading in hits and runs batted in from 1907 to 1909. Strong pitching from Wild Bill Donovan, George Mullin, Ed Killian, Ed Willett and Ed Summers helped the Tigers edge out the Philadelphia Athletics by one and a half games for the pennant in 1907. The White Sox were in third place. Chicago's National League team faced the Tigers for the Series that year.

In the first game the two teams fought to a 3-3 standstill when the game was called on account of touched second, and insisted Merkle was therefore out – and the run didn't count. The umpire agreed, but as the crowd was already running wild around the field, the game was left at 1-1 and a re-match called for if necessary by the final standings. Sure enough, the Cubs and Giants ended up the season tied for first place, and in the required playoff game, the Cubs won and thus claimed the pennant.

The National League won the Series once more in 1909 before the American League took over. This time the Tigers met the Pittsburgh Pirates, whose secret weapon was John Peter 'Honus' Wagner, considered by many to be the best all-around player in the history of baseball. This 1909 Series would prove more exciting than the last, since the Tigers had an all-new infield consisting of Tom Jones at first, Jim Delahanty at second, George Moriarty at third and Owen Bush at shortstop. As for Wagner and Cobb, each was the top batter in his league – Wagner with .339 and Cobb with .377. Each was the opposite of the other in temperament; and each held the bat with his hands nearly half a foot apart. Even though he was already in his mid-thirties, the Flying Dutchman, as Wagner was often called, outplayed Cobb, outhitting him .333 to .231, and stealing six bases to Ty's two. Cobb was also outclassed at bat by Delahanty, who hit .346. The Pirates took the Series, but not without a fight from the Tigers. It was the first time the World Series went a full seven games. Cobb and Wagner never played opposite each other again.

If the public was beginning to wonder just how major the American League was – it had won only a single World Series in nine years – the World Series itself nevertheless had become the nation's biggest sports event. By the end of the first decade of the new century and of American League existence, many of the game's pioneering heroes were ready to retire. Among them were the Cleveland Naps' (later called the Indians) celebrated second baseman Nap Lajoie, who finished his career with a lifetime batting average of .339. King of the pitchers Cy Young would soon retire with 511 wins. The new generation was already warming up: Philadelphia Athletics second baseman

Above: Boston catcher Bill Carrigan, Cleveland second baseman Nap Lajoie and the famous pitcher Cy Young pose for the camera.

Left: Jack Barry, the Philadelphia Athletics' shortstop from 1908 to 1915, played in four World Series with that team, winning three of them.

Eddie Collins, Boston center fielder Tris Speaker, and Washington pitcher Walter Johnson.

Connie Mack's Philadelphia Athletics were the cream of the American League in 1910. In addition to Eddie Collins and veteran first baseman Harry Davis, Mack had a stable of promising new players, especially with Jack Barry at shortstop and Frank Baker at third base. They came to be known as Connie's $100,000 infield – an estimate of their worth at the time. Veteran pitchers Jack Coombs and Chief Bender gave the Athletics a win-loss record of 54-14.

Second-place New York was 14 and a half games behind the pennant-winners, and Detroit came behind them in third, despite Ty Cobb's title-winning .385 average. Already one of the most disliked of players, Cobb was the target of an attempt on the part of the St Louis Browns to throw Nap Lajoie the title as the season's top hitter. When Ban Johnson heard about the goings-on, he kicked the participants, Browns' manager Jack O'Connor and coach Harry Howell, out of the American League for life. Despite the attempted manipulation, Cobb beat out Lajoie by a hundredth of a point. In the World Series, the Athletics steamrolled the National League's Cubs four games to one. It was the first in a winning streak that would see them win the American League pennant four out of the next five years.

The Athletics took the Series with Collins, who had broken his leg, on the sidelines. Heinrich 'Heinie' Zimmerman replaced him. For the first time since 1906, the Athletics (with Chief Bender and Jack Coombs pitching) won the opening game of the Series, 4-1. It was superb hitting that clinched the Series, with the A's batting .316 overall, a record that held until 1960.

Mack's Philadelphia team repeated in 1911, the year Frank Baker earned his title as Home Run Baker. Although the A's didn't move into first place for the pennant until late in the season, they still topped the Tigers by 13 and a half games. Ty Cobb had his best hitting season yet, with .420, and he and Sam Crawford racked up 465 hits. That still wasn't enough to stop Connie Mack's wonder team, though.

An American League star for Cleveland who premiered that season was 'Shoeless' Joe Jackson, said to be illiterate. The South Carolinian had a .408 batting average for the Naps with 233 hits, 45 doubles and 19 triples. The rookie was known as the greatest natural hitter who ever lived.

The Athletics met McGraw's New York Giants in the 1911 World Series. Baker hit two home runs in two days during the second and third games, convincing New York's catcher Chief Meyers that the American League team must have some mysterious access to the Giants' signals. While Home Run Baker's overall record of 100 home runs does not seem spectacular by today's standards, the game was different then. It was the era of the 'dead' ball, and while the cork-centered ball had just been introduced, the emphasis was on place hitting, bunting and base stealing. Judged by the standards of the times, Baker's record of nine homeruns that year was indeed outstanding.

In 1912 it was a Boston Red Sox player who won the kudos. Fenway Park was opened that year, and Smokey Joe Wood, a 22-year-old pitcher, gave the Sox a 34-5 season to mark the occasion. He struck out 258 batters, pitched 10 shutouts and batted .290 to boot. Washington's Walter Johnson was close behind with a 32-12 record, 303 strikeouts and a 1.39 ERA. He also posted a record-breaking 16 consecutive wins.

Third baseman John Franklin 'Home Run' Baker slaps an infield hit for the Philadelphia Athletics. Home Run Baker earned his nickname in the 1911 World Series, smashing a two-run homer in game two, and a ninth-inning homer in game three. The A's took the Series against the Giants, four to two.

The two American League pitchers got to face each other on 12 September 1912, with fans overflowing Boston's new ball park. The game ended 1-0 in Boston's favor when the Sox scored in the sixth inning on consecutive doubles by Tris Speaker and George 'Duffy' Lewis. With George 'Duffy' Lewis in left field, Speaker playing center, and Harry Hooper covering right, the Sox's outfield was as solid as its pitching. They went on that year to win the pennant, and Washington finished second ahead of the Philadelphia Athletics, despite Connie Mack's claim that they were the best team he'd ever managed.

The World Series that year has been characterized as sloppy but excitingly close, with the Boston Red Sox competing against the New York Giants. When the seventh game of the Series had to be called for darkness at a tie, an eighth game became necessary. The final game went ten inning. Pitchers Christy Mathewson (New York) and Hugh Bedient (Boston) battled till the seventh innings, when Bedient was replaced by Joe Wood. The score was 1-1 at the end of nine innings. The Giants scored another run in the tenth, but when the Red Sox came to bat, the Giants' center fielder committed the celebrated error called 'Snodgrass's $30,000 Muff' by dropping an easy fly

Above: Ty Cobb and Nap Lajoie are each awarded a '30' motorcar by Hugh Chalmers in a ceremony witnessed by 20,000 spectators. Although Cobb beat out Lajoie for the 1910 batting championship by a fraction of a point, the two players received equal awards.
Left: Two Hall of Fame managers, Connie Mack of the Philadelphia Athletics and Clark Griffith of the Washington Senators, shake hands.

Above: Boston Red Sox pitcher Smokey Joe Wood and New York Giants pitcher Jeff Tesreau shake hands before the first game of the 1912 World Series. Wood won this contest for Boston, striking out 11 batters, and Boston went on to win the Series four games to three.

Right: John Phalen 'Stuffy' McInnis played first base for the Philadelphia A's as part of Connie Mack's $100,000 infield. During his nine years with the A's (1909-17), Stuffy McInnis maintained a .304 batting average.

McInnis at first base, along with Eddie Collins, Jack Barry and Frank Baker. Injuries kept the Giants from operating at full strength. The Giants' Mathewson, who had pitched in eleven World Series games and won five, of which four were shutouts, went down in defeat in what was to be his last World Series performance.

1914 launched the Great War in Europe and the battle against the Federal League in American baseball. More a spoiler than a serious threat, the Federal League didn't have much success in wooing players, and within two years it was just a memory. It's possible, however, that because of the Federal League, the Philadelphia A's lost the Series that year. With Connie Mack's $100,000 infield in full swing, the A's won the pennant with ease. The second-place Red Sox were eight and a half games behind them, but they picked up a 19-year-old rookie – in a deal with the Baltimore Orioles for three players – who was

ball. The Sox racked up two runs to win by a final score of 3-2. Before the game was over, the Giants had chalked up 16 errors and the Sox, 14 for the Series.

The 1913 season saw Smokey Joe Wood, the Red Sox's brightest star the year before, vanish from the firmament almost as quickly as he had appeared when he injured his arm during spring training. Washington's legendary pitcher Walter Johnson had his best season in 1913. He pitched 36-7 and topped the league in wins, in ERA's with 1.09, in strikeouts with 243 and in shutouts with 12. For more than a month, early in the season, he kept all batters at bay and allowed no runs at all, pitching 55 and two thirds scoreless innings. It took Don Drysdale to top that record in 1968.

Despite Johnson's brilliance, Washington finished six and a half games behind the Athletics, in second place. Ty Cobb took his seventh batting crown in a row at .390, and Shoeless Joe Jackson was right behind him with a .373.

Connie Mack's A's were matched against McGraw's Giants in the World Series that year, and the A's had an easy win, 4-1. Mack's infield had added Stuffy destined to become one of baseball's greatest players. His name was George Herman Ruth, soon to be nicknamed 'Babe,' and that first season he batted .200, with one double.

The Tigers' powerhouse Ty Cobb took the honors again with .368, and the Senators' pitcher Walter Johnson had a 25-18 season, something of a high-low record. Even winning their fourth pennant in five years, the A's stood on the brink of disaster. Chief Bender and Eddie Plank had succumbed to the blandishments of the Federal League and were playing their last season for Connie Mack. Morale was low and what should have been an easy win in the World Series turned into a rout.

They faced the Boston Braves, who had earned the nickname 'Miracle Braves' for their spectacular rise from the bottom of the National League to first place. Spurred to victory by manager George Tweedy Stallings, the Braves were on a roll. Stallings used two sets of outfielders, one for right-handed pitchers and one for left-handers. Chief Bender lost the opener to the Miracle Braves, 7-1, and never pitched for the A's

again. The rest of the games were close, but the Braves took them one after another, 1-0, 5-4 and 3-1. With his .545 batting average, Braves player Hank Gowdy became the first to hit over .500 in the World Series, while Home Run Baker led the A's with .250.

As if that defeat were not enough, Connie Mack then sold off the team's best players and sent the Athletics to last place in the league. Eddie Collins went to the White Sox, Jack Barry and Herb Pennock to the Red Sox and Bob Shawkey to the Yankees. Frank Baker retired, and Jack Coombs was released. It took many years for the team to recover.

The Red Sox replaced the Athletics as the American League's leading team for the next few years, taking three pennants from 1915 to 1918. Particularly strong was the Boston team's pitching. The outfield, featuring Tris Speaker at center, Duffy Lewis at left and Harry Hooper at right, was a defensive powerhouse. In 1915, Babe Ruth played his first full season in the majors, batting .315 and hitting four home runs.

The Phillies were the National League entry against Boston in the World Series that year. It was the

New York Highlanders' manager William Edward 'Wild Bill' Donovan and Washington Senators' manager Clark Griffith shake hands before a game. Also known as 'The Old Fox,' Griffith managed a first-place team only once during his 20-year career, although his 1491 wins places him tenth on the all-time list.

Phillies' first shot at the Series and their last pennant until 1950. The magic ingredient that took them to the World Series in 1915 was right-handed pitcher Grover Cleveland Alexander. He had won 31 games that season, 12 of which were shutouts. The Phillies took the first game in the Series, but even Alexander couldn't stop Boston, and the Red Sox cinched the rest – all with a 2-1 score. It was Babe Ruth's World Series debut. He played his first World Series game at Baker Bowl, the Phillies' home park, where 21 years later he played his last major league game.

Once the Federal League threw in the towel,

players' salaries, which had risen to stave off the contenders, took a nosedive. Players who refused to cooperate found themselves traded, like Tris Speaker, who ended up in Cleveland. Even without Speaker, though, the Red Sox won the pennant again in 1916. Pitching was the key, with Babe Ruth turning into the league's top left-hander. Winning 23 games, he helped bring a speedy defeat to the Brooklyn Dodgers, who opposed the Red Sox in the 1916 World Series.

The next year brought a pause in the Red Sox sweep, as the White Sox took the pennant. The White Sox had a strong infield, pitching on a par with the Red

Above: The formidable pitching staff of the 1917 Boston Red Sox. From left to right: Ernie Shore, Dutch Leonard, George Foster and Babe Ruth.
Below: Detroit Tigers Ty Cobb (left) and Sam Crawford (right) talk with Chicago's Shoeless Joe Jackson.
Opposite: Hall of Fame catcher Ray Schalk played for the White Sox (1912-28).

Sox, and Shoeless Joe Jackson in the outfield. The highlight of the World Series between the White Sox and the Giants was one disastrous inning that cost the Giants the Series.

Chicago won the opening game, 2-1, after a stand-off in which each pitcher gave up seven hits and struck out two batters. With five runs in the fourth, the Sox racked up their second win, 7-2. Then the Giants rallied and won 2-0 in the third game and 5-0 in the fourth. The two teams went neck and neck through the seventh inning of the fifth game, with the score tied at 5-5, until the Sox pulled ahead to win 8-5.

The Giants' infamous blunders came during the fourth inning of the sixth game. White Sox player Eddie Collins sent a grounder to Heinie Zimmerman, but Zimmerman's throw missed first base and so Collins was able to get to second. Shoeless Joe Jackson then hit an easy fly into right field – but the Giant Dave Robertson dropped it. Now Collins was on third, and when Happy Felsch's hit was caught by the pitcher, Collins was caught between third and home. Collins got past the Giant catcher while Zimmerman had the ball and since no one had bothered to back up at home plate, Collins beat Zimmerman there. The White Sox won the game, 4-2.

America's entry into the War in 1918 made it questionable whether there would even be a World Series that year. The pennant went back to the Red Sox, despite the continued strength of Chicago. The leagues had orders to end play by Labor Day because of the war; then a 15-day grace period was allowed so the Red Sox could play the Cubs in the World Series. Although Red Sox manager Ed Barrows had begun to use Ruth increasingly in the field in order to take advantage of his hitting talent in more games, Ruth pitched two games of the Series, winning the first 1-0, and the fourth, 3-2. The star of the series, though, was George Whiteman, an aging outfielder from Toronto whom the Red Sox had picked up in midseason. His fielding and hitting helped the Sox in all six games. In the series-winning game his hit gave the Red Sox the winning run in their 2-1 victory, and his spectacular catch in the eighth inning stopped a Cub rally dead. The next year Whiteman was back playing in Toronto.

The year 1919 stands out in baseball history, but not for good reasons. It was the year of the White Sox scandal. Babe Ruth spent the season in the outfield, setting a new home run record of 29 and a new batting record of .657. Despite the Babe's brilliant play, the Red Sox finished fifth and the pennant went to the White Sox. Comiskey's team had a reputation for being outstanding – when they wanted to be. The problem was gambling, and they threw the 1919 Series to Cincinnati, earning the ignominious title for themselves of the Black Sox.

Eight players were involved in the scandal: outfielder 'Shoeless' Joe Jackson, third baseman George 'Buck' Weaver, first baseman Arnold 'Chick' Gandil, shortstop Charles 'Swede' Risberg, pitchers Eddie Cicotte and Claude 'Lefty' Williams, center fielder Oscar 'Happy' Felsch and utility infielder Fred McMullin. Eddie Collins was one of those who remained untainted. The Sox had been said to be split into cliques for some time, and the split was along the lines of who was crooked and who was straight. Weaver, it was argued by some, was guilty only by association, having sat in on the negotiation over the fix, but having decided not to participate in it.

The ringleaders were Cicotte, Gandil and Williams, who approached the gamblers (including the notorious Arnold Rothstein) in New York at midseason to set the stakes. The players were promised $100,000, most of which they were never to see. It must have seemed like a lot of money in those days, when a player was doing well if he earned $6000. Comiskey contributed to the trouble in the sense that he was notoriously tight, paying the lowest salaries in either major league.

Betting odds before the Series began went from 3-1 in favor of the White Sox to 8-5 in favor of Cincinnati, a sure clue to the shenanigans going on. The pre-established high sign was for the White Sox pitcher to hit the first batter in the first game. Eddie Cicotte performed on cue, and Cincinnati won, 9-1.

Claude Williams walked three batters in a single inning in the second game, an unheard of feat for him, and the Reds won again, this time 4-2. When Comiskey got wind of what was going on, he passed the word to John Heydler, president of the National League, who informed Ban Johnson. Johnson, who by now had fallen out with Comiskey in a personal feud, dismissed it as 'the yelp of a beaten cur.'

The Sox won the third game, 3-0, possibly because the gamblers were reneging on their promise to pay the players $10,000 of the $100,000 total after each game. Two errors by Cicotte gave the Reds a 2-0 win in the fourth game, and they won again, 5-0, in the fifth. The Commission had temporarily lengthened the Series to a best of nine that year, so the Reds needed one more win to take the Series.

Cicotte talked Manager Kid Gleason into letting him pitch again, and the Sox won 4-1. Then Claude Williams lost to the Reds, 10-5, and the Series was over. It broke all records in receipts and attendance, and the Reds were the first to earn more than $5000 in a series. Nothing was said publicly about the fix until the following September, but rumors flew fast and furious. Boxer Abe Attell confessed to being involved in the deal and named the eight players. The *Chicago Tribune* called for a grand jury investigation.

When confronted by Gleason and Comiskey, Cicotte broke down. He, Jackson and Williams gave the details of how the games were rigged to a grand jury, and Comiskey suspended all eight. As Shoeless Joe Jackson was leaving the courthouse after the grand jury hearing, a small boy supposedly came up to him with tears in his eyes, and as the legend has it, cried, 'Say it ain't so, Joe.' Criminal indictments followed, but by then the players' written confessions had disappeared, and they all were acquitted. According to the letter of the law, they could have been reinstated.

The three-man National Commission was replaced

that year, however, by a single Commissioner of Baseball. Judge Kenesaw Mountain Landis, named for a Civil War battle, took quick and decisive action: 'Regardless of the verdict of juries, no player that throws a game, no player that entertains proposals or promises to throw a game, no player that sits in conference with a bunch of crooks and gamblers where the ways and means of throwing games are discussed, and does not promptly tell his club about it, will ever again play professional baseball.'

The 'Black Sox' scandal seriously undermined the confidence of many in the game that had become the national pastime, but Landis's firm handling of the scandal helped mitigate the disgrace. Some felt some of the players deserved a pardon. Buck Weaver never shared in the ill-gained profits, and played .324 ball in the Series. Ten thousand fans signed a petition calling for his reinstatement, but Judge Landis sternly turned a cold shoulder.

Shoeless Joe Jackson got no fix money either and averaged .375 for the Series, the best in both leagues, but he was never allowed back in baseball. In fact when word got back to Judge Landis that Jackson had been hired to coach a class D minor league team, he ordered him fired. It took the legendary Babe Ruth to wipe the slate clean in the roaring twenties and make the crowds forget about the dirty deeds their heroes in Chicago had done.

'Shoeless' Joe Jackson (left) and Oscar 'Happy' Felsch were both suspended from baseball forever by Commissioner Landis for their involvement in the Black Sox scandal.

CHAPTER TWO

The House that
Ruth Built

" . . . they fixed up a ball that if you
don't
miss it entirely it will clear the fence."

—Ring Lardner

Through his dramatic commissionership, Judge Landis provided a symbol that reassured the public of baseball's honesty and integrity, and made it a respected and admired sport. As the new decade began, a rising interest in baseball was further enhanced by the advent of the lively ball, by rule changes that encouraged hitters, by post-World War I affluence, and above all by Babe Ruth, whose rising popularity and playing style revolutionized the game. All these elements combined to usher in an age of unprecedented prosperity for the American League.

During the twenties, the fast and colorful new game of home run baseball emerged to draw crowds in increasing numbers and set the style for years to come. The American League, after two decades of struggling to survive league wars, scandal and its own magnates, at last achieved an element of stability and maturity. The greatest stars the league had ever known – Ty Cobb, Tris Speaker, Walter Johnson, Eddie Collins, Lou Gehrig, Lefty Grove, Babe Ruth, George Sisler, Harry Heilmann, Jimmie Foxx, Al Simmons, Goose Goslin – were assembled as the new power game competed successfully in the unrestrained, fast-moving, action-oriented postwar society.

Beginning with President Taft, who originated the custom of throwing out the first ball on opening day, presidents continued to preside over key games, and baseball regained its status as the national sport. As if

to prove that the revitalized game could keep American League fans from turning to other sports and the lure of such stars of the twenties as Red Grange, Jack Dempsey, Gene Tunney, Walter Hagan and Bill Tilden, in 1920 American League attendance jumped by one and a half million as American League fans, supposedly disillusioned by the Black Sox scandal, stormed the gates. In 1920 the American League became the first to top the five million mark.

Crucial to the creation of the more popular, more exciting game was the elimination of trick pitches. In February 1920, both leagues outlawed all tampering with the ball, banning the application of sandpaper, emery, licorice, mud and particularly spit to the baseball's surface, although 17 pitchers in the major leagues who used the spitball as their primary weapon were permitted to continue to do so. In the American League this included five-time 20-game winner Cleveland Indian Stanley Coveleski, Red Faber of the White Sox and Jack Quinn, who pitched for several teams from 1909 to 1933. For the first time since the early days, when batters could call for their pitches, hitters had the edge over pitchers.

On 16 August 1920 popular Cleveland shortstop Ray Chapman was hit on the head by an inside fastball thrown by Yankee pitcher Carl Mays at a Yankee-Cleveland game. Chapman collapsed at the plate and died the next day from the effects of a blow that put a three-and-one-half-inch fracture in his skull. After his death, which remains the only fatality in major league

Spitballer Jack Quinn warms up before a game. John Picus Quinn pitched for several teams during his 23-year career (1909-33), ending up with a 3.27 ERA.

But the introduction of the lively ball was probably even more significant. Despite repeated assurances by baseball officials and manufacturers that the only change in the manufacture of the ball was a better quality wool yarn (made available from Australia after the war), which was more tightly wound on improved machinery, a baseball officialdom obsessed with wooing back fans after the Black Sox scandal could not have helped but notice that more home runs and higher scoring games drew more spectators to the park. Undoubtedly Babe Ruth was the catalyst in this great revolution, just as surely as his bat was the lever that changed the game.

Left: Spitballer Stan Coveleski pitched brilliantly for the Cleveland Indians from 1916 to 1924, achieving the 20-game mark four times during those years. He was elected to the Hall of Fame in 1969.

Below: Henry Louis Gehrig poses in his Columbia University baseball uniform. Lou Gehrig played his entire 17-year career for the New York Yankees (1923-39).

baseball history, precaution was taken to reduce the danger of a batter getting beaned by substituting a new ball whenever the ball in play became even slightly scuffed or soiled. A pitched ball with rough spots or scrapes is more affected by air currents than a smooth one, and can sail unpredictably. This use of new balls protected the batter, but even further handicapped the pitcher, who found it more difficult to put stuff on a smooth, tightly-covered ball. On the other hand, a new white ball is more visible, more predictable in flight, easier to hit, and goes farther and faster when it is hit.

'Gorgeous George' Sisler played first base for the St Louis Browns from 1915 to 1927, then played briefly for Washington before ending his career on Boston's National League team. In 1922 his .420 batting average, with 246 hits, 134 runs and 51 stolen bases earned him the league MVP title.

In 1919 Ruth broke all existing records by hitting 29 home runs for the Boston Red Sox. The Red Sox were a mediocre team, finishing the season in a tie for fifth place, but large crowds came out to see Ruth wherever he appeared in the league. The lesson was not lost on the baseball owners. As Ring Lardner so eloquently put it:

. . . the master minds that controls baseball says to themselfs that if it is home runs that the public wants to see, why leave us give them home runs, so they fixed up a ball that if you don't miss it entirely it will clear the fence, and the result is that ball players which used to specialize in hump back liners to the pitcher is now amongst our leading sluggers.

By the 1920 season, with trick pitches outlawed and the ball juiced up, the stage was set for the change in the game. The substitution of new balls whenever the one in play was even slightly soiled ran up the curtain, and players and fans performed beautifully. In 1920, Babe Ruth, by then with the New York Yankees, hit 54 homers, and Yankee attendance of 1919 doubled, setting a league record of 1,289, 422 which stood until the Yanks themselves broke it in 1946.

It was a new game. Combined major-league batting averages for 1920 were almost 30 points higher than in 1915. By 1925, they were 45 points higher. In 1915, nine batters in the majors hit above .300; in 1927, 35 major-leaguers hit over .300. Although only four batters hit .400 between 1901 and 1920, from 1920 through 1930, eight batters hit .400 – twice as many in

Left: Heinie Groh of the New York Giants puts Cleveland Indian Tris Speaker out at third during a spring training game in Lakeland, Florida.

Elmer Smith played outfield for Cleveland from 1914 to 1921, with a short stint for Washington in 1916 and 1917. His moment in the sun occurred on 10 October 1920, when he smashed the first World Series grand slam ever.

half the time – including in the American League's Ty Cobb, Harry Heilmann and George Sisler (twice).

Major leaguers hit 384 home runs in 1915. In 1920 they hit 631, in 1925 they hit 1167 and in 1930 they hit 1565, four times the number of homers hit in 1915. In 1930 the ball was hotter than ever. Twenty major-leaguers hit above .350 and nine teams averaged above .300, with American League teams averaging better than five runs per game each. Repeated official assertions that the ball was the same as it had always been are difficult to reconcile with the all-time record National League 1930 average of .303 (after the 1930 season the ball was made *less* lively) and the knowledge that only six batters in the National League hit above .300 in 1968.

Somewhat overshadowed by the breaking Black Sox scandal, a Cleveland team powered by playing manager Tris Speaker's .388 average and pitcher Jim Bagby's 31 victories took the pennant in 1920. It was a tight three-cornered race with the Yankees and the White Sox, the Indians finishing two games ahead of a White Sox team that saw most of its regular players suspended as the season progressed. Only three games separated the three clubs at the close of the season.

Hitting .303 as a team, the 1920 Indians were the first club in the century to have three men hit 100 RBI's. Two Indian pitchers besides Bagby had 20-game years, and their sluggers led the league in runs scored as Cleveland took its first pennant after 20 years of struggles and near misses. Their two-game finish over Chicago suggests that they might not have taken the pennant without the demise of the White Sox, but the Indians themselves had had to scramble to find a replacement for star shortstop Ray Chapman after he was killed at the plate by Carl Mays's pitched ball.

Cleveland faced the Brooklyn Dodgers in a precedent-setting World Series. In the fifth game, with the teams tied at two games each, the Indians' outfielder Elmer Smith hit the first grand-slam Series homer, the Indians' Jim Bagby hit the first Series homer by a pitcher, and the Indians recorded the first unassisted Series triple play, made by second baseman Bill Wambsganss (who in the next year set the still-standing record of seven consecutive extra-base hits). The Dodgers were so demoralized by that fifth game that they remained scoreless from then on, and Cleveland took the Series, 5-2

1920 was in every way a year of shocks and superlatives. Babe Ruth hit a record 54 homers and slugged an all-time record .847. The White Sox became the first team in history to have four 20-game winning pitchers. It was also the first year that the Brown's George Sisler hit above .400, leading the league with .407. But above all, it was the year that Babe Ruth came to the Yankees. Not without coincidence, New York won six out of the next ten pennants. The arrival of the Babe signalled the beginning of a Yankee dynasty that would take 29 pennants and 20 World Series championships in the next 44 years.

The players who formed the backbone of the Yankees' first winning teams came almost entirely from the Boston Red Sox. Boston owner Harry Frazee, who liked to invest in Broadway productions, frequently found himself in need of cash, and found a ready buyer for his star players in wealthy Yankee owner and brewery tycoon Jacob Ruppert. The first of the purchases which eventually became known as the

'Rape of the Red Sox' and resulted in the 'Dead Sox' began in July 1919 with New York's acquisition of fastballer Carl Mays for two players and $40,000. In December 1919, Boston was shocked to learn that its best player, Babe Ruth, had been sold to New York for $125,000 and a loan to Frazee of $300,000 (for which Fenway Park was mortgaged as security).

Over the next four years, this startling deal was followed by a steady flow of players from Boston to New York as Frazee gradually liquidated his loan. By 1923, Boston had given the Yankees Mays and Ruth, catcher Wally Schang, shortstop Everett Scott, third baseman Joe Dugan and pitchers Herb Pennock, Waite Hoyt, Joe Bush and Sam Jones. In 1920 the Yankees also acquired Bob Meusel. Red Sox field manager Edward G Barrow came to the Yankees from Boston late in 1920, filling the vacancy left by the death of business manager Harry Sparrow. Joining forces with shrewd, diminutive field manager Miller Huggins and Ruppert's bucks, general manager Barrow deserves much of the credit for New York's era of success. Not surprisingly, the Red Sox spent eight of the next nine years in last place.

The Yankees finished three games out of first place in 1920, but Babe Ruth batted .376, hit more home runs than any American League team had ever hit (54), racked up the all-time record .847 slugging average and batted in 137 runs. Unschooled, uncouth, lovable, and incredibly talented, George Herman Ruth by this performance did more to revive interest in baseball than Commissioner Landis or anyone else inside or outside baseball, and made it the game we know today.

No athlete in this country has ever achieved greater reknown. Trying to write about Ruth, Arthur Daley of *The New York Times* once remarked, is like trying to paint a landscape on a postage stamp. His popularity was such that he packed the house almost anywhere he appeared. When the Yankees played an exhibition game in March 1921 in Lake Charles, Louisiana, the town declared a holiday, banks and businesses closed, and townsfolk who couldn't get in the park climbed trees and telegraph poles to watch the game.

Ruth's slugging accomplishments are so great that his skill as a pitcher is sometimes overlooked. Red Sox manager Ed Barrow switched him permanently to the outfield in 1919 in order to take advantage of his batting in every game, but until that time he compiled a record as a pitcher which leads many to believe that if he had stayed with pitching he would have established himself as the best left-hander in American League history.

In 1915, his first full season on the mound, Ruth won 18 and lost 8. In 1916 he was 23-12, and led the league with a 1.75 ERA with nine shutouts. In 1917 he was 24-13, and in both 1916 and 1917 he allowed only about 6.5 hits per nine innings. At age 22, Ruth had recorded two 20-game years and a total of 67 major-league victories, a win total Lefty Grove didn't reach until he was 28. He was considered in some quarters the best pitcher in the league.

Ruth won six out of eight pitching contests with the great Walter Johnson in his brief career as a hurler, three by 1-0 scores. He never lost a World Series game. His record of 29 and two-thirds scoreless Series innings stood until it was broken by New York's Whitey Ford in 1961. After he was removed from the mound, Babe Ruth, quite likely the greatest all-around player in baseball history, continued to be an alert and aggressive base-runner and a skillful outfielder with surprising grace.

Waite Charles 'Schoolboy' Hoyt pitched for a number of teams during his 21-year career, turning in ten solid years for the Yankees from 1921 to 1930. During that time he pitched in five World Series, winning six games and losing three. He was elected to the Hall of Fame in 1969.

But it is of course for his hitting that he will always be best-remembered. The Big Guy's 54 home runs in 1920 were twice what anyone else had ever hit, and more than any other team except the Yankees. His personal magnetism and swaggering style made even his strikeouts memorable, but all statistics fall short of revealing how he dominated the era, how he out-distanced his contemporaries, and how much more incredible his exploits were in the context of his times than they seem now.

In 1921, probably his best all-around season, he broke the home run record for the third straight year with 59, totalled 204 hits, and achieved an .846 slugging percentage, a .378 batting average, 170 RBI's, 177 runs scored and 144 walks. In 1927, when he set a home run record that stood for 34 years, his 60 homers represented 13.7 percent of all the home runs hit in the American League that season, and again surpassed the individual totals of most major-league teams.

Throughout his long career the Babe hit a home run every 11.7 times at bat. He was the first to hit 30 home runs, the first to hit 40, the first to hit 50, and the first to hit 60. Before Ruth, the career home run record was 136. He surpassed this record in 1921, and his lifetime total of 714 was more than twice that of anyone else.

Ruth averaged 50 home runs a season for six years (1926-1931) and 47 homers a season for twelve years (1920-1931). The Sultan of Swat was one of those rare power hitters who also hit for average. His lifetime

Bottom: A contemporary cartoon illustrates the effect Babe Ruth's extraordinary hitting had on gate receipts.

During his six years as a left-handed hurler for the Boston Red Sox, Babe Ruth's diverse talents were evident in his won-lost record of 89-46 and his 23- and 24-win seasons, and his simultaneous batting average of .309.

Copyright by the Press Publishing Company (New York World), 1927

THE GREAT TURNSTILE WHIRLER
—Cassel in the New York World.

Above: Ty Cobb at bat in 1922. He hit .401 that year, scoring 99 runs and driving in 99 to account for about 23 percent of the Tigers' runs.

Right: After 12 years with the Boston Red Sox, Harry Hooper played right field for the Chicago White Sox from 1921 to 1925. Although he batted a blazing .325 in 1921, his team came in seventh.

average of .342 has been surpassed by only a handful of players. In eloquent testimony to his home-run-hitting threat, Ruth also holds the lifetime record for being walked.

As surely as his style revolutionized baseball and made it the foremost spectator sport of the twenties, Ruth also changed the way the game was paid. Perhaps no one sums up Ruth's influence on salaries better than Yankee pitching great Waite Hoyt: 'Wives of baseball players, when they teach their children their prayers, should instruct them to say: "God bless Mommy, God bless Daddy, God bless Babe Ruth! Babe has upped daddy's paycheck by 15 to 45 percent!"'

The Babe was receiving $10,000 a year from the Red Sox in 1919. This doubled when he came up to the Yankees in 1920, and tripled the next year. In 1922 he signed a five-year contract for $52,000 a year, an astounding and precedent-setting amount. In 1927-1929 he got $70,000, and in 1930 he hit $80,000. The story goes that in 1930 the Bambino was asking for more money than President Hoover was getting. Confronted with this statistic, Ruth replied, 'I had a better year than he did.' Baseball salaries, like the game, would never be the same again.

1920 also saw the flowering of American League slugging great George Sisler, ace first baseman for the St Louis Browns. Like Ruth, Sisler had begun his career in baseball as a left-handed pitcher, although with much less success. Sisler hit a league-leading .407 in 1920, the same year he achieved the still-standing major-league single-season record of 257 hits. Sisler also drove in 122 runs, scored 136 and stole 42 bases.

After slumping to .371 in 1921, Sisler reached his season peak with .420 in 1922. A persisting eye ailment prevented him from sustaining these heights – he missed the entire 1923 season – but he hit respectably after his return, compiling a classy .340 lifetime average. Sisler's 1922 mark left Ty Cobb, with .401, in second place. Although Cobb kept playing until 1928, hitting .323 in his last season, Babe and the home run hitters made his kind of strategic game a thing of the past.

Most of the outrageous slugging in the new hitters' game took place in the American League. Outstanding American League sluggers of the era also included Al Simmons of Philadelphia; Heinie Manush, who played for several teams and registered a .330 lifetime average; Hall of Famers Sam Rice and Goose Goslin of Washington; and Charley Gehringer, the 'Mechanical Man,' who had a .320 lifetime average while playing second base for Detroit with flawless mechanical efficiency.

Harry Heilmann of the Tigers, tutored by playing manager Ty Cobb, took the league honors with a .394 average in 1921. An otherwise undistinguished player, Heilmann took league batting titles in the first four odd years of the twenties – trading off with Sisler, Ruth and Manush – and never fell below .346 during those years. But it was Babe Ruth, in what remains the single greatest offensive season in major-league history, who really held the magic wand in 1921. That season he hit 16 triples and 44 doubles, had 170 RBI's, scored 177 runs and averaged .378. With a slugging percentage of .846, Ruth set a new home run record for the third year in a row with 59.

Faced with this slugging onslaught, pitchers' ERA's ballooned correspondingly. Detroit as a team hit the still-standing American League record average of .316 in 1921, topping four clubs that batted over .300. But despite the still-standing league record of 1724 hits churned out by Heilmann and the Tigers, Detroit, cursed with dismal pitching, finished the year in sixth place.

Propelled by Ruth's 59 homers and a league-leading team total of 134, the Yankees took the first of three consecutive pennants in 1921. While the team was blessed with great sluggers, the first three flags of the dawning New York dynasty owed much to the pitchers the Yanks harvested from the Boston Red Sox. In 1921, Carl Mays won 27 games for the Yankees, and young Waite Hoyt took 19.

In January 1921 the owners of both leagues signed a new National Agreement which bound players, umpires and owners to Commissioner Landis's decisions, and empowered him to levy fines of up to $5000. In baseball matters, the owners even waived their rights to seek justice in civil courts. In the eventuality that the commissioner should die before a successor had been chosen, the president of the United States was designated to appoint his successor. Landis immediately demonstrated that he was worthy of the authority vested in him by ordering the owner and the manager of the New York Giants to sell their gambling-related enterprises in Cuba or get out of baseball.

Yankee slugging at the plate enabled the Yankees to take the pennant again in 1922. The season saw a tight race between the Yankees and the St Louis

Below left: Hall of Famer Harry Edwin 'Slug' Heilmann takes a few swings. Harry Heilmann played right field and first base for the Detroit Tigers from 1914 to 1929, winning the batting title in 1921 with 237 hits, 139 RBI's and a .394 batting average.

Below: Right-hander Urban James Shocker loosens up before a game. Urban Shocker pitched for the St Louis Browns from 1918 to 1924, turning in four 20-game seasons during that time. In 1921 he won 27 games and lost only 12, striking out 132 batters.

Above: Bob Shawkey pitched for the Yankees from 1916 to 1927, compiling a won-lost record of 164-124. He pitched in four World Series for the Yankees, including the controversial game on 5 October 1922, which was called for darkness.

Right: The flags are flying and people are gathering outside Yankee Stadium on opening day – 18 April 1923.

Opposite top: Hall of Famer Herbert Jefferis Pennock moved from the Red Sox in 1923 and pitched for the Yankees for 11 years. He won all five of the Series games he pitched, and played his last year in 1934 back with Boston, ending his career with a won-lost record of 241-162.

Browns. Spearheaded by George Sisler's MVP year, in which he led the league with a .420 average and also set a league record by getting hits in 41 consecutive games, the Browns finished only one game behind New York. Once again the Yankees owed much to pitchers acquired from the Red Sox. Joe Bush won 26 games and Waite Hoyt won 19.

Babe Ruth, limited to 110 games because of repeated suspensions caused by protracted squabbles with umpires (he threw sand in one umpire's face) hit only 35 homers, and failed to take the home run title for the first time in five years, 1922's honors going to St Louis' Ken Williams. This was one of only two years in the 14-year span between 1918 and 1931 in which Babe Ruth did not win or tie the home run title. But his lesson was apparently learned, and he steered clear of serious quarrels with umpires for the rest of his career.

The Yankees were again frustrated in the Series, however, suffering their second straight defeat at the hands of the New York Giants. The 1922 loss was even more devastating than the previous year's, with the Yankees managing only one tie in five games. The great Babe Ruth hit .118 for the Series, collecting one single and one double in 17 times at bat. After the Series was over, half-owner Colonel T L Huston was so disgusted that he called for the dismissal of manager Huggins, a move which widened the rift between Huston and co-owner Jacob Ruppert, resulting in Huston selling out to Ruppert over the winter.

With the Yankee team and manager now receiving the undivided support of success-oriented Ruppert, the New York club skated to their third straight pennant in 1923, finishing a remarkable 16 games ahead of second-place Detroit. Former Red Sox pitchers Joe Bush and Herb Pennock won 19 games each, and Sox transplants Sam Jones and Waite Hoyt won 21 and 17 respectively. Seven of the 13 Yankee front-line players in 1923 were former Red Sox. Of the formidable New York pitching staff of Mays, Hoyt, Jones, Bush, Pennock and Shawkey – known to sportswriters as the 'Six-Star Final' – all were former Red Sox except Shawkey. Former Red Sox pitcher George Pipgras was now waiting in the Yankee wings.

Babe Ruth had a good year in 1923, hitting his best-ever average of .393, although league honors went to Detroit's Harry Heilmann, with .403. In a year in which nobody else even broke 100, Babe set the league record for bases on balls, with 170 walks. Most appropriately of all, he hit a game-winning home run on opening day at the Yankees' new Yankee Stadium.

New York was baseball's biggest market, and Yankee Stadium was the biggest, most modern park in baseball. Before the 65,000-plus seat landmark was opened in 1923, the Yankees had used the Polo Grounds as their home field, renting from the Giants. The new park, built largely from the proceeds of Ruth's success, was also largely built to order for Babe Ruth. Although 'Ruth Field' was ultimately rejected in favor of 'Yankee Stadium,' the right field bleachers in 'The House that Ruth Built' soon became

Below: Walter Johnson with Captain Edith Ivings of the Salvation Army. The great pitcher's gentle and unassuming nature is as legendary as his exploits on the mound.

Below right: Left fielder Charles Jamieson played for Cleveland from 1919 to 1932. In 1923 he smashed 222 hits, with a .345 batting average.

known as 'Ruthville.' As a left-handed batter, most of the Babe's hits went to right field, and Yankee management insured that there would be an ample number of Ruthian round trips by locating the right field bleachers only 296 feet from home plate, behind a fence only 43 inches high. Constructing ballparks to benefit hitters was not an uncommon practice in this era. The arrangement and seating capacity of Yankee Stadium insured that the American League in general and the Yankees in particular would gain an edge on attendance and profits for some time to come.

Babe Ruth redeemed himself for his Series showing of the previous year as his team chalked up their first world championship ever in 1923, defeating the Giants 4-2 in their third straight Series in as many years with that club. Babe's .368 Series average included three homers – two in a row in the second game – a triple, a double and three singles – as well as eight walks. Former Red Sox hurlers Pennock and Bush accounted for three victories, and Shawkey took the fourth. Bob Meusel set a Series record by driving in eight runs. Babe Ruth's slugging and the excitement of the home run game – each team hit five homers – continued to pay off at the box office, where all attendance and financial records were broken. The Yankee share of $6143.49 was not topped until 1935.

The Washington Senators took their first pennant in 1924, preventing the Yankees from winning four pennants in a row by a two-game margin. Their victory made them the third American League club to take their first pennant in the twenties, and left St Louis as the only club in the league yet to take a league championship.

The well-balanced and determined Washington team featured hurler Walter Johnson, now 36, again demonstrating why he was called the greatest pitcher in American League history by compiling a 23-7 record in his 18th year with the Senators. Johnson also led the league in strikeouts, shutouts and ERA's. Firpo Marberry broke all relief records with 15 saves. 'The Boy Wonder' – playing manager Stanley 'Bucky' Harris – 27, who with Peckinpaugh led the league in double plays, spurred his team on to victory with a spirit so tough even Ty Cobb thought twice about sliding into second base. Herold 'Muddy' Ruel, a Yankee castoff who reached the Senators via Boston, provided excellent catching.

For once, Johnson received solid support from his hitters. Goose Goslin hit .344 to lead the league in RBI's (the first Senator ever to do so), Sam Rice came back with .344 and Joe Judge hit .324. The Senators' victory was greeted with an emotional reaction that was extraordinary even for the twenties, including a cup and a special commendation from President Coolidge, in part because it enabled Walter Johnson to compete in a World Series for the first time in his magnificent career.

President and Mrs Coolidge attended three of the games played in Washington in what turned out to be

Left: Second baseman Bucky Harris played for the Washington Senators for ten years, ending his career with Detroit in 1931. In the 1924 World Series, he batted .333 and slammed two home runs to help the Tigers win the title. He was elected to the Hall of Fame in 1975.

Below: Hall of Famer Leon Allen 'Goose' Goslin spent most of his 18-year career with the Senators, but played for the St Louis Browns and the Tigers as well. His superb batting helped bring the Senators to four league pennants, beginning with their first ever in 1924, in which Goslin hit three home runs.

Johnson turned in a 20-7 season, his 12th and last 20-game year, but for once (only the second time in his 19 years with the club) he was aided by another 20-game winner. Spitballer Stanley Coveleski was 20-5 as he registered his fifth consecutive 20-win year in 1925, his first year with the Senators.

Both pitchers received solid support from their batters, but even after a 3-1 lead in the Series, the Senators dropped the championship to the Pirates. Johnson won the first and fourth games, holding the Pirates to one run in each of these contests, but gave up 15 hits in the final deciding game. Bucky Harris was severely criticised for not pulling Johnson from this game by league president Ban Johnson, who accused the Washington manager of losing the Series for the sake of 'maudlin sentiment.'

Primarily because Babe Ruth suffered from an intestinal abscess which required surgery – 'the stomach-ache that was heard round the world' – and didn't return to the lineup until June, the Yankees finished seventh in 1925. This was the second and only other time in 14 years that the Great Man did not win or tie the league home run championship. Teammate Bob Meusel led the league in 1925 with 33, leading also in RBI's with 138. The best Ruth could do was 25, with a .290 season average (statistics that would cause modern players to ask for a raise).

The Bambino, who returned to his dangerous high-living as soon as he was able and sooner than he should have, aggravating his health problems and jeopardizing the Yankees' bid for the pennant, faced a serious showdown with manager Huggins, who sus-

Above: During the ten years that outfielder Robert William 'Long Bob' Meusel played for the New York Yankees (1920-1929), he played in six World Series.

Right: Brothers Joe and Luke Sewell played shortstop and catcher for Cleveland during the twenties.

the most exciting World Series in years. The hard-fought contest between the Senators and the Giants was not settled until the 12th inning of the seventh game. Sir Walter lost the two games he started, but performed heroically in the seventh game. Called in from the bull pen to face the Giants in the ninth inning, Johnson held them at bay until a string of bad luck for the Giants enabled Muddy Ruel to score the winning run from second in the 12th inning.

Washington repeated easily in 1925, finishing eight and a half games ahead of the Athletics, a team Connie Mack was patiently rebuilding. Walter pended him indefinitely and fined him $5000 (a new record). Outraged – more at the suspension than the fine – Ruth vowed that either he or Huggins must go ('either he quits or I quit'), but owner Ruppert stood behind his manager, forcing Ruth to back down and clean up his act.

Ill-health and suspension combined, Ruth missed about one-third of the 1925 season, playing in 98 games. It is a remarkable testimony to his popularity that in 1925 Yankee attendance also fell by about one-third, from slightly over one million in 1924 to just under 700,000 in 1925. Estimates of losses to the club due to his illness ranged as high as $500,000.

In 1926 Babe Ruth came back strong, hitting 47 home runs and averaging .372, and the Yankees began their second string of three consecutive pennants. Washington finished fourth as the great Walter Johnson, now 38, proved he was mortal and slumped to 15-16 in his last full season. It was a tight race, the sixth-place Tigers finishing only 12 games behind the Yankees. Third, six games behind, were Mack's Athletics; and second, finishing three games behind the Yankees, were the Indians, whose right-hander George Uhle completed 32 of 36 starts for a 27-11 record. Indian shortstop Joe Sewell, the man who couldn't be struck out, had an off year in 1926 with six strikeouts, a figure double his 1925 total.

The Yankee resurgence in 1926 owed much to some serious team rebuilding. Aging veteran Whitey Witt was replaced by outstanding center fielder and leadoff batter Earle Combs, and shortstop Everett Scott ended his record 1307 consecutive games in

May, replaced by rookie Mark Koenig. Rookie Tony Lazzeri, who had never even seen a major-league game before he came up to the Yankees from the Pacific League to play second base in 1926, quickly became known as 'Push Em Up Tony' for his ability to hit with men on base, and in his rookie year registered an RBI total in the American League second only to Babe Ruth's. With Ruth, Meusel and Joe Dugan still in top form, the winning combination was completed by the addition of 23-year-old New Yorker Lou Gehrig.

In a story that has now become legend, Gehrig got his start as a Yankee regular on 2 June 1925 when

Hall of Famer Earle Bryan Combs – 'The Kentucky Colonel' – played center field for the Yankees from 1924 to 1935, ending his 12-year career with a .325 batting average and a .350 Series batting average.

When he retired due to an illness rare enough to be named after him, Gehrig's 493 home runs and 1991 RBI's were second only to Babe Ruth's career totals. Only Ruth and Hank Aaron have ever surpassed his RBI's; and only Ruth and Ted Williams have ever bettered his lifetime slugging percentage of .632. Gehrig's lifetime batting average of .340 places him among the very best hitters in baseball. If he had not been cut down in his prime at 34, some statistics might now be written differently.

Despite four homers by Ruth, including three in one game, and a .300 Series average, complemented by a .348 average from Gehrig in his first Series appearance, the Yankees lost the 1926 championship to the Cardinals in one of the most dramatic Series on record. Pitching for the Cards, National League great Grover Cleveland Alexander turned in a virtuoso performance, fanning Tony Lazzeri in a memorable seventh-inning, seventh-game cliffhanger to save the day for St Louis.

In 1927 the Yankees were so hot that there was no American League pennant race. Considered by many the greatest team ever, the 1927 Yankees never fell from first place, and ended the season a league-record 19 games ahead of the second-place Athletics. Their 110 wins and .714 percentage remained the best in league history until the amazing Cleveland victory of 1954. Their team total of 158 home runs was almost three times that of the next best, the Athletics' 56. Even Philadelphia's seven future Hall of Famers, with a .303 team batting average and 91 wins, were no match for New York's incredible machine.

Above: Playing in 2130 consecutive games, Yankee Lou Gehrig earned himself the nickname 'The Iron Horse.' More than any other player Gehrig embodied the spirit of baseball at its best. Although disease ended his career tragically in 1939, he was specially honored by being elected to the Hall of Fame that same year.
Right: Lou Gehrig congratulates Babe Ruth as he crosses the plate after hitting his 60th home run in 151 at bats, in 1927. During the 11 years Gehrig and Ruth played together, they averaged 78 home runs a year and boosted the Yankees to five World Series.

veteran first baseman Wally Pipp, who hit .295 and led the league in triples the year before, told manager Huggins he had a headache. Gehrig played as a substitute, and from that day on this great hitter compiled the unsurpassed record of playing in 2130 consecutive games, ending on 2 May 1939, when he benched himself. Two months later he learned he had a fatal illness. Pipp never got in the starting Yankee lineup again, and was soon traded to Cincinnati.

Known as the 'Iron Horse' for his strength, durability and consistency, the courteous Gehrig, whose mother, until he married, sometimes accompanied him on road trips, and who had left engineering studies at Columbia to join the Yankees, was far removed in personality from the flamboyant Babe Ruth, in whose shadow he played for most of his career, but his record needs no apology. In the 11 years 1927-1937, his home run totals were 47, 27, 35, 41, 46, 34, 32, 49, 30, 49 and 37. Gehrig five times led the league in RBI's, twice in homers and hit as many as 52 doubles and 18 triples a season.

Left: Second baseman 'Poosh 'Em Up' Tony Lazzeri played for the Yankees from 1926 to 1937, earning his nickname by averaging 96 RBI's a year during that time. He ended his career with the National League, with a .292 batting average.

Each member of this superb New York team turned in one of his finest individual seasons. Ruth hit 60 home runs, four more than any other team in the league except the Yankees, drove in 164 runs, and batted .356. Lou Gehrig, 1927's MVP, led the league with 175 RBI's, and scored 149 runs for a .373 average. His 218 hits included 52 doubles, 18 triples and 47 homers.

Until late in the season, Yankee fans were gratified to watch an intramural home run contest between Ruth and Gehrig, who together accounted for almost 25 percent of the American League home runs hit that year. As late as mid-August, Gehrig was leading Ruth 38-36. The Yankees' Earle Combs batted .356 and got 231 hits. Lazzeri and Meusel joined Ruth and Gehrig in driving in over 100 runs each – 102 and 103 – and registered averages of .309 and .337 respectively. Gehrig hit behind Ruth in the lineup, the most devastating one-two punch in history, and was followed by Meusel and Lazzeri. This terrorizing Yankee lineup became known to pitchers throughout the league as 'Murderers' Row.'

The Yankee team of 1927 batted a combined average of .307. Ruth, Gehrig and Lazzeri were the top three American Leaguers in home runs; Ruth and Gehrig led the league in slugging; Gehrig, Ruth and Combs led in total bases; Gehrig and Ruth were first and second in RBI's; Combs and Gehrig were the top two in hits; Ruth, Gehrig and Combs were the top three in runs scored; Gehrig led in doubles; and Combs and Gehrig were the top two in triples.

The Yankees failed to secure only two offensive categories in 1927. George Sisler led the league with 27 stolen bases, and Harry Heilmann took the batting championship in an exciting duel with Al Simmons

that was not resolved until the final day of the season. Going six for eight in a doubleheader against the Indians, Heilmann finally passed Simmons and ended the season with a .398 average, only one hit short of .400.

The Yankee sluggers were supported by one of the strongest pitching staffs of the era. Waite Hoyt went 22-7, Herb Pennock 19-8, spitballer Urban Shocker 18-6, Dutch Ruether 13-6, and George Pipgras 10-3. Sinkerball artist rookie Wilcy Moore turned in a sensational never-repeated year as the league's leading relief pitcher, 19-7, and led the league with an ERA of 2.28. Only the Yankees' catching, which was average, was less than outstanding in 1927.

The Bronx Bombers crowned their pennant success by flattening the Pirates four straight in the

World Series, the first time an American League club had taken the Series without a loss. The story goes that before the first game, the Pirates came out as the Yankees were taking batting practice, and were so awed by watching Ruth, Gehrig, Meusel and Lazzeri knock successive balls into the bleachers that they never recovered.

The Yankees repeated in 1928 but not without a struggle. Despite another outstanding season from both Ruth and Gehrig, the Yankees' early July lead of 13 and a half games slowly dissipated as Lazzeri, Dugan, Meusel and Koenig suffered injuries and missed games. Strong seasons from Hoyt and Pipgras, who won 23 and 24, saved the day, but Pennock, with 17 wins, developed arm trouble late in the season and never again performed as well as he had.

On 8 September Connie Mack's rebuilt Athletics pulled into first place with a half-game lead. But on 9 September, before a record crowd of 85,264 fans at Yankee Stadium, the Yankees proved they were still champions by taking both games of a doubleheader from the Athletics, 3-0 and 7-3. After taking another game from Philadelphia the next day, they stayed on top for the rest of the season, clinching the pennant two days before the season ended. The Red Sox finished last again.

Ty Cobb and Tris Speaker closed their active careers at the end of the 1928 season. Another era of sorts had ended the year before when American

League President Ban Johnson resigned after losing his long power struggle with Commissioner Landis, and all-time great pitcher Walter Johnson quit the game with a lifetime total of 416 wins.

Cobb and Speaker and the third member of their famous batting trio, Eddie Collins, now relegated to pinch-hitting, were all playing for Connie Mack in 1928. Once again the Athletics lost to the Yankees despite seven future Hall of Famers, but this year they narrowed the Yankees' lead from 19 to two and a half games. If age had not caught up with Cobb in the final weeks of the season and if Mack had figured out exactly where to put twenty-year-old slugger Jimmie Foxx in the lineup, the story might have been different.

The Yankees vanquished the Cardinals 4-0 in the 1928 Series. Following their sweep of the Pirates the year before, this gave the club the new record of eight consecutive victories in two consecutive Series. But the real story of the Series was the still unequalled hitting of Ruth and Gehrig, who dominated the championship as no two men ever have. In an incredible display of slugging, Ruth hit .625, still the highest batting average in World Series history, launched three homers in one Series game, drove in four runs, and scored nine. Gehrig hit .545, banged out four homers, drove in nine runs and scored five.

In 1929 the team that had made the amazing Yankees sweat in 1928 was unstoppable. Connie

Ty Cobb and baseball commissioner Judge Landis. Cobb retired in 1928 with a still-unsurpassed career batting average of .367. His record of 4191 hits remained unbroken until 1985, when it was bested by Pete Rose. Ty Cobb was elected to the Hall of Fame in 1936.

Mack's Athletics took their first pennant in 15 years, beating out the second-place Yankees by a comfortable 18-game margin. The Yankees could muster only one league leader in 1929, Babe Ruth, who took the honors in homers and slugging. To complete the sad picture, New York manager Miller Huggins fell ill and died in September.

The team painstakingly assembled by Mack and the Shibes was the last dynasty formed exclusively from players purchased from minor-league clubs. Branch Rickey's farm system, which had done so well for the Cardinals, was well on its way to becoming accepted practice in the big leagues. The players Mack purchased from the minors finished second in 1925, third in 1926, second in 1927 and second in 1928 before all the pieces fell into place, and the Athletics took three pennants in a row.

Robert Moses 'Lefty' Grove and George Earnshaw, the mainstays of the Athletic pitching staff, both came from Jack Dunn's Baltimore club. Grove, possibly the best left-hander in history, threw a ball so fast it looked 'like a piece of white thread coming to the plate.' He came to Philadelphia in 1925 and quickly proved he was worth his $100,600 purchase price (Dunn wanted more than the $100,000 he'd received for Ruth) by leading the league in strikeouts for seven straight years, beginning in 1926.

In the Athletics' 1929-1931 championship seasons, Grove won a total of 83 games and lost only 15. When

Hall of Famer Lefty Grove pitched for Philadelphia from 1925 to 1933. 20-, 28- and 31-game seasons in 1929, 1930 and 1931 helped bring the A's to the Series all three years.

At 6' 11" and 210 pounds, righthander George 'Moose' Earnshaw was an imposing pitcher. During the six years he pitched for the A's, he had three 20-game seasons, winning 98 games and losing 58.

he did lose, which was rare, he was famous for smashing up the locker room and throwing anything that wasn't tied down. The 300-game-winning Hall of Famer was what was called a 'great competitor,' meaning he was mean. Grove had no compunction about throwing at opposing batters, including Babe Ruth, and even at his own teammates in batting practice. He did say that he never aimed for the head, and he never shaved Lou Gehrig, asserting 'It was best not to wake him up.'

George Earnshaw did not have the staying power of Grove, but at his peak he was right behind him, winning 67 and losing only 28 games in the A's three consecutive pennant years. Big left-hander Rube Walberg, another purchase from Dunn, also won

Catcher Mickey Cochrane leaps for a tag in a close play. An essential component on one of Connie Mack's most laudable teams, 'Black Mike' played for the A's from 1925 to 1933, then for Detroit from 1934 to 1937. He was elected to the Hall of Fame in 1947.

many games. Max Bishop, regular second baseman during Mack's winning years, came from Dunn's Baltimore club, as did regular shortstop Joe Boley, who gave up his position in 1931 to the younger Dib Williams.

Catching for Grove in his heyday was Gordon 'Mickey' Cochrane. A Hall of Famer considered by many the best catcher of all time, Cochrane still holds the all-time highest lifetime average for a big-league catcher, at .320. Fast enough to bat third and occasionally first on a team with exceptionally good hitters, during the A's pennant-winning years Cochrane hit .331, .357 and .349, three of his nine .300-plus seasons. Even when he didn't hit outstandingly, as in his MVP year of 1928 when he hit .293, Cochrane's natural leadership inspired the team. His fire and dash – and occasional rage – were in every way on a par with Grove's.

Following Cochrane in the batting order were outfielder Al Simmons and first baseman Jimmie Foxx, a lineup almost as lethal as the Yankees' Murderers' Row. Foxx, a natural athlete with a temperament and outlook on life much like Ruth's, was perhaps the strongest man ever to play the game, crushing the balls he connected with out of shape. Known as 'The Beast,' his professional career began at age 16, and he was only 21 in 1929 when he finally became the

regular on first base and turned in his first great season. That year Foxx hit .354, drove in 118 runs and launched 33 homers, the first of 12 consecutive seasons in which he hit at least 30 homers, a record unequalled even by Ruth. Only twice in those 12 years did his average fall below .300. In 1932 Foxx came close to breaking Ruth's 60-homer record, hitting 58; and in 1938, he hit 50, leading the league with 175 RBI's, a .349 batting average and a .704 slugging percentage. Foxx twice led the league in batting, and was three times elected Most Valuable Player. When he retired in 1945, one of the very few to hit over 500 homers, his 534 lifetime record was second only to Ruth's 714.

Testy Al Simmons, for whom Mack traded several players and $40,000 in 1924, paid out handsomely as a superb left fielder and one of the best right-handed hitters in baseball history. In his prime during his eight years with the A's from 1925 to 1932, Simmons four times topped .380, averaging .364, and drove in over 100 runs each year. He drove in over 100 runs in each of his first 11 years (as many as 165 per season), amassing a reputation as a great run-producer, and hit over 30 homers three times in the four years from 1929 to 1932. Simmons did all this with a batting style that was technically all wrong, breaking a cardinal rule of batting by stepping away from the pitch while playing in a park that was notoriously friendly to hitters.

Mack got off to a surprising start in the Series by using Howard Ehmke, instead of one of his regulars, to open against the Cubs. Ehmke kept the Cubs off-balance with his slowballs, winning 3-1 and setting a record of 13 Series strikeouts – a record that stood until Carl Erskine broke it in 1953. In the fourth game, Al Simmons banged out a homer to open a record-breaking Series inning in which the A's scored ten runs. Mule Haas, one of 15 A's who came to bat that inning, hit an inside-the-park three-run homer.

Two days later, with President Hoover in attendance, Haas hit another homer, and Bing Miller drove in the winning run with a double to clinch the Series. With Jimmy Dykes hitting .421 for the Series, Cochrane hitting .400, Miller hitting .368, and Foxx hitting .350 and slugging two homers, Mack crowned his first pennant of the decade with a 4-1 Series win, and showed that his boys had the stuff to move into the next decade with continuing dominance.

Right-hander Howard Ehmke pitched for the Athletics from 1927 to 1930. Ehmke struck out 13 batters in the first game of the 1929 World Series, which the A's won 3-1. Philadelphia went on to defeat the Cubs four games to one.

Aloysius Harry 'Bucketfoot Al' Simmons played left field for the Philadelphia Athletics from 1924 to 1932, winning the league batting title twice during those years and averaging .357. In the three Series he played for the A's, he smashed six homers, five doubles and 12 singles. Simmons was elected to the Hall of Fame in 1953.

instead of into it, supposedly robbing himself of power by 'putting his foot in the bucket.' His long bat and unorthodox style helped him to two league batting championships, the Hall of Fame, and a respectable .334 lifetime average.

Outfielders Bing Miller and Mule Haas also hit .300 for Mack's winning teams. Jimmy Dykes, a good fielder and solid hitter who had been with the club since 1918, held down first base, and the Athletics were well-supplied with reserves. All in all, the A's combination of Grove, Cochrane, Foxx and Simmons compares favorably with Yankee Hall of Famers Hoyt, Pennock, Ruth, Gehrig and Combs.

Beside the awesome ascendancy of the A's, what finally derailed the Yankee train in 1929 was the collapse of their pitching staff. Ruth was still hitting home runs and Gehrig was swinging into his prime, but Pennock was permanently weakened by his sore arm, Wilcy Moore never repeated his outstanding 1927 season and Hoyt just lost it. Other things being almost equal, Grove's 20 wins and Earnshaw's 24 did the trick. Finishing in second place, 18 games behind the A's, the Yankees, who introduced the use of numbers on players' uniforms in 1929, a helpful device soon adopted by all clubs, were still better off than the Boston Red Sox, who finished last again and scored fewer runs than any other club that season

Lou Gehrig, batboy John McBride and Babe Ruth at the 1933 All-Star game.

CHAPTER THREE
Heroes of
the Depression

"To be considered great,
a team must repeat."

Connie Mack

Repeat is what Mack's men did in 1930, and again in 1931. The Athletics who finished eight games ahead of the Senators in 1930 were the same team that left the Yankees 18 games behind in 1929, with Jimmy Dykes now playing third base on a regular basis. Al Simmons led the league with a .381 average, and he and teammate Jimmie Foxx together drove in 321 runs for Philadelphia – six runs less than the Gehrig-Ruth total – as they pushed their team to 102 victories in this hit-happy season.

In 1930 the owners, in response to the fans' enthusiastic reception to the hitting game, pumped more life into the ball than ever before. The American League batted .288 overall, with teams averaging better than five runs per game each – only the Red Sox failed to average over four runs per game. Three players registered slugging percentages over .700. Over in the National League, six clubs posted team batting averages of over .300. (By comparison, in 1968 only six players in the National League hit .300 or better.)

In the midst of this hitting carnage, the A's Lefty Grove won 28 games, lost five, and struck out 209 batters, posting a league-leading ERA of 2.54. Grove's ERA, remarkable for 1930, led Cleveland's Wes Ferrell, who posted a 3.31 ERA and won 25 games on his way to setting a record by winning over 20 games in each of his first four years in the majors, beginning in 1929. Ferrell, who with Detroit's 'Mechanical Man' Charlie Gehringer and Washington's shortstop Joe Cronin, turned in an outstanding performance in 1930, would take two more 20-game seasons, both with the Red Sox.

Right-hander Wesley Cheek Ferrell pitched for the Cleveland Indians for seven seasons (1927-33), then for the Boston Red Sox, Washington Senators, New York Yankees, Brooklyn Dodgers and Boston Braves, ending his career in 1941. The tall Southerner pitched six 20-game seasons during his 15-year career.

Babe Ruth, with 49 round trippers, was still the league's home run king in 1930. Hitting .359, his 153 RBI's were fourth-ranked in the league, following Philadelphia's Al Simmons (165) and Jimmie Foxx (156). Yankee teammate Lou Gehrig led the pack with 174 RBI's and hit .379. Combs hit .344, and catcher Bill Dickey, proving himself to be in the same league as catching great Mickey Cochrane, hit .339 in his second season with the Bombers. Once again it was the failure of New York's pitching staff that kept the hard-slugging Yankee club out of the race.

The Athletics followed up their 1929 Series victory by taking the 1930 Series from the Cardinals, 4-2, after dropping the first two games. This was the third time an American League club took four games in a row from their National League opponents. For Connie Mack, the win was his fifth world title, a record for a manager up to that date, but it was also to be his last. Despite an outstanding team that would repeat again in 1931, no one could have chosen a worse time to establish a dynasty. With the Wall Street failure cutting incomes everywhere, Mack found himself squeezed between the high salaries of his stars and a steadily declining attendance.

As the Depression deepened, attendance declined with the nation's financial health. Total baseball receipts of $17 million in 1929 slid to a low of $10.8 million in 1933, then climbed slowly to $21.5 million in 1939, followed by a wartime slump, then a new height of $68.1 million in 1948. During the hard years, baseball provided the public with a chance to at least temporarily forget the harsh realities of its economic winter and supplied superstars to fire the imagination. But this must have been small consolation for Connie Mack, who watched his team's attendance fall from 830,000 in 1929 to only 300,000 in 1933, the third straight year of serious decline. Mack also lost heavily in the market crash of 1929. Desperate for cash, he once again began dismantling his team and selling his stars.

In 1931, however, the Athletics were still intact. Spearheaded by an incredible MVP year from pitcher Lefty Grove, the club gave Mack his ninth and last pennant, placing him in position to become the first manager to win three straight World Series. The A's 107 victories were the highest win total of Mack's career, and their 1931 percentage of .704 was the second best in American League history. Al Simmons, chief accomplice to the A's star pitcher, led the league for the second straight year with a batting average of .390.

Lefty Grove won 31 games and lost only four. Not since Smokey Joe Wood's 34-5 season in 1912 and Walter Johnson's 36-7 record in the following year had an American League pitcher so outdistanced and outclassed all the competition. Grove's 16-game winning streak that season in fact tied the league record set by Wood and Johnson. Only one other pitcher in the league, New York's Lefty Gomez, with 2.63, posted an ERA under 3.00 in 1931. Grove's ERA was 2.05. He also led the league in wins, percentage (.886), complete games (27) and strikeouts.

The scores of the four games he didn't win were 7-5, 4-3, 2-1 and 1-0. His attempt at 17 straight victories was crushed when outfielder Jim Moore misjudged a fly ball. In a classic display of the Grove rage, the great competitor commemorated the occasion by ripping up his uniform and tearing steel lockers off the wall.

The Athletics of 1931 featured winning streaks of 17 straight in May and 13 in July. The Yankees, in their first season under manager Joe McCarthy, saw continued outstanding slugging from Ruth and Gehrig, who tied for league home run honors with 46 each. Gehrig set the all-time American League RBI record with 184. Teammate Lefty Gomez's 21 wins and 2.63 ERA helped keep the Yanks in second place, but with Red Ruffing having trouble adjusting in his first year after arriving from Boston, New York still fell short of the pitching it needed.

Despite some solid hitting from Al Simmons and Jimmie Foxx in the World Series, the Athletics dropped the championship to the Cardinals in a thrilling

Below: In the 17 years he played catcher for the New York Yankees (1928-46), Hall of Famer Bill Dickey played in eight World Series.

Above: Charlie Gehringer played for the Detroit Tigers for his entire 19-year career (1924-42). His outstanding defensive talent at second base was complemented by his superb batting. Gehringer won the league batting title in 1937 with a .371 average, and finished his career with a batting average of .320.

Above: Johnny Allen pitched for the New York Yankees from 1932 to 1935, then for Cleveland for five years. He finished up his career in the National League.

Opposite: Third baseman and sometime-shortstop Cecil Howell Travis joined the Washington Senators in 1933 and played his entire 12-year career with that team, finishing up in 1947 with a .314 batting average.

seven-game contest. In addition to the defeat of Mack's powerhouse team, 1931 was also marked, sadly, by the sudden deaths of American League president Ernest S Barnard and former president Ban Johnson. After 20 years of service as league secretary, Will Harridge became the new league president.

After the 1930 season, even the owners realized that their formula for success had been mixed a little too rich, and over the winter they squeezed some of the juice out of the ball. Not surprisingly, in 1931 team, league and individual batting averages declined dramatically. With the Great Depression tightening its grip on the land, contraction was felt everywhere. By 1933 American League attendance was off at least one and a half million from 1929, only 60 percent of what it had been in the heyday of the twenties. Forced

to sell his stars to survive, Connie Mack began by shipping Al Simmons, Mule Haas and Jimmy Dykes to the White Sox for $150,000. By the 1936 season, practically all of his big names were gone except Jimmie Foxx, and Foxx soon went to the Red Sox, where he had some of the best years of his career.

The demise of the Athletics brought about a change in the balance of power in the American League. 1932 saw the Yankees back on top, ending the Athletics' three-year reign, just as the Athletics had ended the Yankees' three-in-a-row in 1929. Continuing the theme of reversal, the 1932 Bombers posted 107 wins – the same as Mack's boys in 1931 – and led the A's by 13 games, half a game less than the second-place A's had bested the Yanks in the preceding year.

The team Joe McCarthy steered to the championship in his second year of managing the Yankees was built largely of regulars from the Huggins regime, fortified with the pitching that had been lacking the three years previous. Babe Ruth, now 37, managed 41 home runs and a .341 average; Lou Gehrig continued to blast away with consistent excellence; and Combs, Lazzeri, Pennock, Pipgras and the more newly arrived Bill Dickey continued to turn in solid performances. But it was McCarthy's careful handling of the pitching that made all the difference. Vernon 'Lefty' Gomez compiled a 24-7 year, Red Ruffing went 18-7 and rookie Johnny Allen pitched 17-4.

Jimmie Foxx established himself as the league slugging king, hitting 58 home runs, and also led the league in runs (151) and RBI's (169). In 1932, the first of his three MVP years, he got 213 hits and averaged .364, just three points shy of league-leading Dale Alexander, (whom the Red Sox acquired from Detroit in mid-season). Philadelphia's Lefty Grove, who was 79-14 for the previous three years, actually lost 10 games in 1932, winning 25, and posting a league-leading ERA of 2.84.

The Yankees demolished the Cubs in the Series four games straight, the third straight Series sweep for the New York club. For Yankee manager McCarthy, who had been dropped by the Chicago club in the last week of the 1930 season for failing to bring owner Philip Wrigley a world championship, the victory must have been particularly sweet. The Yankees, hitting .313 as a team, averaged nine runs per game in their devastation of the Cubs.

Lou Gehrig turned in the greatest individual Series performance ever in 1932, hitting .549 for the championship games, his nine hits (he struck out once and walked twice) including three home runs and a double. He scored nine runs and drove in eight. New York's Lazzeri launched two homers too, but as usual it was Babe Ruth, hitting two homers in his tenth and last Series appearance, for a lifetime total of 15 Series homers, who really stole the show.

In the fifth inning of the third game, Ruth pointed to the most distant part of Wrigley Field, and after two strikes launched a homer into the center field bleacher at which he had apparently pointed. Manager McCarthy later insisted Ruth had merely pointed to the Cubs' dugout to silence hecklers, and the truth about the Babe's famous 'called shot' may never be known.

Although McCarthy's Yankees finished second the next three years, New York's purchase of the Newark team in the International League set the stage for a second era of Yankee domination. Placed under the gifted administration of George M Weiss, the Yankees' new farm system was to generate excellent Yankee replacements for years to come.

Batting .287 as a team, the Washington Senators surprised everyone in 1933 by finishing seven games ahead of a Yankee club torn by dissension, and 19 and a half games ahead of an Athletic club which was disappearing on the auction block. In New York, Babe Ruth, in his last season as a .300 hitter and seeking management of the Yankees, led a clique which refused to speak to McCarthy or to any player who did. Meanwhile, youthful Washington playing manager Joe Cronin spirited his club to a victory reminiscent of the Senators' 1924-1925 victories under 'boy wonder' Bucky Harris.

Pitching for the 27-year-old Cronin, a gifted leader who would one day become president of the American League, was Alvin 'General' Crowder, with 24 wins, and Earl Whitehill, with 22, backed up by the

Above: Right-hander Lynwood Thomas 'Schoolboy' Rowe pitched for the Detroit Tigers for nine years, moving to the National League in 1942. He helped the Tigers to three league championships, turning in season wins of 24, 19 and 16 during those years.

Right: Catcher Luke Sewell played for Cleveland from 1921 to 1932, for Washington for two years, for the Chicago White Sox from 1935 to 1938, for Cleveland again in 1939, and ended his playing career in 1942 with the St Louis Browns. As manager of the Browns from 1941 to 1946 he won one league championship, then managed four more years for the Cincinnati National League team.

best infield Washington had ever seen. Joe Kuhel covered first, Buddy Myer second, Cronin was at short, and Ossie Bleuge covered third with a dazzling display of defensive efficiency. Luke Sewell was solid behind the plate.

Cronin, batting .309 and driving in 118 runs, showed the way to the hard-hitting outfield of Heinie Manush, Goose Goslin and Fred Schulte. The Washington whackers launched few spectacular homers, but hit with a regularity and consistency sufficient to compile the league-leading team average.

Jimmie Foxx took another triple crown in 1933 and repeated as the league's Most Valuable Player, hitting 48 home runs, batting in 163 runs and scoring 125 runs. His batting average was .356. Teammate Lefty Grove, in his last year with the A's, led the league in wins for the last time with a 24-8 season, and former teammate Al Simmons, now with the White Sox, became the last American Leaguer to record 200 hits five years in a row in what was his last 200-hit season. The Philadelphia Athletics had already won their last flag. Despite the presence of President Franklin Delano Roosevelt at the third game of the World Series to throw out the first ball, the Senators, who would never win another pennant, dropped the world championship to the New York Giants, four games to one.

In 1934 the Detroit Tigers took their first pennant in

25 years, a win that marked the first time a club outside the eastern division had taken an American League championship since Cleveland in 1920. The key to the Tigers' success was the purchase of catcher Mickey Cochrane from cash-hungry Connie Mack in 1933. As playing manager, Cochrane justified his $100,000 price tag by solving Detroit's pitching problems, turning Lynwood 'Schoolboy' Rowe and Tommy Bridges into certified stars. Rowe took 24 games in 1934, including a 16-game winning streak in midsummer that tied him for the league record with Johnson, Wood and Grove. Bridges, featuring the league's best curve ball, added 22 wins to the Tigers' tally.

Cochrane's hurlers were backed up by the flawless Charlie Gehringer at second, Billy Rogell at short, Marv Owen at third and the hard-hitting outfield of Goose Goslin, Pete Fox, Jo-Jo White and Gerald 'Gee' Walker. Veterans Gehringer and Goslin churned out base hits, but the batting of a young first baseman named Hank Greenberg proved instrumental in compiling the team's .300 average.

Big (6′ 3½″ tall and weighing 210 pounds), awkward, slow and never more than adequate at his defensive position, Hank Greenberg nevertheless realized his boyhood ambition and became one of baseball's all-time great sluggers. Rising above his physical limitations through unremitting hard work, Greenberg as a youth practiced batting until his hands bled, and in the majors once stayed after a night game for more batting practice.

His first season in the big leagues was relatively undistinguished, although he hit .300 or better for each of the first seven seasons of a career interrupted by four and a half years of military service. In 1934, his second year with Detroit, he began to show his stuff, knocking out 26 homers and 63 doubles, only four below the major-league record. The RBI totals for which he was known also began to swell. In 1935, he led the league with 170 RBI's, tied Foxx for home runs with 36, and averaged .328. Playing with Detroit from 1933 to 1946 (he ended his career with Pittsburgh in 1947), Greenberg four times led the league in home runs, socking 58 in 1938, and ended his career with 331, then fifth on the all-time list, and a .313 average. After playing in only 12 games in 1936 because of a broken wrist, Hank turned in his best year in 1937. His 200 hits that season included 40 homers, 14 triples, 49 doubles, 137 runs scored, 183 RBI's – one less than Gehrig's league record – and a .337 average.

The Yankees, who finished seven games behind the Tigers in 1934, featured a triple crown year from Gehrig (49 homers, 165 RBI's, a .363 average), and a fizzle-out from Babe Ruth. For anyone else, 22

Tiger first baseman 'Hammerin' Hank' Greenberg smashes a liner through the gap. During the 12 years he played for Detroit, Henry Benjamin Greenberg helped bring his team to four league championships and two Series victories. Apart from his batting achievements during the season, he turned in a career post-season batting average of .318, with a .624 slugging percentage.

The sparkling shortstop Joe Cronin played the last 11 years of his 20-year career with the Boston Red Sox, and managed the team from 1935 to 1947. He was elected to the Hall of Fame in 1956.

Opposite: Joe DiMaggio touches the plate after blasting a homer out of the park. The legendary 'Joltin' Joe' DiMaggio hit in 56 consecutive games, was named the league's Most Valuable Player three times, clinched the batting title twice and led the league in home runs twice. The Yankee Clipper boosted his team to nine World Series victories. He ended his career with a .325 batting average, and was elected to the Hall of Fame in 1955.

A gifted comedian who attributed his success to 'clean living and a fast outfield,' Gomez was troubled by a sore arm throughout his career, but pitched with excellence when his ailment left him alone. After retirement he did well on the banquet circuit with a great stock of baseball stories, and teammates recall he used to speak of inventing a revolving goldfish bowl to save fish the bother of doing all the work.

919,000 enthusiastic spectators jammed Detroit's Navin Field in 1934, setting baseball's season attendance mark (and tripling the Tigers' 1933 total), but Detroit was unable to follow through in the Series, losing to the Cardinals, 4-3. In the final game, which Detroit dropped 11-0, Commissioner Landis was forced to remove Cardinal Joe Medwick from action after an incredible display of vegetable-throwing by loyal Tiger fans who disapproved of Medwick's aggressive slide into third baseman Marv Owen.

Detroit repeated with the same team in 1935. Over one million loyal fans filled Navin Field, a display of support unmatched by any other club in the dark decade. In a close struggle with the Yankees, Detroit's pitching staff paved the way. Bridges was 21-10, Rowe 19-13, Eldon Auker 18-7 and General Crowder 16-10. Hank Greenberg's league-tying 36 homers and league-leading 170 RBI's helped push his team to a .290 overall average. Charlie Gehringer, who rattled pitchers by not swinging until he had two strikes, struck out only 16 times in 610 at bats, hit .330 and drove in 108 runs. Manager Cochrane and outfielder Pete Fox both had .300 seasons. Despite owner Yawkey's outlay of $250,000 for manager-shortstop Joe Cronin and 45 wins from Wes Ferrell and Lefty Grove, the Red Sox finished fourth.

Detroit faced the Chicago Cubs in the 1935 World Series. Both clubs had lost their last four Series matches and were determined to win, but even with the loss of Hank Greenberg due to a broken wrist in the second game, Detroit was victorious this time, 4-2, setting off a celebration in Motor City that did not end until the following morning.

Even without Ruth, the Yankees had finished only three games behind Detroit in 1935. In 1936, with Greenberg's wrist keeping him out for the season, Schoolboy Rowe experiencing a sore arm, and manager Cochrane suffering a nervous breakdown, the Tigers fell 19 and a half games behind New York, and the Yankees took the first of four consecutive pennants. In this string, they would finish 19 and a half, 13, nine and a half, and 17 games ahead of their runners-up. New York manager Joe McCarthy, a perfectionist who had rankled under his three second-place finishes since 1932, put together a team in 1936 that had six men batting over .300 and five men achieving over 100 RBI's, and was propelled by the first of four consecutive 20-win seasons from hurler Red Ruffing. In the next eight seasons, the Yankees would take seven pennants and four consecutive World Series. To the solid Yankee lineup of Lou Gehrig, Tony Lazzeri, Frank Crosetti and Red Rolfe in the infield, with catching great Bill Dickey behind the plate, and George Selkirk and Ben Chapman in the outfield, McCarthy in 1936 added the final ingredient to one of the greatest clubs of all times, a young outfielder named Joe DiMaggio.

In his rookie year, 1936, on a team that averaged seven runs per game and clinched the pennant on 9 September, the earliest date in American League history, Joseph Paul DiMaggio, son of a fisherman, got 206 hits, including 44 doubles, 15 triples and 29 home runs. He scored 132 runs and had 124 RBI's. His batting average was .323, and his virtuoso performance

homers, 84 RBI's and a .288 average would have been nothing to sneer at, but for the Babe these numbers spelled the end of the line. After the season, the Yankees let him go, and he ended his career with the National League's Boston Braves in June 1935, after three more homers. Across town, in tribute to the expense and energy lavished upon the club by new owner millionaire Tom Yawkey, the Red Sox, Babe's first major-league team, finished in the first division in 1934 for the first time since 1918.

But the real news in the Yankee camp in 1934 was the performance of four-time 20-game winner Lefty Gomez, who led the league with a 26-5 season and a 2.33 ERA, and also led in winning percentage, complete games, innings pitched, strikeouts and shutouts.

style and grace, which still captivate spectators on Old-Timer Days, created a following and a mystique second only to that of Babe Ruth, who must remain the most idolized ballplayer of all time. But DiMaggio, whose chemistry with the crowd contained nothing of the salt-of-the-earth appeal of Babe Ruth, must rank as a close second to the Bambino, and he was the object of such hero worship as only a handful of sports stars is ever likely to receive.

Above: Luke Appling, the quiet and efficient shortstop for the Chicago White Sox, played for them his entire 20-year career, during which time he clinched the batting title twice. For a shortstop, his 2218 games and 1424 double plays are second only to Luis Aparicio's record. He ended with a .310 batting average and was elected to the Hall of Fame in 1964.

Right: Speedster and center fielder Ben Chapman played for the Yankees from 1930 to 1936, when he moved to the Senators, then played for several different teams.

in left field, which he played most of the season, revealed a throwing arm that enabled him to lead all American League outfielders in assists, an unusual accomplishment from this position. The next year he improved, hitting .346, driving in 167 runs, scoring 151 times and launching 46 home runs.

In 1933 DiMaggio had been the most desired minor-league player in the country. His San Francisco Seals club decided to hold onto him for another year, figuring his price could only rise, but DiMaggio suffered a knee injury which scared off most would-be purchasers. Yankee scout Bill Essick convinced the Yankees to gamble $25,000 to acquire the 21-year-old player, and in 1935 DiMaggio proved he was not quite damaged goods by batting .398 and collecting 270 hits in 172 Pacific Coast League games.

McCarthy and DiMaggio, who eventually joined Ruffing, Gomez, Gehrig and Dickey in the Hall of Fame, together revamped the Yankee image from one of Ruthian brute strength to one of cool, efficient dominance. McCarthy not only expected his Yankees to win, he expected them to be dignified as well, and got rid of Ben Chapman, a southerner who played outfield with DiMaggio, because he was too emotional.

DiMaggio didn't need to be told to be cool. No one has ever been able to determine whether DiMaggio's enigmatic off-the-field behavior was attributable to snobbishness or insecurity, but his performance on the field renders such considerations inconsequential. His seemingly effortless mastery of the game, his

It is appropriate that the Yankees' precedent-setting four consecutive pennants and four consecutive world championships should begin with the arrival of DiMaggio, but in 1936 he had a lot of help. Most Valuable Player Lou Gehrig led the league with 49 home runs and 130 RBI's; 'Push Em Up Tony' Lazzeri, in his last big year, pushed in 109 runs; and right fielder George Selkirk knocked in 107. Hurler Monte Pearson added 19 wins to Ruffing's 20. The Yanks' ace catcher Bill Dickey knocked in 107 runs and set the American League season record for hits by a catcher, posting an average of .362.

Hitting was heavy throughout the American League in 1936, with five teams hitting over .290, and 18 players driving in over 100 runs. Luke Appling of Chicago led the league with a .388 average, the highest by a shortstop in the century. Leading in RBI's with 162 was Hal Trosky, a regular on first with Cleveland, the American League's strongest second divi-

sion team, whose Earl Averill led the league in hits and was second only to Appling in batting.

The Yankees lost the first and the fourth World Series games to the New York Giants, but came out on top to take the first of four consecutive Series. They would lose a total of only three games in all four Series, sweeping their last two championship contests. In 1936 the Yankees took one game from the Giants 18-4, and another 13-5, with seven-run innings in both these lopsided contests. To add insult to injury, the second seven-run inning was the last inning of the sixth and final game. In the second game, Tony Lazerri became the second player ever to hit a World Series grand slam.

Not all the news in the American League in 1936 came from New York. That year also saw the debut of a young player named Bob Feller, pitching for the Cleveland Indians. On 23 August Feller started his first big-league game, and made headlines when he struck out 15 batters, two short of the then-major-league record. On 13 September he struck out 17 Philadelphia Athletics, setting a new American League record and tying Dizzie Dean's major-league record. According to Feller, 'I guess that's when people began to realize I was for real.' Then Feller, at 17 the only real prodigy in baseball history, went home to Van Meter, Iowa, to finish high school.

Feller was mid-America personified, a product of the Iowa corn belt and a former semipro father who tutored him on a baseball diamond he and his father carved out of their farm when Feller was 12. By 1935

Above: First baseman Hal Trosky swung a heavy bat for Cleveland for nine years (1933-41), averaging .310 and 113 RBI's a season during that time.

Left: Hall of Famer Bob Feller, who took four years out of his brilliant career for combat duty in World War II, became baseball's leading pitching prodigy when he signed on with Cleveland in 1936, at the age of 17. The strong and self-confident farmboy struck out 15 batters in his first major league appearance and broke the major league record for strikeouts with 18 the following year, quickly earning the nickname of 'Rapid Robert.' He pitched 3 no-hitters and finished up in 1956 with a career won-lost record of 266-162.

Right: Tommy 'Old Reliable' Henrich played outfield for 11 years for the Yankees.

Below: Third baseman Pinky Higgins turned in a .303 batting average and batted in 106 runs during his two years with the Red Sox in 1937 and 1938. Although he played mainly for the A's and Tigers, he ended his career in 1946 with Boston, who came up with the pennant that year.

Feller was pitching semipro ball in Des Moines. In a sequence of events that has since become legendary, Cleveland general manager Cy Slapnicka, in town to look at another player, finally gave in to months of pestering by Feller fans, went to Van Meter to see him play, and wired back that he had just signed 'the greatest pitcher he had ever seen.' The on-the-spot deal was sweetened with an autographed baseball and a dollar bill.

Feller later claimed it took him three years to learn how to pitch in the big leagues. In 1936 he walked 47 men in 62 innings, but he also struck out 76, and recorded his 15- and 17-strikeout games. Two years

later, when he was 19, he set a major-league record by striking out 18 men in one game. His fastball was called by many better than Johnson's, and he also had a curve which moved nearly as fast. By the time he was 22 he had won 107 games, including his first no-hitter.

Although four years in the service robbed him of spectacular career statistics, Feller recorded more low-hit games than any pitcher in baseball, including 11 one-hit games. No other pitcher has recorded more than five. His three no-hitters tied Cy Young's record. In his day he set major-league records for most strikeouts in a season (348 in 1946) as well as for most strikeouts in a single game. Ranked with the greatest American League pitchers, Johnson and Grove, Feller was one of the most exciting players since Babe Ruth, and a major draw. Fellow players considered him in a class by himself, and held him in particular awe. According to Ted Williams, 'He had more stuff than anybody.'

The Yankees repeated in 1937, winning 102 games for the second straight season and finishing 13 games ahead of the Tigers. Despite outstanding individual players who led the majors in hitting – including MVP Charlie Gehringer, who took league honors with a .371 average – the Tigers suffered from pitchers who skidded after manager-catcher Mickey Cochrane was severely beaned in May. The incident, reminiscent of Chapman's death, ended Cochrane's playing career. Elsewhere in the league, the Browns stirred memories of their 1922 power as each of their three regular outfielders hit above .325.

But it was the Yankees all the way. Gehrig had his last great year with 37 homers, 159 RBI's and a .351 average, and DiMaggio, in his second year with the Yanks, led the league with 46 home runs. New to the Yankees' indelible cast of characters was Tommy Henrich, an outfielder who personified the solid Yankee players who stood behind their superstars and gave the team its depth. Acquired as a free agent after a fierce bidding war, 'Old Reliable' Henrich was always capable of making the big play or getting the clean hit when it was needed. He hit .320 in 67 games in 1937, and played through 1950.

Although the Giants took one game from the Yankees in the 1937 Series, McCarthy's boys breezed to a 4-1 victory that ranks as one of the easiest Series wins ever for an American League team. Chalking up a total of 20 victories out of 22 Series games since 1927, the Bombers became the first club to take six world championships. Tony Lazzeri, in his last World Series with the Yanks, led both teams with a .400 average, including one homer, and Lou Gehrig hit his tenth and last homer in World Series play. For many, the highlight of the Series was Lefty Gomez's pause on the mound to observe a plane pass overhead.

Hank Greenberg, one of the greatest in Detroit's long history of great hitters, riveted attention throughout the 1938 season by methodically compiling a total of 58 homers. With five games left to play in the season, he was only two round trips short of Babe Ruth's 1927 record total. Big Henry failed to hit any long ones in the first three of these games, and had the misfortune to face Bob Feller in the fourth, the opener of a doubleheader against the Indians. Although Feller lost the game 4-1, he set a major-league record by fanning 18 players, and kept all of Greenberg's balls in the park. In the second game, Hank managed three singles, but that was all he wrote. Jimmie Foxx, now with Boston, also turned in an outstanding year, winning his third MVP, launching 50 home runs, and leading the league in average (.349), RBI's (175) and in slugging percentage (.704).

The 1938 Yankees, in manager McCarthy's opinion the best team he ever fielded, finished nine and a half games ahead of the Red Sox. Once again they had little on their minds through September. The Yankee farm empire, patiently assembled by George Weiss, began to pay off, adding such players as Joe Gordon to New York's durable veterans. In fact, some felt the Yankees' Newark farm team was so good it belonged in the majors. In his rookie year, Gordon, who replaced Lazzeri at second, hit 25 homers and established a great double-play combination with Frankie Crosetti. Henrich was now a starter in right field, and

pitching was solid throughout, with Red Ruffing winning 21, Lefty Gomez 18, Monte Pearson 16 and farmer Spud Chandler 14. Relief pitcher Johnny Murphy recorded his first big year with 11 saves.

Lou Gehrig, who had complained of lumbago at the 1937 World Series and had for the first time turned in a championship performance that was less than extraordinary, recorded his weakest year since his first with the Yankees. Lou's 29 homers, 114 RBI's and .295 average were considerably more than a feeble effort, but were ominously low by his standards.

Hall of Famer Red Ruffing pitched 14 years for the Yankees (1931-46), achieving four consecutive 20-game seasons from 1936 to 1939.

Above: Spud Chandler worked his right-handed magic for the Yankees for 11 years, ending with a .717 winning percentage.

Left: Outfielder Doc Cramer played mainly for the A's, Red Sox and Tigers, finishing with a .296 career batting average.

The Yanks, who swept the Cubs 4-0, experienced difficulty only in the second game, when Dizzy Dean pitched his club to a 3-2 lead in the eighth inning. McCarthy, who now had the satisfaction of taking the world championship from his former team twice, also became the first manager in baseball history to win three consecutive World Series. Bill Dickey and Joe Gordon both hit .400 for the Series, with Gordon, in his first Series appearance, driving in six runs.

For the first time in Series competition, Lou Gehrig did not get an extra base hit or drive in a run. At spring training in 1939, his clothes hung on him like a sack, and his reflexes were shot. In the eight games he played at the start of the season, he managed only four singles in 28 at bats. When his teammates praised him for handling a routine play without error, Gehrig considered his .143 average and asked manager McCarthy to take him out of the game. McCarthy, who feared Gehrig wouldn't be able to get out of the way of a pitched ball, had been unwilling to take captain Gehrig out of the lineup. When the crowd at the stadium on 2 May 1939 heard that Gehrig was ending his record of 2130 consecutive games, they gave him a standing ovation. Lou sat down and wept, as did some of his teammates, until Lefty Gomez rallied them out onto the field. Gehrig remained in uniform for the rest of the season, but never played another game.

Two months later Gehrig learned he was suffering from amyotrophic lateral sclerosis, a rare neuro-muscular disease with no known cure. On 4 July 1939 before a crowd of 60,000 which had gathered at

Yankee Stadium for a doubleheader and a special occasion called Lou Gehrig Appreciation Day, the Iron Man received a bear hug from Babe Ruth, and announced in a simple speech that despite the doctors' predictions, 'I consider myself the luckiest man on the face of the earth.' He lived to see himself voted into the Hall of Fame, and was the first Yankee to have his number retired. Lou Gehrig died on 2 June 1941.

The arrival of Charlie Keller from the Yankees' Newark farm team helped somewhat to replace the gap left by Gehrig. Hitting over .300 in his rookie season, 'King Kong' Keller took up position in left field, and with DiMaggio in center and Henrich in right formed one of the great outfields in baseball history. By midseason the Yankees were back on track, ending the year with 106 wins – the most of any year of their

four-year streak – and a finish 17 games in front of a strong Red Sox team.

Strong on offense, the 1939 Yankees had five .300 hitters, and four players – DiMaggio, Gordon, Dickey, and Selkirk – who each hit more than 20 home runs and drove in more than 100 runs. MVP DiMaggio led the league with a .381 average, his first title and lifetime best, and after flirting with .400 became the last right-handed hitter to clear the .380 mark. Ruffing won 21 games, but with Gomez suffering a sore arm and slumping to 12, New York lacked a solid number-two starter, making it impossible for McCarthy to establish a set rotation. Individual performances made the difference, strong contributors including farm system sprouts Atley Donald – who won 13 games, including his first 12 – and Spud Chandler.

Left fielder Charlie 'King Kong' Keller joined the Yankees in 1939, contributing to a strong defensive outfield which was also tough on pitchers. He went to the Series four times with the Yanks, collecting his share of runs, homers, hits and RBI's along the way.

In early July a Red Sox team strong on slugging took five games straight from the Yankees at Yankee Stadium. Speaking for Boston that year was Jimmie Foxx, with a league-leading 35 homers, 105 RBI's, and a .360 average; Joe Cronin with 107 RBI's and a .308 average; Doc Cramer with a .311 average; Bobby Doerr with a .318 average, and a 20-year-old rookie named Ted Williams who batted .327, achieved a league-leading 145 RBI's, launched 31 homers, and nearly overtook Harlond Clift for the lead in walks – a remarkable testimony to the rookie's eye. Not to be forgotten was Lefty Grove, throwing a 15-4 season for

the Red Sox, and taking his record ninth ERA title. Only lack of pitching depth prevented the Red Sox from giving New York a better run for its money.

The Yankees followed up their fourth consecutive pennant with a 4-0 sweep of Cincinnati in the Series, becoming the first club ever to win four consecutive world championships. No other club had ever been able to take more than two championships in a row. Charlie Keller exhibited a real Gehrig Series touch, batting .438, and driving in six runs with seven hits that included three home runs, a triple and a double.

The Yankees, with four pennants and four World

Red Rolfe scores for the Yankees in the 1939 World Series, while Joe DiMaggio, the batboy and umpire look on, and Cincinnati catcher Ernie Lombardi waits for a late throw. The Yanks blanked the Reds four games to none.

Series victories in as many years, were now in the middle of a period of dominance that would see them take seven pennants in eight years. They failed to repeat in 1940, but their third-place finish found them only two games behind the league-leading Tigers. That is how close they came to eight straight pennants. Most significant of all, in none of the years they won was there ever any question of their dominance after midseason.

With the steadily increasing use of radio and night games raising attendance and interest across the country, by the end of the decade baseball had not

only recovered from the decline of the Depression, but had established itself on the American scene more securely and profitably than ever before. Stars like Joe DiMaggio, Jimmie Foxx, Hank Greenberg, Bill Dickey, Ted Williams and Bob Feller propelled the American League to what was probably the peak of its supremacy, a dominance that extended not only to the playing field but to the box office. By the first year of the new decade, the American League outdrew the National League by over one million paying spectators, outhomered the senior circuit by almost 200 runs, outscored it by over 700 runs, and outbatted it by an average of seven points. Not until a second world war and a social revolution called Jackie Robinson would its supremacy slacken.

Hall of Famer Jimmie Foxx, who played first base for the Philadelphia A's from 1925 to 1935, played for Boston from 1936 to 1942. In 1938 'The Beast' took the batting title for the second time, with a .349 average, leading the league in RBI's and bases on balls as well. Foxx's statistics are a testament to his power: during his 20-year career he belted 534 homers and batted in 1921 runs, ending up with a .609 slugging percentage.

On 29 April, 1944 a number of former major leaguers serving in the
Navy played against a Hawaiian All-Star team (and won in 12
innings, 4-2), raising over a million dollars in war bonds.

CHAPTER FOUR
The Fighting Forties

"I don't think either of them can win."
Warren Brown, *Chicago Tribune* **sportswriter, asked to pick a winner in the 1945 World Series.**

As major league baseball embarked on the 1940s, things never looked better – assuming, that is, that baseball stadiums could be isolated from the world around them. In fact, various events beyond the confines of the stadiums were going to infringe heavily upon baseball before the decade was over. The most important event in the mainstream of history was, of course, World War II, but in retrospect it had relatively little effect on organized baseball as a whole, although it undeniably affected the careers of individual players. Much is made of the fact that World War II disrupted major league baseball, but in fact its impact was mainly confined to three or four seasons. Although Europe was at war by 1940, it was only in 1942 that American ballplayers began to go into the armed services in any numbers, and by 1946 almost all of them would return with just about as much talent as before.

Another event that would have a more far-reaching impact on baseball had actually occurred on 27 August 1939. A doubleheader at Ebbets Field in Brooklyn between the Dodgers and the Reds was the first televised major league game, and although there were only a handful of sets to receive it, the newspaper account marveled over the fact that people 'as far away as 50 miles viewed the action and heard the roar of the crowd.' That televised game, even more so than the bombing of Pearl Harbor, would be the 'shot heard round the [baseball] world.' Television would wait until after World War II was over to make its pitch, but once it began to deliver in the late 1940s, baseball would never be the same.

Night baseball, too, which had been played only occasionally since the first night game on 24 May 1935, began to catch on after the war. By 1948 every major league club's stadium would have lights – except for Wrigley Field in Chicago. And 40 years later Chicago's North Side ball club would still be defying the trend to 'produce' baseball for the convenience of the television audience.

World War II was bigger than baseball, it was irresistible. Television was also bigger than baseball, but baseball chose to get aboard. But there was still another event in the 1940s that major league baseball, to its everlasting credit, may take some little pride in helping to bring about: that is, the acceptance of black Americans into the mainstream of society. Regrettably, it was not the American League that commenced the process: that honor belongs to the Brooklyn Dodgers and their owner, Branch Rickey, who in 1947 brought up Jackie Robinson from the Montreal farm team and put him in the lineup. But during the 1947 season, Bill Veeck, owner of the Cleveland Indians, put the second black player on the field, Larry Doby, and before the season was out the St Louis Browns fielded two blacks, Henry Thompson and Willard Brown. It must be admitted that thereafter the American League fell behind the National League in signing on black players – the Boston Red Sox waited until 1959 – but major league baseball can take some satisfaction in knowing that it helped to speed up the long overdue process of integrating America.

But as the 1940 season got underway, none of these revolutionary events was on the minds of most Americans, whether ballplayers or fans. In fact, the world seemed to be going on as usual, which meant that among other things the Yankees would probably win the American League pennant for the fifth consecutive year. Joe DiMaggio was as hot as ever – his .352 average would lead the league for 1940 – and there was Charlie Keller and Joe Gordon and Spud Chandler. The Indians, however, signaled a tight race to come when their 21-year-old ace, Bob Feller, pitched against the White Sox the first and only no-hitter on an opening day. Feller also went on to have a superb season, winning 27 games and leading all other pitchers in the league in virtually every category.

But in the end, the Yankees could only come in third, two games out, and Cleveland could only come in second, one game out, as the Detroit Tigers surprised everyone and took the pennant. Manager Del Baker had cleverly shifted the team's home run producer, first baseman Hank Greenberg, to left field in order to move backup catcher Rudy York into the starting lineup; Greenberg's 41 homers and 150 RBI's and York's 33 homers and 134 RBI's more than justified the switch. Charlie Gehringer and Barney

Right-hander Bobo Newsom pitched for the Detroit Tigers from 1939 to 1941, winning two games (including a fifth-game shutout) and losing one for them in the 1940 World Series.

McCoskey also hit over .300, while Bobo Newsom (21-5) and Schoolboy Rowe (16-3) provided the necessary pitching skills. Newsom was a colorful character of the old school of baseball. His real name was Louis Norman Newsom, but he was known only as 'Bobo' because of his own habit of addressing everyone else as just that. (He is said to have called even the Olympian 'Mr Mack,' 'Bobo' on first meeting him.) Whether it was his rough manners or his lack of discipline, Newsom would pitch for 18 different teams during 26 years in the majors, but the fact is he won many games for those teams, finally retiring with a career total of 211-222.

In the World Series, the Tigers found themselves facing the Cincinnati Reds. Newsom pitched and won the first game, 7-2, with his father watching in the stands; the very next day, Mr Newsom died of a heart attack. The teams were tied, two games each, when Newsom returned to pitch in the fifth; he gave up only three hits, while his teammates gave him 13, so the Tigers went ahead in the Series. The Reds tied up the Series in the sixth game, so Newsom was asked to pitch the seventh (after only one day's rest – the teams' cities being so close that no travel days were allowed). Newsom did wonders, giving up no runs through the sixth inning while the Tigers tiptoed along on one unearned run; then in the seventh, when the Tiger shortstop cut off a throw that might have been a putout at home, the Reds tied up the game and a sacrifice fly brought in a second run. The Reds won game seven, 2-1, and the Series.

During the 1941 season, the war in Europe loomed ominously, but interfered with American baseball players very little. The notable exception was Hank Greenberg, who enlisted in the Army shortly after the season began. For two all-time greats of the American League, 1941 was a banner year. For one, it began on 15 May: Joe DiMaggio got one single in his four at bats – hardly much for any player, let alone the Yankee Clipper, to write home about. But he hit in the next game, and the next game, and the next game.... By 29 June he had hit in 42 consecutive games, breaking George Sisler's old American League record. A few days later he broke the all-time record for hitting in consecutive games, 44, set by Wee Willie Keeler back

Above: Catcher Rollie Hemsley played for Cleveland from 1938 to 1941, turning in four solid years out of his 19-year career before moving to the Reds, Yankees, and finishing up with Philadelphia's National League team.

Left: Birdie Tebbetts taps one into center field. Catcher George Robert Tebbetts played for the Tigers from 1936 to 1947, then moved to the Red Sox, and finished his career with the Indians.

Theodore Samuel Williams – 'The Splendid Splinter' – played left field for the Red Sox for his entire 19-year career, with three years out for military service. Named the league's Most Valuable Player twice, in 1946 and 1949, and winning the Triple Crown twice, in 1942 and 1947, Teddy Ballgame ended his playing career in 1960 with a home run in his last at-bat. He was elected to the Hall of Fame in 1966.

in 1897. By now the whole country was waiting for each day's news report – and fans were showing up in record-breaking numbers at each Yankee game. Then on the night of 17 July, the Yankees played the Indians and 60,000 fans showed up in Cleveland. It took two pitchers, Al Smith and Jim Bagby, Jr, and some incredible catches by the Indians' third baseman Ken Keltner, to shut the mighty Joe down. Yet his hits in 56 consecutive games remains as of this day one of the most secure all-time records.

Meanwhile, another American League player was enjoying a good year at the plate, a 22-year-old in his third year with the Red Sox – Ted Williams. Williams was hardly an unknown; in his first season with the Sox, Williams had batted .327, hit 31 homers and led the league with 145 RBI's. Indeed, great things had been expected of Williams almost from the moment the Red Sox's general manager Eddie Collins had

discovered him in San Diego in 1936. Collins had gone to California primarily to seek out a promising second baseman, Bobby Doerr, but Collins had been so impressed with the tall, 17-year-old, left-handed hitter that he signed up Williams too. It was 1938 before the Sox brought Williams to spring training, and even then he was confident to the point of cockiness. (One story goes that when someone said to him, 'wait till you see Foxx hit,' Williams' cool retort was, 'wait till Foxx sees me hit.')

But Williams had an eye and a bat that could more than support his mouth and his manner. The Sox had such a strong outfield in 1938 that he was sent to Minneapolis for another year of seasoning, but in 1939 he joined the Red Sox and proved that Eddie Collins had not been seeing double. And then in 1941, Williams was truly hot. By the time he came into the final day of the season, his average was .3995 – good

Left: Outfielder Sam Chapman played for the Philadelphia Athletics for 11 years, turning in his best year in 1941, with 106 RBI's and a .322 batting average.

Below: Ken Keltner played third base for Cleveland for 12 years, and ended his career in 1950 with the Red Sox.

the fourth game with the Yankees leading two games to one, and it was considered either team's Series to win. The Dodgers were leading 4-3 in the top of the ninth and relief pitcher Hugh Casey had set down the first two Yankees and then gone to a full count with Tommy Henrich. Casey pitched a curve (which some would insist was a spitter), Henrich swung and missed and Dodger fans were about to celebrate – when their usually fine catcher, Mickey Owen, let the ball get away. Henrich sprinted safely to first and before the inning was over, the Yankees picked up four runs. The Yankees won that fourth game, 7-4, and then went on to take the fifth, 3-1, and win their ninth World Series.

By the time the 1942 season got underway, America had formally and fully entered the war, and players were beginning to go off to the armed services. Bob Feller was one of the first of the stars to enlist. Just as

enough to go into the record books as .400. The last major leaguer with a season average .400 or better was Bill Terry of the Giants, who had ended up with .401 in 1930. The Red Sox manager, Joe Cronin, told Williams he could sit out the doubleheader against the Athletics and preserve his .400 average, but Williams insisted on hitting his way into the record-book. In the first game, he went 4 for 5, and in the second game he went 2 for 3, ending the season with a .406.

In team play, however, the Red Sox could not match the Yankees. By 4 September and their 136th game, the Yankees were setting their own record by clinching the league pennant on the earliest date ever. The Yankees then went into the Series to face none other than the Brooklyn Dodgers; the Yankees and the Giants had met in five World Series but this was a first for these two New York rivals. The teams went into

Above: Yankee shortstop Phil 'Scooter' Rizzuto makes a putout at second base. Rizzuto played in nine Series contests during his 13 years with the Yankees. Phil Rizzuto continued in baseball after retiring from his playing career in 1956 by becoming a well-known and well-liked announcer.

Right: Right-hander Tex Hughson turned in a .640 winning percentage and a 2.94 ERA after his eight-year career with the Red Sox, including two 20-game seasons. He led the league in strikeouts in 1942, and averaged 125 strikeouts per season during his most active years.

in World War I, there was some suggestion that perhaps it wasn't right for grown men to be playing and watching a game while others were dying in battle. But President Franklin Delano Roosevelt himself wrote to the Commissioner of Baseball, Judge Landis, not long after Pearl Harbor: 'I honestly feel that it would be best for the country to keep baseball going.' In general, everyone agreed that major league baseball would help to keep up morale at the homefront and overseas, so the teams continued playing. But in the next two years, over 300 major league players would go into the armed services, and those who stayed had legitimate exemptions. Although many of the players were put into 'safe' positions, this was mainly because their commanding officers wanted to keep celebrities on their staffs. Many players refused such cushy assignments and found themselves sent off to the frontlines. Meanwhile, ball park attendance gradually declined as the public declined in numbers and had less time available for sports. Several teams began to suffer financially, but the major leagues continued.

There was little surprise when the Yankees came back in 1942 to take the pennant for the sixth time in seven years. The Yankees had such oldtimers as Joe DiMaggio, Charlie Keller, Joe Gordon, Bill Dickey, Red Ruffing and Lefty Gomez, but they also had some newcomers from their own farm system, including Phil Rizzuto at shortstop and a pitcher, Ernie Bonham, who would end the season with 21 wins. Forty-one-year-old pitcher Ted Lyons of the White Sox, however, won 14 and lost 6, leading the league with his 2.10 ERA. The Red Sox's Ted Williams won the triple crown, batting .356, with 36 homers and 137 RBI's. (Both Lyons and Williams would enter the armed forces after this season.)

The Yankees went into the World Series in 1942 highly favored to beat the inexperienced St Louis Cardinals, whose superb farm system, built up by general manager Branch Rickey, had yielded a crop of fine rookies. In the first game the Cardinals couldn't even get a hit off Yankee Red Ruffing until the eighth inning, and they lost 7-4. But the Cards came back in the second game to win 4-3. In the third game, before 70,000 fans at Yankee Stadium, everyone assumed that the Yankee bats would come alive, as they did – but Cardinal outfielders Terry Moore, Stan Musial and Enos Slaughter took turns making spectacular catches and the Cardinals upset the Yankees, 2-0.

Below: A future Hall of Famer, White Sox hurler Ted Lyons turned in a league-leading 2.10 ERA in 1942.

Washington outfielder George Case led the league in stolen bases six times, and scored a league-leading 102 runs in 1943.

Game four seesawed back and forth but the Cardinals ended up beating out the Yanks once again, 9-6. In the fifth game, still in New York, Yankee fans assumed that the world would be set right by a Yankee win; instead, rookie Whitey Kurowski hit a two-run homer with one out in the ninth, and the Cardinals had defeated the mighty Yankees, 4-2 – the Yanks who had not lost in their last eight straight Series appearances! In fact, the last Series they had lost was to the Cardinals in 1926.

The Yankees had already lost Johnny Sturm and Tommy Henrich to the armed forces during the 1942 season; then in 1943 they lost Joe DiMaggio, Phil Rizzuto, Red Ruffing and Buddy Hassett. But all the other teams were losing players, too. Still, 1943 seemed like a season 'on hold' and it was probably no coincidence that both the Yankees and the Cardinals repeated in their leagues and met again in the World Series. And just as in 1942, the Cards lost the first game and then won the second. The Cardinals' Mort Cooper pitched in this game – with his brother Walker Cooper catching. Even more extraordinary was the fact that their father had died that very morning. In the third game (played in Yankee Stadium to cut down on travel during the war) the Yankees came back and won, 6-2, to make the game count 2-1. The teams then moved on to St Louis where the Yankees repeated with a 2-1 win. In the fifth game Mort Cooper gave up only a two-run homer to Dickey, but Spud

Right: The St Louis Browns' shortstop Vern Stephens led the league in RBI's with 109 in 1944, helping to boost his team to the league and world championships that year.

Opposite top: Pitching great Bob Feller poses with Walker Cooper at the Great Lakes Naval Training Center.

Opposite bottom: First baseman George McQuinn demonstrates his stretch. McQuinn, who played in the Series for both the Browns and the Yankees, finished his 12-year career in 1948.

Below: Nelson Potter pitched for the Philadelphia A's until 1941, when he went to Boston and St Louis, finishing his career in 1949 with the Boston Braves.

Chandler shut down the Cardinals, and the Yankees won the Series four games to one, the seventh time they won it under manager Joe McCarthy.

The 1944 season was probably the nadir for major league baseball as far as the available talent was concerned. It was in this year, for instance, that the Cincinnati Reds actually used a 15-year-old pitcher, Joe Nuxhall. Virtually all the great players were off in the armed forces by now, so at least all teams were playing at about the same level. The Tigers and Yankees found themselves racing for the pennant, however feebly, with the St Louis Browns in hot pursuit. The Browns had never won a pennant, but in 1944, managed by Luke Sewell, and aided by veteran hitters Mike Kreevich and Vern Stephens, and pitchers Jack Kramer and Nelson Potter they defeated the Yankees and clinched the pennant on the last day of the season.

As if to cooperate with the wartime restrictions on travel, the Cardinals won again in the National League, so there was to be not even a subway series but a staircase series, as both St Louis teams played in Sportsman's Park. The Cardinals, of course, were veterans at Series play, but the Browns surprised everyone by taking the first game, 2-1, on a two-run homer by George McQuinn. The Cardinals came back in the second game but the Browns once more astonished everyone with a win in the third game, 6-2. Then the Cards took the next three games, although hardly by routs – the scores being 5-1, 2-0 and 3-1. The Cardinals got to fly the World Series flag above Sportsman's Park, but the Browns could be

first and only championship the team would win in
St Louis.

The war would not end until August 1945, so the
1945 season was almost as devoid of the big stars as
1944 had been. No All-Star game was held in 1945,
both because of the lack of all-stars and the wartime
restrictions on travel. During the season, though, as
the war was winding down first in Europe and then in
the Pacific, several players were able to rejoin their
teams. One of these was Hank Greenberg, who had
been among the first to go into the armed forces. He
rejoined the Tigers in June after completing his service with the Air Force in Europe, while pitcher Virgil
Trucks got out of the Navy after the Japanese sur-
rendered in August and also got into a Tiger uniform –
just in time to pitch the final game of the season
against the Yankees. And it was this final game that
clinched the pennant for the Tigers, who had also
relied on the talents of Rudy York and left-hander Hal
Newhouser.

The Tigers went into the Series against the Chicago
Cubs, and both teams were regarded as so light on
talent that sportswriter Warren Brown quipped, 'I
don't think either of them can win.' In fact, it was an
exciting Series, with the lead swinging back and forth
and taking the teams into a seventh and deciding
game. Hal Newhouser gave up 10 hits to the Cubs but
spaced them so that they produced only three runs,
and the Tigers won the last game, 9-3, to become
World Champions.

Right: One-armed Pete Gray appeared in 77 games for the St Louis Browns in 1945 and batted .218.

Below: Senator catcher Rick Ferrell puts out Yankee second baseman George 'Snuffy' Stirnweiss in a close play at home. Stirnweiss led the league in hits, triples, runs and stolen bases in 1944 and 1945.

The year 1945 will also be remembered as the year that the St Louis Browns fielded a one-armed outfielder, Pete Gray. Gray had lost his right arm in an accident at the age of six, but he had taught himself both to catch and bat with his one good arm. He manipulated a glove with such dexterity that he could make a catch and throw almost as fast as the average outfielder. As for his batting, by 1944 he was hitting .333 for Memphis in the Southern Association, so the Browns decided to bring him up. Gray played in 77 games during 1945 and hit .218 – an amazing feat even allowing for the fact that he wasn't facing the best pitchers of all time.

Another unique figure in the history of major league baseball was conspicuous in 1945 – but by his absence: Judge Kenesaw Mountain Landis, the first, most colorful and most powerful of the commissioners of baseball. He had died in November 1944 after having served since 1920, and for his occasionally autocratic ways, he was generally conceded to have made modern major league baseball a respectable institution. His successor was Albert Benjamin 'Happy' Chandler, a former governor and senator from Kentucky.

The year 1945 in baseball history will always be remembered as the year that Branch Rickey signed Jackie Robinson – although Robinson did not actually

1918. But Williams had plenty of help from such players as Dom DiMaggio, who hit .316, Johnny Pesky, with .342, Rudy York and Bobby Doerr. For the World Series, the Red Sox had to wait until the Cardinals and Dodgers went through a three-game play-off to break the tie – the first in major league history – for first place in the National League. The Cardinals emerged the winner, then promptly lost the first game in the Series to the Red Sox on a tenth-inning homer by Rudy York. The Cardinals took the second game, but the Red Sox, now on their home field, took the third – again paced by Rudy York's three-run homer. The Cards took the fourth game, 12-3, but the Red Sox took the fifth, 6-3, so the teams headed back to St Louis with the Cardinals needing to win two straight. They did win the sixth, so now it came down to the final game. Murray Dickson who had been so crucial in the Cardinals' wins, pitched this last game and went into

Left: Second baseman Bobby Doerr played for the Boston Red Sox for 14 years, ending his career in 1951. In the 1946 World Series, Doerr had nine hits, a home run and three RBI's.

Below: Rudy York played catcher and first base for the Tigers from 1934 to 1945, when he went to the Red Sox, then the White Sox, and ended his 13-year career with the A's. During his year with the Tigers York averaged 27 home runs a season.

play for the Dodgers until 1947 – and true students of the sport will remember 1946 as the year of the Mexican League. A fabulously wealthy Mexican, Jorge Pasquel, decided to start a league that would compete with the two in the United States, and he went about building it up the way new teams and leagues had always tried to break into the bigtime – by offering players more money. Relatively few major league players went for the offers and most of these were from the National League – Sal Maglie, Max Lanier, Mickey Owen and others. The new Commissioner, 'Happy' Chandler, showed that he could be unhappy when someone intruded on his territory and immediately declared that any players who went down to Mexico would be barred from the two major leagues for five years if they tried to return. The players, in fact, were soon dissatisfied with conditions in the Mexican League and began to come back (the league soon folded). Chandler relented somewhat by letting them back in the majors in 1949.

The 1946 season also saw the return of almost all the prewar stars and major league baseball once again expressed the spirit of the country, as the fans turned out in record-breaking numbers to cheer on their teams. Hank Greenberg was back in form for the Tigers and hit 44 homers, while Bob Feller, after four years of service in the Navy, not only led the league in all kinds of pitching statistics, he set an all-time league strikeout record of 348. (Although research would later establish that Rube Waddell had actually struck out 349 in 1904.) Feller also completed 36 games, the most in the American League since Walter Johnson completed 38 in 1910.

But neither of these stars were enough to carry their teams to the top of the league. That honor fell to another returned serviceman, Ted Williams, whose .342 average, 38 homers and 123 RBI's led the Boston Red Sox to win the pennant for the first time since and the Dodgers. The Yankees had set a record-equaling (to that of the 1906 White Sox) 19-game winning streak, thanks to some old veterans such as Joe DiMaggio and Tommy Henrich, and a new young pitching staff that included Allie Reynolds (19-8) and reliever Joe Page.

The 1947 World Series produced three instant stars and two unforgettable plays by the Dodgers. Going into the fourth game, the Yankees were leading two games to one. The Yankees started Bill Bevens on the mound, despite his 7-13 record for the season, and although he was occasionally wild he came into the bottom of the ninth with a no-hitter and the Yankees leading 2-1. Bevens' ninth walk of the game put Carl Furillo on, but Bevens then got his second out. Yankee manager Bucky Harris signaled for Bevens to walk

Above: Shortstop Johnny Pesky played for the Red Sox from 1942 to 1951, then for the Tigers and Senators. During his first three years with the Sox he led the league in hits, and he finished his career in 1954 with a .307 batting average.

Right: 'Fireman' Joe Page pitched for the Yankees for seven years and went to the Series with them twice. In 1947 he set relief pitching league records in all three categories by winning 14, losing 7 and saving 17.

the eighth inning with a 3-1 lead; then he allowed Boston to tie it up and had to be relieved by Harry 'The Cat' Brecheen. In the bottom of the eighth, Cardinal Enos Slaughter led off with a single – a remarkable feat, considering that his elbow had actually been broken during the fifth game. The next two Cardinals went down, and then Harry Walker hit what was probably a reasonable single; Boston's Leon Culberson fielded it and threw to shortstop Johnny Pesky – who hesitated just long enough to allow Slaughter to go for broke and beat the throw to home plate. The Cardinals kept their 4-3 lead and won the 1946 World Series. For years afterwards, Pesky would be hounded by this split-second hesitation, but it seems fairer to just accept that Slaughter's gutsy running beat the throw.

Although Ted Williams enjoyed another outstanding season in 1947 – becoming the first American League player to take the triple crown of batting for the second time – the Red Sox could not repeat. The season started with a verbal war between the Yankees and the Dodgers – who were furious when the Yankees hired their coach Chuck Dressen – that led to a series of penalties from Commissioner Chandler, the most extreme being the suspension of Dodger manager Leo Durocher for the entire season, for 'conduct detrimental to baseball.' And the season ended with a baseball series between the Yankees

Pete Reiser in order to bring up the lighter-hitting Eddie Stanky, and Dodger manager Burt Shotton then put in a pinch hitter, Cookie Lavagetto, who promptly hit a double off the right-field wall and drove in the winning runs.

The Yankees came back and won the fifth game, so now the Dodgers had to do or die. In the bottom of the sixth, the Dodgers had a fairly solid 8-5 lead, but the Yankees got two men on base. Then Joe DiMaggio hit what looked like a sure homer toward the left-center bullpen, but Al Gionfriddo – who had just entered the

game as a replacement – snagged the ball with a spectacular catch against the fence. The Yankees lost 8-6, but with Joe Page pitching five shutout innings in relief, the Yankees took the seventh and deciding game. Everyone agreed that the heroes of the Series had been Bill Bevens, Cookie Lavagetto and Al Gionfriddo – yet they never played in a single major league game again.

The Cleveland Indians led off the 1948 season as the only American League team with a black player, Larry Doby, who had played 29 games for the team in 1947.

Larry Doby forged the way for black players in the American League, joining the Cleveland Indians in 1947. He played outfield for them until 1956, when he went to the White Sox. Doby led the league twice in home runs, and ended his career with a .285 batting average.

Satchel Paige's pitching helped the Indians win a league pennant in 1948. Leroy Robert Paige pitched for the St Louis Browns from 1951 to 1953. He was elected to the Hall of Fame in 1971.

Then in midseason 1948, the Indians signed on a living legend from the old black leagues, 41-year-old Satchel Paige (his nickname coming from the fact that he had carried satchels, or luggage, as a boy). Even allowing for a certain amount of exaggeration, there was no denying that Paige was one of the fastest and most effective pitchers who had ever played the game. Paige was clearly well past his prime, but he would appear in 21 games for the Indians and end up 1948 with a 6-1 record and an ERA of 2.47. This was

also the year that the Indians went all the way to take the pennant. Their shortstop-manager Lou Boudreau led the way with his .355 average and although Bob Feller ended up with only a 19-15 record, rookie Gene Bearden had a superb 20-7 record while Bob Lemon pitched ten shutouts to end up with a 20-14 season.

But it was hardly a walkaway for the Indians. As they came into the final weekend of the season, they appeared to have the pennant nailed down with their one and a half game lead over both the Red Sox and

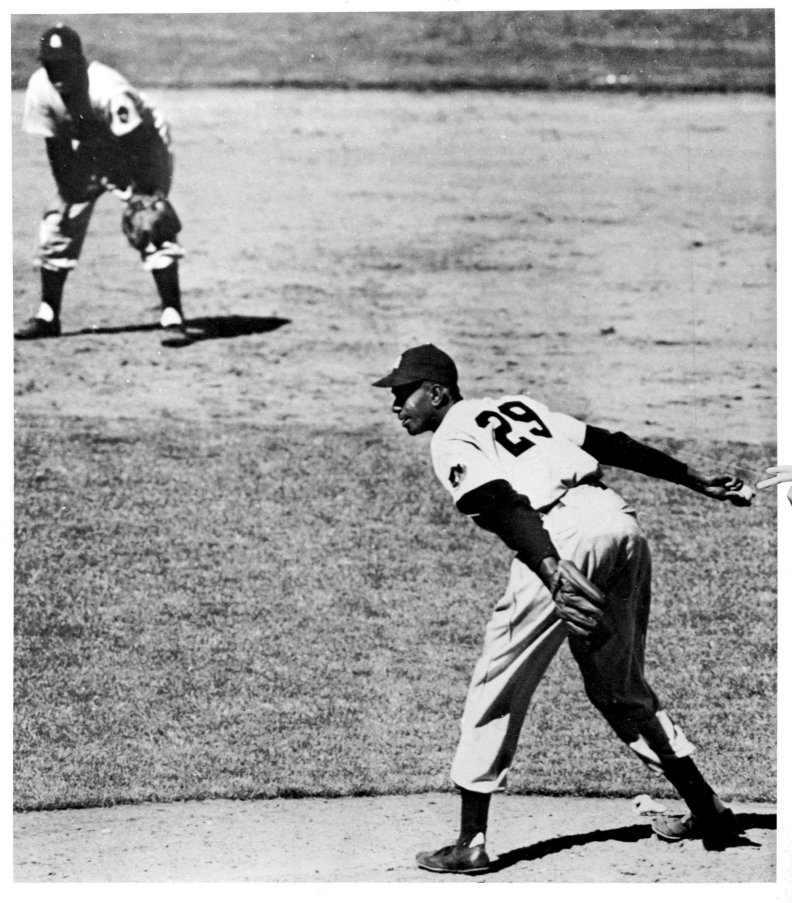

the Yankees. The Red Sox eliminated the Yankees, but then on the final day of the season, the Red Sox won and the Indians lost – forcing the first play-off in American League history. The league used a single-game play-off, to be played in Boston's Fenway Park. Ted Williams, with his .369 average, was looked to as the potential tie-breaker, but it turned out to be Lou Boudreau who hit two homers and two singles, and behind the cool pitching of Gene Bearden the Indians won 8-3, and went into the Series for the first time since 1920.

In the Series the Indians found themselves confronting another team that were a bit rusty in Series play – the Boston Braves, who hadn't been there since 1941. The first game featured a hotly disputed call when the umpire ruled that pitcher Bob Feller had not picked off Phil Masi at second base – and then Masi went on to score the one run of the game and leave the Braves the winner, 1-0. As if to revenge themselves for what they regarded as an unearned win, the Indians came back and took the next three games straight. A record-setting crowd of 86,288 fans showed up in Cleveland's stadium for the fifth game to

Right: Hall of Famer, shortstop and clutch hitter Lou Boudreau played for Cleveland from 1938 to 1950.
Below: Indian pitcher Gene Bearden doubled and scored in the shutout he pitched in the 1948 Series.

watch Bob Feller pitch what everyone assumed would be the decisive fifth game, but the Braves were able to hit him and ended up beating the Indians, 11-5. In the sixth game the Indians went ahead 4-1, but the Braves scored two more in the bottom of the eighth and had the tying run on third. Then Indian reliever Gene Bearden got the last out and the Indians took their first World Series in 28 years.

Second baseman Joseph Lowell 'Flash' Gordon blasted a home run for Cleveland in the sixth game of the 1948 Series. Gordon played for the Indians for four out of his eleven years in the majors.

The Yankees had finished in third place in 1948, and that was enough to cost manager Bucky Harris his job. In his place the Yankees hired Charles Dillon 'Casey' Stengel. Hardly a household name at the time, Stengel had played as an outfielder with National League teams between 1912-25. He had gone on as a not very successful manager of the Dodgers and Braves during the 1930s, then had had considerable success managing the Oakland Oaks of the Pacific Coast League. Even so, Stengel hardly seemed to fit the Yankee 'image'; for those familiar with his public image thought of him as a slightly garrulous clown who spoke his own brand of English, dubbed 'Stengelese.' But Stengel wasted no time in demonstrating that if he was a clown, it was Pagliacci – a serious man behind the exterior. He had some veterans to draw on, although both DiMaggio and Berra were lost in the early season to injuries, but to the likes of Tommy Henrich and Phil Rizzuto he added new talents such as Hank Bauer, Jerry Coleman and Bobby Brown. For pitching Stengel could count on Vic Raschi, Allie Reynolds, Eddie Lopat and reliever Joe Page. Up the coast, though, another savvy manager, Joe McCarthy, had a powerful team in the Red Sox, with Ted Williams, Bobby Doerr, Dom DiMaggio, Johnny Pesky and Vern Stephens. As so often, though, the Red Sox couldn't come up with the pitching, so even though they led the Yankees coming into the final weekend, the Yankees beat them twice and took the pennant on the final day of the season.

And so the Yankees went into the 1949 Series to face their now archrival, the Dodgers, whom the Yankees had beaten in 1947. The Yankees took the first game, 1-0, but the Dodgers won the second by the same score. The third game went into the ninth inning with the score tied, 1-1. In the top of the inning the Yankees scored three runs, but then the Dodgers came back with two homers to make it 4-3; then Joe Page got them out before the score could be tied up. In the fourth game, Eddie Lopat and Allie Reynolds kept the Dodgers from winning again, and in the sixth game, the Yankees won 10-6, taking the first of ten

pennants they would win under Casey Stengel and the first of five consecutive World Championships.

The 1940s had begun with the clouds of war hanging over major league baseball; they were ending with only the cloud of the Yankees hanging over the American League. A lot of good baseball had been played between those two thresholds, and although some statistics had been slightly skewered by the interruption of wartime service, this was a small enough price to pay to keep the world safe for baseball.

Right-handed hurler Allie Pierce 'Superchief' Reynolds threw for the Yankees from 1947 to 1954 and won seven out of nine World Series games – including two shutouts – during that time.

In the 12 years he managed the Yankees, Casey Stengel brought his team to ten league pennants and seven World championships. He was elected to the Hall of Fame in 1966.

CHAPTER FIVE
The Fabled Fifties

"I have one helluva ball club but it's underrated. And we're going to get better."

Casey Stengel referring to his 1953 Yankees.

The American League's 1950s were dominated by the New York Yankees. They won nine pennants and eight world championships. For much of the decade the other American league clubs were like fodder feeding the Yankees' championship stampede. There were years of challenge and disappointment for New York, and great performances from athletes of other clubs. Nonetheless, it was the rise and fall of the seemingly unbeatable New York franchise which stands out the most. The Yankees won the world championship seven times in the decade. From 1949-1953 Casey Stengel led the Bombers to five straight championships – a new record in the annals of the game. This was the same Stengel who was found deficient as manager of the Boston and Brooklyn clubs in the National League.

The first bang of the 1950 season took place off the field. Club owners refused to renew Happy Chandler's contract as Commissioner of Baseball. This opened the way for Ford C Frick to become baseball's third commissioner. Frick enjoyed a three-year contract at $65,000 a year. This was also the year that the Yankees introduced a sensational new southpaw,

Whitey Ford. The year 1950 saw the end of one of the longest careers in the game. Connie Mack managed his beloved Athletics for the last time.

Mack's final stint in the Philadelphia dugout took place on 1 October 1950, as the A's closed out the season by beating the Senators at Shibe Park, 5-3. Mack's lifetime record of managing the same major league team for 50 years may never be broken. Although 17 of his later teams wound up in a disappointing last place, in his career Mack had experienced the thrills of glory, winning a total of nine pennants. It seemed that an era was ending when, on 16 October, Mack announced his resignation as manager. Although he continued as club president, Jimmy Sykes replaced him on the field.

The closing out of the 1950 season found New York struggling for the pennant. They finally took it in the last two games of the season. The best Boston's Red Sox could do was second place again, as Yankee rookie pitcher Whitey Ford provided his team with their winning edge. The club's management had plucked him from the Kansas City farm team and brought him to the varsity; Ford responded by winning nine out ten games. Sluggish hitting by Joe

Left-hander Whitey Ford – The Chairman of the Board – pitched for the Yankees for 16 years, turning in a won-lost record of 236-106 for an all-time second-best winning percentage of .690. Charles Edward Ford led the league in games won and in winning percentage three times, and twice in games saved and innings pitched.

DiMaggio contributed to the difficulty the Yankees faced in winning the league championship. The usually dependable batter had been temporarily benched because of weak hitting, but later picked up and ended the season with an average of .301.

The Yankees faced the Philadelphia Phillies in the 1950 World Series. The National League champs had just beaten out the Brooklyn Dodgers for the pennant. Delaware millionaire Bob Carpenter had invested heavily in the Phillies, signing a number of prospects with hefty bonuses on the order of $50,000 each. The Philadelphia 'Whiz Kids' won their first pennant in 35 years and, wrote a New York baseball scribe, 'will now prepare to play a World Series against men who

smoke cigars and chew tobacco.' The tough guys soundly spanked the kids in four straight, but the games were in fact very close. Philadelphia lost by only one run in each of the first three games 1-0, 2-1 and 3-2. Only in the final game in this pitchers' series was there any show of power. Even then the score was low by Yankee standards, 5-2, behind the 21-year-old rookie Whitey Ford.

This was the second straight World Series win for Casey Stengel, the 'wise old clown' who substantially changed professional baseball. He strengthened the bench by eliminating the old utility player – the 'jack of all trades, master of none' – from his club. In the off season he worked on developing a dozen or so of the

Big Vic Raschi contributed to the Yankees' much-feared pitching staff from 1946 to 1953, with a won-lost record of 120-50 for those years, and an impressive career winning percentage of .667.

In 1951 Yankee pitcher Allie Reynolds won 17 games – including seven shutouts – and lost only eight. The following year he would whiff 160 batters to lead the league in strikeouts. Reynolds finished up with a career ERA of 3.30 and a .630 winning percentage.

best minor league players in the Yankee farm system. Casey concentrated on the most apt youngsters, a distinct departure from Rickey's assembly line approach. In line with this philosophy, Stengel founded the Yankees' first 'instruction school' in 1951, staffed by a distinguished faculty, including baseball deans Frank Crosetti, Ed Lopat, Bill Dickey and Ralph Houk. These old pros were assisted by Johnny Neun, Bill Skiff, Steve Souchak and Randy Gumpert. Although Casey delegated the drilling and most of the teaching, he kept a sharp eye on his students and teachers, overseeing the whole processs as well as the details. Dickey, Houk and Skiff worked with the catchers, Lopat and Gumpert with the pitchers, and Souchak and Crosetti taught the infielders.

Casey hoped to polish future superstars quickly in order to move them from the farm team circuit to the majors in the fastest possible time. The 1951 school, which was held in Phoenix, Arizona, included such luminaries as Mickey Mantle, Gil McDougald and Tom Morgan. Two American League Rookies of the Year, Bob Grim (1954) and Tony Kubek (1957), came directly into the majors from Casey's course of instruction. Mickey Mantle's Cinderella experience owes much to Casey's career-building approach. Practically overnight he was transformed from an unheralded shortstop on the Joplin, Missouri farm squad in the Class C association to playing next to Joe DiMaggio in the Yankee outfield.

Coach Bill Dickey remembers the 18-year-old's arrival at Phoenix. 'I was pitching batting practice when he took his first swings,' related Dickey. 'The kid hit the first six balls nearly 500 feet, over the lights and out of sight.' Mantle was later asked to take spring training with the varsity. He jumped overnight from Class C to Triple A and then to the major leagues.

Stengel turned many long-established baseball conventions inside out. This maverick studied people and situations while many of his opponents followed static guidelines with an almost biblical faith. In tight situations Casey astounded the pundits. He used left-

handed batters against southpaws, and vice versa. The cherished 'percentages' mandated doing otherwise; Casey knew better. 'People alter percentages,' Stengel countered in defense of his moves against the book. 'Johnny Fredericks and Andy High were two left-handed batters with the Dodgers who could wear out a southpaw. And Carl Hubbell, one of the greatest left-handers in history, had more trouble with left-handed batters than he did with the right-handed ones.' Casey pulled things apart and put them together in new, exciting forms which effectively devastated a generation of opponents. He knew both his players and his opponents better than anyone else.

The St Louis Browns found their off-field excitement in the person of Bill Veeck, who purchased the club from Bill and Charlie DeWitt. Veeck added spice to the league's 1951 season in ways that were more exotic than some of Casey's most unconventional decisions. The club owner stationed contortionist Max Patkin to whoop it up on the coaching lines. Veeck's most famous stunt, filled at first with comedy, probably broke the heart of the man wearing uniform number '1/8,' Eddie Gaedel.

Gaedel's day in the sun occurred on 9 August 1951. The American League was celebrating its golden jubilee with gala festivals in all the parks. A crowd of 18,369 turned out to see St Louis play a double-header against Detroit. Gaedel, the Brown's first batter, strode to the plate. He stood three feet seven inches tall and weighed 65 pounds! Pitcher Bob Cain looked wide-eyed in astonishment and the plate umpire Ed Hurley glared suspiciously. Gaedel proudly stood his ground, holding a strong batter's stance. Zack Taylor, the Browns' manager, walked to the plate with a copy of Gaedel's playing contract and Hurley told everyone to play ball. Cain couldn't zero his pitches in the strike zone between the neophyte batter's shoulders and knees. The pitcher launched four balls. Triumphant, Gaedel trotted to first base. Jim Delsing went in to run for him.

Unfortunately Eddie Gaedel's career as a big league utility man ended there. The next day American League President Will Harridge refused to honor Eddie Gaedel's contract. According to Harridge, Gaedel's 'participation in an American League Championship game comes under the heading of conduct detrimental to baseball.' Gaedel responded that 'this is a conspiracy against little people,' but Harridge's decision held and Gaedel lost his $100-a-game job.

Not even the Eddie Gaedel affair could distract fans from the fact that the Yankees were on their way to winning their third straight pennant in 1951. The highlights of the season included the pitching feats of the 'Superchief,' Yankee Allie Reynolds, who further emphasized the fact by blazing a pair of no-hit games. The first occurred on 12 July in Cleveland, with George Woodling connecting for a Yankee home run to win the game 1-0. The second came against the Red Sox at Yankee Stadium, by a score of 8-0. Reynolds walked the first three batters in the first game and four in the second. These were the first no-hit games pitched by a Yankee since a Monte Pearson triumph in 1938. Reynolds' second win captured the pennant and a place in history: no other pitcher had thrown a no-hit game to nail down the pennant.

The Yankees squared off against the Giants in the 1951 World Series – but it might well have been the Dodgers for the National League except for one of the most exciting moments in baseball. The Giants and Dodgers had finished the regular season in a tie, and in the third play-off game, the Dodgers were ahead, 4-2, with the tying runs on second and third in the bottom of the ninth. Bobby Thomson came to bat and the Dodgers put in relief pitcher Ralph Branca, but Thomson sent his second pitch out of the field for a three-run homer that gave the Giants the series and the pennant. At first it seemed as if the Giants would continue their 'miracle' drive and sweep past the Yankees, as they won two of the first three games. Then they began to lose steam. The Yankees went on to win three straight and the title. During the strenuous pennant drive the Giants heavily relied on two 23-game winners, Sal Maglie and Larry Jansen. Worn out from the battle to the Series, neither pitcher won a game against the Yankees. Yankee rookie Mickey Mantle, however, didn't perform especially well either, batting an even .200. Willie Mays, the future Giant great, performed meagerly, batting only .182 during the Series. Veteran Joe DiMaggio, whose batting average during the regular season had reached a new low of .263, tapped in a modest .261 in the championship bouts.

DiMaggio did achieve yet another distinction in 1951. Playing in his tenth World Series had tied Babe Ruth's record for participation in championship games. His greatness on the field, however, was beginning to fade, and the Yankees needed some transfusions in their lineup. Added power came not only from Mantle but from a more sensational rookie, Gil

Left: Left-hander Ed Lopat warms up before a game. Edmund Walter 'Steady Eddie' Lopat performed consistently well for the Yankees, turning in 109 wins and only 51 losses during the seven years he pitched for them.

Below: Sportsman's Park, home field of the St Louis Browns since their entry into the American League in 1902, and of Chris van der Ahe's famous St Louis Browns even before that.

Above: Joe DiMaggio bids farewell to Casey Stengel and Yankee Vice-President Del Webb in Yankee offices in December, 1951.
Right: First baseman Mickey Vernon takes a cut during practice. James Barton Vernon played for the Senators for 13 and a half years, ending his 20-year career in 1960 after two years in the National League. His hitting won him the batting title twice, and he led the league in doubles three times.

McDougald. Gil, who was primarily a second baseman in his rookie year in 1951, moved to third base in 1952. Despite his rather strange batting stance, he led the team in batting with .306 in 1951. He also tied a record during the Series for the most runs batted in during an inning – four, by hitting a grand slam home run. He was the only rookie ever to hit a grand slam in the Series. In addition to hitting, McDougald proved an effective fielder.

Mickey Mantle, of course, was another young blood who was to revitalize the Yankee organization. The former shortstop on the Joplin farm team could hit the baseball a proverbial mile from either side of the plate. Mantle proved an apt replacement for Joe DiMaggio, although his powerful style was more reminiscent of the fabled Babe Ruth than of DiMaggio. The latter, slowed by injuries, decided to retire despite an offer of $100,000 from the Yankees in return for wearing the team uniform while viewing most of the next season from the dugout. Joe had collected over $700,000 in his 13 years with the team and now felt ready to move on to other careers. Naturally, a place had been reserved for him at the Baseball Hall of Fame in Cooperstown, New York.

At the press conference announcing his retirement, DiMaggio was asked who was the greatest hitter he had ever seen. 'That's an easy one,' he replied. 'Ted Williams, without a question.' One of the greatest players of all times, Ted was known as 'Mr Baseball,' or the 'Splendid Splinter.' During the 1950s he enjoyed the highest lifetime average for any active player. In nine All-Star games he held a .409 batting average. He

also captured the batting and RBI crowns four times. He stood six foot three inches tall and weighed in at 205 pounds. Batting left-handed, he threw with his right.

In 1952 Ted Samuel Williams left the Red Sox to fly as a Marine jet pilot in Korea. His last game of the 1952 season was against Washington on 30 April 1952. As a farewell gesture he blasted a two-run game-winning homer against Detroit. The fighting and turmoil on the Korean Peninsula decimated other American League contenders. The Bronx Bombers lost Whitey Ford, infielders Gary Coleman, Bobby Brown and hurler Tom Morgan to the draft. Coleman was a sparkling second baseman, especially adept as an acrobatic pivot man in exciting double plays. For the 1952 season, scrappy Billy Martin replaced Coleman on the Yankees and Mantle opened his first full season by hitting the ball where it had never gone before, over the left-center wall in Washington. In his first full season with the Yankees he led the club with a batting average of .311 and was the team's second-best home run artist with 23. The 20-year-old blond wonder boy was a switch hitter who could slug, not slap from either side of the plate. He also struck out often from either side, sometimes kicking the water

Above: Shortstop Phil Rizzuto and second baseman Billy Martin polish up on their double-play maneuvers in a Yankee infield practice session.

Left: The great Mickey Mantle – 'The Commerce Comet' – began his blazing 18-year career with the Yankees in 1951. Three times selected as the league's Most Valuable Player, in 1956, 1957 and 1962, Mantle's fiercely competitive nature drove him to win the Triple Crown in 1956 as well. Besides his legendary batting skills – with which he led the league in homers four times, in runs scored six times and in RBI's once – Mantle inspired a great team to even further greatness.

cooler on his return to the dugout. Pitchers, nonetheless, feared him and he soon led the club for free trips to first on balls.

Stengel relished winning the 1952 pennant and Series. The Yankees beat the Cleveland Indians by a narrow two games in the American League race before facing the Dodgers in the Series. Brooklyn battled gallantly, but suffered defeat for the sixth straight time. It took seven games, the Yankees taking the final one, 4-2, with a home run by Mickey Mantle clinching it.

Competition for the batting title in 1953 turned into a race between rookie slugger Mantle and the returning veteran Ted Williams. On 29 July, the discharged Marine Corps jet pilot zoomed into Fenway Park. Not quite 35 and a veteran of two wars, he returned to Boston with a boyish grin and, as usual, without a necktie. He was in no shape to play in the game against the White Sox that day, but a crowd of 19,083 nevertheless turned out just to catch a glimpse of their Red Sox idol. His first day on the field, 6 August 1953, proved dismal. He popped out while pinch-hitting, thereby ending a rally against the Browns. Three days later he stepped in to hit for Johnny Lipon. Mike Garcia wound up and threw the ball. Williams unleashed his swing and drove the ball into the sky and out of Fenway Park. All who had seen him knew that Ted was off and running. 'It's nice to know I haven't lost my batting eye,' remarked the Boston idol. In the 37 games remaining that season, he batted a searing .407 and smashed 13 home runs. Neither age nor the time in Korea adversely affected his performance.

Around the time of Williams' return, Mickey Mantle, 13 years his junior, was photographed chewing bubble gum while playing center field. By 1953 Mickey Mantle was fully at home. The Yankees rolled over the rest of the American League to take an unprecedented fifth straight pennant. It was the easiest of the five championships. The Bombers had one 18-game-streak that practically ended the race. In the final standings they led second-place Cleveland by eight and a half games. In the Series the Yankees met the Dodgers again and beat them again, four games to two. The exciting finish came in the sixth game, bottom of the ninth, when Billy Martin singled to score Hank Bauer and win the game 4-3. 'I have a helluva ball club, but it's underrated,' remarked Stengel following the game. 'And we're going to get better.' A week later the Yankees' front office underlined the comment by announcing the team would introduce its first black player. His name was Elston Howard and he could both catch and play the outfield.

Two startling moves would soon leave St Louis and Philadelphia without American League representation. Although Bill Veeck, in his first full season as owner of the Browns, managed to increase attendance from 293,790 to 518,796, the enlarged gate still wasn't enough to pay the bills, and Veeck desperately tried to get permission to move his club to Baltimore. Twice fellow club owners turned down his request for the new venture. During the 1953 season, hard up for cash, he stopped promotion and was reduced to selling players.

Something had to happen, and it did. On 29 September 1953 the American League announced that

Mickey Mantle slides in a close play at homeplate.

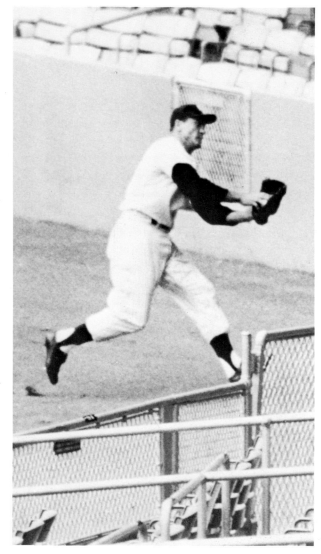

attorney Clarence W Miles and a syndicate had purchased the Browns and were moving the club to Baltimore (the team name was changed to the 'Orioles'). The reported price was $2,475,000. A year later Arnold Johnson would buy the Philadelphia Athletics for $3,500,000 and move them to Kansas City. Both clubs drew well in their initial season, the Orioles pulling 1,060,910 fans in 1954, and the sixth-place Athletics attracting 1,393,054 in Kansas City the next year.

Baltimore opened the 1954 season with the greatest parade in the city's history. Vice-President Richard Milhouse Nixon rode in an open car as did Connie Mack and Clark Griffith. An estimated 500,000 people turned out to watch the floats, marching bands and celebrities. Mrs John J McGraw, widow of the Orioles' manager a half century before, had a place of honor among those present. The season-opener saw the Orioles face off against Detroit. Baltimore was blanked 3-0 before a disappointed crowd of 46,354 fans. Baltimore lost 100 games that season, winning only 54. That, however, was good enough to land them into seventh place, leaving the cellar to the stumbling Athletics. In September, Baltimore managed to lure Paul Richards away from the White Sox to take over as the Baltimore manager. From then on the Orioles began to strengthen their wings for the eventual flight to the top.

The year 1954 proved momentous in the world of sports. England's Roger Bannister broke the most important track barrier by running the mile in under four minutes. His exact time was three minutes, 59.4 seconds. In baseball the Cleveland Indians achieved something of similar greatness. They shattered the nearly universal belief that baseball belonged to the Yankees. Author Douglas Wallop's novel *The Year the Yankees Lost the Pennant* was published that year. It was supposed to be a humorous fantasy with a

In their last meeting the Indians defeated the Yankees twice on a balmy Sunday afternoon. After the drubbing, Hal Lebovitz, the baseball writer for the Cleveland *News*, offered Stengel a ride from the park to his hotel room. Stengel gruffly refused and was snappish in answering the reporter's questions. 'Stengel is a poor loser,' declared Lebovitz. After all, he and the Yankee club had never learned how to accept defeat.

The Indians faced Willie Mays and the Giants in the 1954 World Series. In the first game the score stood at 2-2 in the top of the eighth when Indian first baseman Vic Wertz stepped to the plate. Wertz, who batted .500 in the Series, faced a game-winning opportunity with two runners on base. He blasted a pitch high and long down the Polo Grounds' deep center-field alley. Willie Mays turned his back on the infield and ran like a gazelle. He seemed destined to crash against the out-

Above: Right-hander Early Wynn warms up before a game. A future Hall of Famer, Wynn pitched for the Cleveland Indians for nine years (1949-1957) during his 23-year career, turing in four 20-game seasons during that time.

Right: Power-hitter Vic Wertz played first base for Cleveland from 1955 to 1958. Wertz's outstanding performance in the 1954 Series – smashing eight hits, scoring two runs and batting in three more – was not enough to bring his team the championship.

Faustian theme. The seemingly unreal became fact and Mr Wallop was on his way to fame and fortune with *Damn Yankees* eventually becoming a successful Broadway musical and motion picture.

Ironically, the Yankees won more often in 1954 than in any previous term in Stengel's career as manager. They won 103 and lost 51, which was brilliant but not good enough. A fully inspired Cleveland Indian team broke the American League record by winning 111 games, losing only 43. The previous record of 110 games was assembled by the 1927 Yankees, who were considered the mightiest team in the history of the sport. Cleveland manager Al Lopez, who formerly played for Stengel in the National League, beat out his old teacher. The magical Indians simply had a better team. Their fine pitching staff included two 23-game winners, Bob Lemon and Early Wynn. Good performances on the mound from Mike Garcia (19-8) and 35-year-old Bob Feller (13-3) rounded out the pitching staff. Their best hitters were second baseman Bobby Avila and Al Rosen, batting .341 and .300 respectively. The club played excellent defense, particularly in the outfield.

paid their way into Shibe Park in 1953. Owners Roy and Earle Mack, the sons of Connie Mack, were struggling to buy control from each other. Rumors surfaced that the A's were destined for far away places. A 'Save the A's' committee formed in hope of attracting enough local enthusiasm to warrant keeping the franchise in the city of brotherly love.

Then the Mack dynasty came to an end. Fifty-four years earlier, Ban Johnson had moved the A's to Philadelphia, and now another Johnson, businessman Arnold Johnson, was taking them out. Spry 92-year-old Connie Mack flew to Kansas City for the opening game. The crowds adored him, paying tribute with applause at the airport and later with an ovation at Municipal Stadium. Lou Boudreau was recruited away from Boston to manage the team. He stopped the A's almost certain fall to the basement, bringing them up to sixth place.

Facing the pennant-winning Indians was not the only challenge the Yankees had in the 1955 season. Their biggest trouble appeared in the depletion of their pitching staff. Both Allie Reynolds and Vic Raschi were gone and Eddie Lopat was clearly slipping. To reconstruct their pitching staff, the Yankee

Far left: Cleveland third baseman Al Rosen (1947-56) stands ready at bat.

Left: Cleveland's Mike Garcia – 'The Big Bear' – pitched his way to a league-leading 2.64 ERA in 1954.

field barrier. He caught the ball over his left shoulder in football fashion, a full 450 feet from home plate. The outfielder's grace, speed and precision cost the Indians the game. The Giants went on to win the opener in the bottom of the tenth. Sweeping the Series four games to none, they ended seven consecutive seasons of American League dominance.

The 1954 Series was staged in each league's biggest park. Cleveland's municipal stadium was the largest, with 74,000 seats, and the Polo Grounds had seating for 55,131 fans. Consequently an attendance record was set in this Series with a four-game total of 251,507 paying fans. They proved to be the most lucrative series to date for the players. The winning Giants were paid $11,147.90 for a full share and the Indians got $6,712.50. In contrast, poor attendance was undermining another once-proud team. The westward expansion of the American League began with the move of the Philadelphia Athletics to Kansas City.

In 1952 because of the solid pitching of Bobby Shantz, the A's had pulled up to fourth place. They then lost footing and continued to decline to seventh in 1953, ending up in the basement in 1954. Attendance drooped like performance, as only 362,113 fans

Indian pitcher and future Hall of Famer Bob Lemon won 207 games and lost only 128.

organization would have to pull a rabbit out of the hat. Although the kinds of winners they required were a scarce commodity, the New York front office waved a magic wand and created one of the most massive trade deals in history. The Yankees gave the Orioles Jim McDonald, Harry Bird and Bill Miller, pitchers; Hal Smith and Gus Triandos, catchers; Don Leppert, Willie Miranda and Kal Segrist, infielders; and Gene Woodling, an outfielder. In return the Orioles gave the Yankees Bob Turley, Don Larsen and Mike Blyska, pitchers; Darrell Johnson, a catcher; Dick Kryhoski, a first baseman; Billy Hunter, a shortstop; and Ted del Guercio and Jim Fridley, outfielders. Turley and Larsen were the key men for Stengel. They provided him with the pitching strength he needed. Baltimore gained a future star in Triandos, and Woodling proved very useful in a future trade with Cleveland. The Yankee farm system, in the meanwhile, turned up a pair of good hurlers in the persons of Johnny Kucks and Tom Sturdivant. They joined Ford, Grim, Byrne, Turley and Larsen as Stengel's winning pitchers.

American League fans enjoyed an exciting four-way contest in 1955 between the Yankees, White Sox, Indians and Red Sox. Early in the season, only three games separated the four teams, with the Indians in the lead. The Yankees put on a spectacular finishing run, winning 15 consecutive games and clinching Stengel's sixth pennant flag in seven seasons. At the finish the Yankees led the Indians by three games, although Cleveland had tried hard. Bob Feller was at the end of his career, splitting his eight decisions. A new strikeout ace, left-hander Herb Score, won 16 games and struck out 245 batters, more than one an inning. His wins recalled Feller's earlier glories.

This was not a great season for pitchers. The American League, for the first time in its history, could not boast of a single 20-game winner. Yankee Whitey Ford, Frank Sullivan of the Red Sox, and Bob Lemon of Cleveland won 18. Increased reliance on the use of relief pitchers may have accounted for the shift in statistics. In Cleveland relief specialists Ray Narleski and Don Mossi were considered the most valuable members of the staff after Herb Score. It was, however, another great season for Yankee catcher Yogi Berra. Berra was named the American League's Most Valuable Player for the third time, a distinction he shared with Joe DiMaggio and Jimmie Foxx.

The 52nd World Series finally caught up with Stengel. On the morning of 30 September 1955, only the most dedicated Brooklyn fans gave the Dodgers a chance against their rivals from across the river. The Dodgers were already down by two games, and it seemed yet again that they would be the bridesmaid instead of the bride for the eighth time. Brooklyn manager Walter Alston picked blue-eyed Johnny Podres, with his nine wins and ten losses, in desperation. His two aces, Don Newcombe (20-5) and Billy Loes (10-4), had just flunked the test against the Yankees. Podres' appearance on the mound coincided with his 23rd birthday. He celebrated it in style, holding the Bombers to seven hits as the Dodgers took the game, 8-3.

Thus began a three-game rally that shook the baseball world and brought seemingly limitless joy to the borough of Brooklyn. The Yankees tied the Series, taking game six behind the four-hit pitching of Whitey Ford. Yankee Stadium was the site of the seventh and deciding game. Johnny Podres, now 23 years and four days old, took up the pitching assignment. In a thrilling breathtaking performance, including 'el Catch' by Cuban speedster Sandy Amoros, Podres and the

Bums from Brooklyn blanked the Yankees 2-0. Tommy Byrne was the losing pitcher. Stengel characteristically accepted blame for the loss. 'Podres hadn't pitched a complete game since July,' remarked Casey, 'and I figured he couldn't last, so I had the hitters taking pitches. But he lasted so I guess I should've had the boys swinging.'

The American League was spreading out and reached a new attendance record with the comple- tion of moves to Baltimore and Kansas City. The 1955 gate surpassed the 1953 gate by more than two mil- lion. The Washington Senators, however, were seri- ous losers; the number of paying fans dropped from 595,594 in 1953 to 425,238 in 1955. In 1956, attendance at Washington's Griffith Stadium plunged even further. More and more commentators raised the question of whether the national capital could sup- port a major league franchise.

The great leftie Whitey Ford pitched 18 Series games for the Yankees, winning a record 10 games. He was elected to the Hall of Fame in 1974.

Big Milt Pappas pitched for Baltimore for nine years and went to the Cincinnati Reds in 1966. He then pitched for Atlanta and for the Cubs, ending his career in 1973 with a won-lost record of 209-164 and a 3.40 ERA.

The Yankees opened in Washington on 17 April 1956. President Eisenhower threw out the season's first ball. But it was Mickey Mantle who proved to be the day's commander-in-chief by unleashing his batting arsenal. Up against veteran Camilo Pascual, he hit two home runs over the centerfield fence, the first time any batter had slugged two in the same game in that direction. Yoga Berra smacked four hits that game, including a homer, and the Yankees destroyed hapless Washington, 10-4.

Hall of Famer and former Yankee Bill Dickey had this to say in the clubhouse after the game: 'Mantle's got more power than any hitter I ever saw, including Babe.' By now the 24-year-old slugger was a national celebrity more for his potential than for what he had actually accomplished. Mantle had not won the American League batting honors in the 1955 season, those kudos going to Detroit sophomore outfielder, Al Kaline. Mantle, however, hit more home runs than anyone in the league that year with 37, and some rocketed farther than a ball had ever flown before. Yet he remained green and continued to struggle. He had not developed the consistency or the confidence needed to reach his full potential.

On that same opening day of 1956 Ted Williams showed that he planned to stay in the batting contest. He splashed two doubles and a single to the left side of second base, signaling that the baseball veteran was still out to break a few records of his own. But as the season progressed, it became clear that the batting honors would belong to Mickey Mantle. The homers he started hitting in Washington continued in profusion. Mantle set his sights on the Triple Crown – leading the league in batting percentage, home runs and runs batted in. Batting right- or left-handed he elicited fear in the hearts of pitchers. His strikeout percentage declined. He increasingly drew walks as pitchers fretted about throwing in the batting zone while he stood at the plate.

By the time of the All-Star game, the Yankees held on to first place. The White Sox, however, were having a sensational season and stayed uncomfortably close to the leaders. Freshman shortstop Luis Aparicio breathed life into the club. The team stressed speed with Aparicio, Minnie Minoso and Jim Rivera. The

Left: Outfielder and powerhitter Gus Zernial played for the Philadelphia, then the Kansas City Athletics from 1952 to 1957.

Below: Baltimore Oriole catcher Gus Triandos tries in vain to catch a ball fouled into the Yankee dugout by Gil McDougald.

Third baseman Ray Boone played for Detroit from 1953 to 1958. He led the league in RBI's with 116 in 1955.

White Sox led the league in steals and boasted an outstanding second baseman in Nellie Fox. Larry Doby and Sherman Lollar generated the team's batting power.

Rocky Colavito led the Indian attack. An outfielder, he had a great arm and fabulous power. Colavito hit 21 home runs that season, showing the promise of his future greatness. The Red Sox, revolving around Ted Williams, were on their way to a fourth-place position for the fourth straight time. On 6 August, Ted tied one of Babe Ruth's records, albeit a dubious one. Having dropped a Mickey Mantle fly ball, Williams fumed on his way to the dugout when the side was retired. He then spat in the direction of the box seats to show his disdain for the jeering fans, and was fined $5000, equaling the one received by Ruth. Williams was repentant and in his next game blasted a home run

against Baltimore as a heroic apology.

In the summer of 1956 Mantle appeared to be threatening another Babe Ruth record. Few players had approached Ruth's 60 home runs in one season before 1956; Mickey had 47 going into September, but at this critical time he entered a slump and only produced five more during the season. He won the Triple Crown with 52 home runs, a .353 batting average and 130 RBI's, helping his Yanks capture the pennant. Mantle, in fact, led both major leagues in all three categories, a feat accomplished only four times.

The Yankees avenged their World Series defeat of the previous year by beating the Dodgers in seven games. With the series tied at two–all, the fifth game proved to be of great significance. Casey decided to gamble on pitcher Don Larsen, whose record was only 11 wins and 5 losses for the season. The burly

Left: Speedster shortstop Luis Aparacio led the league in stolen bases for nine consecutive seasons, including the seven he played for the White Sox (1956-62). He ended his 18-year career in 1973 with 506 stolen bases under his belt, and was elected to the Hall of Fame in 1984.

Below: Second baseman Nellie Fox played most of his 19-year career for the White Sox, leading the league four times in hits.

pitcher stood six feet tall and weighed 230 pounds. His opponent on the mound was Sal Maglie, the veteran former Giant. Both men were pitching flawless games until Mantle belted a home run in the fourth. Larsen, however, continued to down batters like flies.

Earlier Larsen had switched to pitching without a wind-up, after suspecting that third base coaches were reading him correctly and signaling his intentions to batters. Going into the ninth inning not a single Dodger had even made it to first base, and Larsen was only three out from pitching a perfect game. There had never been even a no-hitter in a World Series, and regular season perfectly pitched games had occurred only six times in the 75 years of major league history. Excitement grew as the Dodgers came up to bat.

Carl Furillo opened the inning by flying out. Then Roy Campanella grounded to Billy Martin, who threw the Dodger catcher out at first. Next Dale Mitchell came to bat as a replacement for Maglie. Larsen's first pitch was a ball, the second was called a strike, and

the third was swung at and missed for strike two. Larsen picked up the resin bag, rubbed his hands, and threw. The ball was fouled back. He pitched again, Mitchell half swung, then checked his swing, and the umpire called strike three. Yogi Berra rushed out to the mound and leaped into Larsen's arms. Larsen had made history, pitching a perfect game before 64,519 Yankee Stadium fans in World Series play.

Brooklyn went on to win the sixth game but was clobbered by the Yankees 9-0 in the seventh and deciding game. With men on base, Yogi Berra belted

Yankee right-hander Don Larsen pitched five Series games for New York, but his most memorable was on 8 October 1956, when he pitched the only perfect game in World Series history.

two home runs off Don Newcombe, the outstanding Dodger game-winner who always lost his touch in World Series play. Berra's homers came in the first and third innings, giving the Yankees a 4-0 lead. Manager Alston thought Newcombe would settle down and allowed him to come out and begin the fourth inning as well. But when the first Yankee batter,

Elston Howard, promptly hit one into the seats to make it 5-0, that was all for Don, who later received a telegram of condolence from President Eisenhower. Yankee pitcher Johnny Kucks (18-9) pitched a superb shutout.

The Cleveland Indians threatened the Yankees in the 1957 season. Rocky Colavito performed as one of

Outfielder Rocky Colavito played for Cleveland from 1955 to 1959 and from 1965 to 1967. Rocco Domenico Colavito hammered 21, 25, 41 and 42 homers in consecutive seasons, beginning in 1956.

Rookie of the Year in 1955, left-hander Herb Score pitched two brilliant seasons for Cleveland, leading the league in strikeouts both years, before he was hit in the eye by a line drive in 1957. His winning percentage declined dramatically after that, and he finished his career pitching for the White Sox in 1962.

the league's steadiest hitters, and pitcher Herb Score seemed destined for a legendary career. Pitching with blinding speed and a wicked curve ball, he won 16 games in his rookie year, and 20 in his second year out. He led the league in strikeouts in his first two professional seasons. Then, on 7 May 1957, Score was struck in the right eye by a line drive hit by Gil McDougald. He was 23 years old. The accident ended his season. Although he returned to baseball, he never regained his greatness. McDougald was sleepless after the accident. Not permitted to visit the pitcher in the hospital, he talked to all the doctors caring for the injured pitcher. 'If Score loses his eye, I might quit the game,' McDougald told Cleveland reporter Hal Lebovitz. 'It isn't worth it.'

Ted Williams had a momentous year with the Red Sox. Now 39 years of age and a four-time holder of the Triple Crown, he became the oldest batting champion in American League history. He averaged a searing

.388 for the season. Although early in the season he suffered a slump and had numerous rows with the press, in two games (8 May and 13 June) he thumped three home runs. His previous three-homer game had been 11 years earlier in 1946. Toward the end of the 1957 season it seemed as if the Boston superstar could *not* be silenced. In September he went through six games and reached base 16 consecutive times without being retired. The Senators' Hal Griggs finally ended that remarkable string of successes. Home run honors for 1957 belonged to Roy Sievers, Washington's strongman, who belted 42 of them and had 114 runs batted in. He also led the league in total bases.

The first half of the 1957 season had found the Yankees in a meager third place, playing without verve. Then they came to life, winning ten straight, and moved into first place on 30 June. In the World Series that year the Yankees faced the Milwaukee Braves. Warren Spahn lead the Braves' pitching staff with a 21-win season. Behind him were stellar performers center fielder Hank Aaron, who batted .322, and the league's home run king with 44, veteran Red Schoendienst. Third baseman Eddie Mathews was another Braves' long-ball hitter; he had slugged 32 home runs during the season.

The Yankees had rarely faced a team with such an awesome combination of batting and pitching power. The Series opened at Yankee Stadium, with Spahn facing Whitey Ford. Ford held the Braves to five hits and one run, and the Yanks won 3-1. The battle had begun, and in the Milwaukee locker room later that day the silence bespoke of a grim determination. In the second game Brave Wes Covington's spectacular second-inning catch ended a Yankee rally, and Milwaukee pitcher Lew Burdette held the Bombers to only seven hits, pulling out a 4-2 victory. Then in the first game at Milwaukee County Stadium the Yankees crushed the Braves 12-3 as six Brave pitchers allowed

11 walks. The defeat was even more bitter because of the performance of a home-town boy in a Yankee uniform, Tony Kubek. The rookie led the onslaught with two home runs and four RBI's.

Next it was the Braves' turn, with a 7-5 Warren Spahn victory in an exciting and controversial ten innings. With the Series tied at two games each, game five featured another clutch catch by Covington as Lew Burdette pitched his way to a slim 1-0 victory. Hank Aaron's homer in game six tied the score at two all in the top of the seventh, but New York went on to take the game 3-2. Lew Burdette pitched again in the crucial, winner-take-all seventh game, shutting down the Yanks 5-0. In Burdette's three games, all wins, he had allowed only two runs and 21 hits. The Yankees lost the Series for only their second time since 1942.

The irony for Casey Stengel was that Burdette, only the fourth pitcher to win three games in a World Series, had been traded from New York. He was also

Outfielder and first baseman Roy Edwards 'Squirrel' Sievers played for Washington from 1954 to 1959 and in 1964 and 1965. His best season was 1957, when he led the league in homers with 42, and in RBI's with 114.

Shortstop Tony Kubek hit two home runs in the World Series in his rookie year, and was named Rookie of the Year. He played a total of five Series during his nine years with the Yankees (1957-65).

the only pitcher ever to win three Series games from the Yankees. Casey's reaction was a mixed one, as he commented, 'How many runs did we score off that fellow? Two? Well that's the story.' He was quick to threaten, however, that the Yankees would be 'heard from again.'

Yogi Berra's season's performance raised specula-

tion that he might be sliding toward an early retirement at age 32. At .251, his batting average was the lowest it had been in 12 seasons, although even in this off-year he managed to hit 24 home runs and bat in 84 runs. A colorful and irascible character, Berra had been named the American League's Most Valuable Player in 1951, 1954 and 1955. When he was named

Catcher Yogi Berra played his entire 19-year career for the New York Yankees, beginning in 1946. The 14 World Series he played in brought him four all-time firsts in the Series record books: most games played (75), most at-bats (259), most hits (71) and most doubles (10). His Series career statistics also include 12 home runs, 41 runs scored, 39 RBI's and 32 bases on balls. During the fifties Berra averaged 26 homers a season, and he was a fine defensive player as well, with a lifetime 175 double-plays to his credit. Three-time MVP Lawrence Peter Berra, who managed the Mets from 1972 to 1975 and the Yankees in 1965 and 1984-85, was elected to the Hall of Fame in 1971.

the MVP the third time, an umpire exclaimed 'Most Valuable Player! They ought to call him most voluble player.' For all his nagging about plate umpires' calls, Yogi rarely got tossed out of games and never drew a fine from the league president's office. Fears of his retirement were premature, as Berra quickly bounced back, eventually moving from his catching position to the outfield.

By now the impact of television on attendance was beginning to show at the gate. The Yankees, for example, had the vast New York metropolitan area to themselves after the Dodgers and Giants moved west, yet they were getting fewer fans through the turnstiles. In 1958 their attendance would drop 68,000 from the 1957 totals.

In the winter of 1958, American League president Will Harridge announced his plans for retirement. Seventy-two years old, he had served the League for 28 years. Joe Cronin was elected to the job on 31 January 1959 for a seven-year term of office. Cronin's successful election followed another bonanza season for those 'Damn Yankees.' But the season also featured bright stars throughout the league. The phenomenon of Ted Williams was still batting his way into baseball history. Already the oldest batting champion, Williams won his sixth batting championship in 1958, finishing at .328. Next in line was his Boston teammate Pete Runnels, who hit .322. White Sox slammer Rocky Colavito blasted four home runs in consecutive trips to the plate on 10 June. He managed to do this in Baltimore's Memorial Stadium, the toughest park in the league for home runs. Lou Gehrig has been the first American League player – back in 1932 – to hit four in a game.

In 1958 the Yankees gained their fourth straight pennant, their ninth in ten years. Stengel tied Connie Mack's record for managing nine league championships. Although New York ended up ten games ahead of the second-place White Sox, there were signs that the Yankee dynasty was beginning to crack. Early in the season the club had appeared unbeatable; they even had a 10-game winning streak, which ended when Tiger pitcher Frank Lary beat them. (Lary had an impressive 27-10 record in his contests with the Yankees.) Then the Yankees slowed down, not even maintaining a .500 win-loss margin in the last two months of the season. Their prime hitter, Mickey Mantle, was bothered by a shoulder injury and ended up with a .304 average.

The 1958 World Series was a repeat of 1957 – the Yankees against the Milwaukee Braves. Neither team had faced much serious opposition all season from within their leagues and both were looking forward to this ultimate contest. The Braves quickly moved into the lead by taking the first two games in Milwaukee, but the Yankees came back in their home stadium to win the third game. Then the Braves took the fourth game to gain what seemed like an unsurmountable lead of three games to one. But Yankee Bob Turley pitched a five-hitter, Elston Howard made a spectacular diving catch, and Gil McDougald hit a homer that proved to be the winning run as the Yankees took the fifth game, 7-0. With the Braves ahead three games to two, an exciting sixth game went into the end of the ninth inning with a 2-2 tie. Then McDougald's homer did it for the Yankees again as they won in ten innings, 4-3, tying up the Series at three games each. The seventh game pitted the Yankees' ace Don Larsen

From left to right: Warren Giles, National League President and Ford Frick, baseball commissioner, welcome Joe Cronin as the new American League President.

against the Braves' ace Lew Burdette. Larsen had to be relieved by Bob Turley, but Bill Skowron's three-run homer in the eighth put the Yankees on top, 6-2, and gave them another World Championship.

The 1959 season was distinguished by the Red Sox's introduction of their first black player, infielder Elijah (Pumpsie) Green. Now all 16 major league teams had been integrated. This decade-ending year was also unique in Yankee performance, as the club that had won nine of the previous ten pennants went through a frustrating series of slumps and injuries. By late May the World Champions were in the cellar, and by Labor Day they were eliminated from the American League race.

The fight for top place in the league centered on the White Sox and the Indians. Al Lopez, now with Chicago, relied on outstanding pitching, speed and defense to sweep a four-game series at Cleveland which began on 28 August. That spelled the end for the Indians and the White Sox ended up with a five-game lead. The White Sox went on to lose in a tight Series with the Dodgers.

And so ended the decade. Although subsequent decades brought a seemingly endless march of record-breaking performances, the fifties would be fondly remembered as an era bearing such legendary names as Joe DiMaggio, Ted Williams, Gil McDougald and Willie Mays.

Gil McDougald is congratulated by teammate Tony Kubek, after belting a third-inning solo homer in the fifth game of the World Series. The Yankees won this game and went on to take the Series, four games to three.

President Kennedy throws out the first ball at the All-Star Game on 10 July 1962.

CHAPTER SIX
The Sensational Sixties

"I'll never make the mistake of being 70 years old again."

Casey Stengel, after being fired from the Yankees.

Brooks Robinson graced third base with his sparkling performances for 23 years, playing for the great Baltimore Orioles from 1955-77. In 1964, when he was selected as the league's Most Valuable Player, Robinson led the league in RBI's with 118, and batted for a .317 average. On a team that won two out of four World Series contests and played in five league championships between 1966 and 1974, Brooks Robinson batted .500 and .583 in his first two play-offs, and batted .318 in the 1970 Series. He holds the all-time records at third base for fielding average, most games played, most putouts, most assists and most double plays. He was elected to the Hall of Fame in 1983.

The sixties began with the collapse of the Continental League – an idea whose time had never come. The venture had been the brainchild of attorney William A Shea. Branch Rickey was slated to serve as the league's president. Though stillborn, this challenge woke up the National and American Leagues to the fact that there was no shortage of interest and money for major league expansion. On 2 August 1960 Shea and Rickey announced in Chicago that the existing major leagues would absorb their franchises. The National League had already decided to add New York and Houston to its playing circuit. The American League quickly raced to parity. Calvin Griffith's Washington team was granted permission to relocate in Minneapolis-St Paul and a new franchise for the nation's capital was approved. General Elwood Quesada, chief of the Federal Aviation Administration, led the group investing in the new Washington team. Cowbow Gene Autry and tycoon Bob Reynolds rounded out the process by acquiring the new Los Angeles franchise. All the new clubs then had to scramble for players to field in time for the season's opener just four months away. In order to accom-

modate this, the other American League clubs created a players pool by each contributing 15 players from the 40-man reserve. The new clubs would pay $75,000 for each athlete they selected. The Angels invested in 30 players and the Senators invested in 31.

One gentleman clearly not for sale was Ted Williams, who passed an epic milestone during the 1960 season. Facing Wynn Hawkins, a Cleveland right-hander, he blasted his 500th home run at Cleveland Municipal Stadium, thereby joining the immortal Babe Ruth (714), Jimmie Foxx (534) and Mel Ott (511). Williams' triumph was witnessed by American League President Joe Cronin, who had managed the slugger when he hit his first professional home run. In another Red Sox-Indians match on 10 August Williams passed Ott by hitting number 512, again off a Cleveland pitcher Barry Latman, in the fifth. He slugged another in the sixth off Johnny Klippstein. The Red Sox won, 6-1. Following the game Williams announced that he was leaving baseball at the end of the season. He went out with a bang, batting .316 in his last year and hitting 29 home runs. Ending his baseball career on a fitting farewell note, Williams hit a home run in his last at bat, in Fenway Park on 28 September in a 5-4 Red Sox victory over the Orioles. Williams' career home runs totalled 521.

The 1960 season found the Yankees pulling themselves together after the previous season's slump. The Yankees went on to claim the pennant, completing Stengel's tenth win in 12 years, a feat which tied him with John McGraw for the most championships in a major league career. The Baltimore Orioles came in second place with fine performances by manager Paul Richards' pitching staff. They finished eight games behind the leaders.

The World Series found New York pitted against the Pirates. Although New York had greater cannon power, outhitting Pittsburgh 91 to 60 and outscoring them 55 to 27, the Pirates made their hits count. The Bucs won the first game despite the fact that the Yankees had 13 hits to Pittsburgh's six. The Yankees wreaked revenge in the next two games, however, punishing an assortment of Pirate pitchers. Game two of the Series, with a final score of 16-3, featured two Mickey Mantle home runs, including a blast that soared 478 feet. It was the first time in the 51-year history of Forbes Field that a right-handed batter had hit a homer over the center-field wall.

The Yankees cleaned up in the third game with a score of 10-0, as Whitey Ford held Pittsburgh to four hits – three singles and a double. Despite their two resounding defeats, the Pirates fought their way back in a tense and exciting fourth game, winning by a score of 3-2. With the Series tied at two all, the Pirates went ahead the next day, beating the Yankees 5-2 with sure relief pitching by Elroy Face. But in the next game Casey's boys opened up another slugfest, winning 12-0, the biggest margin for a shutout in World Series history.

The final game, played before 36,683 fans, epitomized baseball at its most dramatic. Rocky Nelson drove in a first-inning homer to put the Pirates ahead, 2-0. The Bucs earned two more runs in the second. Then Bill Skowron broke the ice for the Yankees, hitting a solo home run in the fifth. The next inning New York exploded as Bobby Richardson singled, Tony Kubek walked, Mickey Mantle singled and Yogi Berra belted a homer. The Yankees moved ahead, 5-4, then added two more runs off relief pitcher Elroy Face in the eighth. The score was 7-4 when Pittsburgh came to bat in the eighth. Gino Cimoli, pinch-hitting

First baseman Bill 'Moose' Skowron averaged .294 during his nine years with the New York Yankees (1954-62), and popped more than 20 homers four times in those years.

for Face, singled to right. Then centerfielder Bill Virdon sliced a grounder at Kubek who was ready for the easy double play; the ball, however, took a bad bounce, striking the shortstop in the throat and knocking him to the ground. He required first aid and was forced to leave the game. Dick Groat then singled Cimoli home, a sacrifice and a hit scored another run, and part-time catcher Hal Smith got hold of a low pitch for a three run-homer, putting Pittsburgh ahead, 9-7. The Yankees came back in the ninth to tie the score at 9-9.

The big right-hander Art Ditmar pitched for the Yankees for four and a half years, playing in three World Series, before moving to Kansas City in mid-season 1961.

Ralph Houk replaced Casey as the Yankee manager. Houk was a clear-headed man committed to professional baseball, and an excellent field manager. The club in his charge was so powerful no obstacle could stand in its way. Most serious baseball talk of the 1961 season buzzed about the awesome power of the so-called 'M&M' boys, the Mantle and Maris combination. The Yankees had acquired the talented Roger Maris in 1960. He and Mantle chased Babe Ruth's 60-homer record all summer long, keeping in stride with the master's accomplishments of the 1927 season. Injuries ended Mantle's run in September at 54, but Maris persevered, hitting number 60 on 26 September against right-hander Jack Fisher. He belted record-breaking number 61 on 1 October, the closing game of the season.

Ever since Babe Ruth hit 60 big ones in 1927, baseball theologians weighed the implications of his record being matched or broken. In 1930 Hack Wilson of the Chicago Cubs had walloped 56; Jimmie Foxx and 'Hammerin Hank' Greenberg subsequently nailed 58 outside of the fence, in 1932 and 1938 respectively. Then, when Roger Maris nearly vaporized Tracy Stallard's pitch with his 61st homer, he was not immediately canonized. Instead the high priests and a vocal segment of the baseball congregation were calling for a major league inquisition. Earlier, anticipating a possible schism, Commissioner Ford Frick ruled that Ruth's record would remain exalted unless it was topped within the 154 games of the traditional baseball calendar. Secularists like Joe Cronin reacted against the pontiff, seeing 'no logic to the ruling.' The addition of new clubs had indeed extended the season to 162 games. But Ruth himself took the home run title after playing 44 more games than Ed Williamson who hit 27 during 112 games of the 1884 National League season. Maris himself never suggested that he equalled the greatness of Ruth, who hit his home runs when few other players managed to do so. In 1927 the

Above: Roger Eugene Maris played right field for Cleveland and Kansas City before joining the Yankees in 1960. When he hit next to Mickey Mantle in the line-up, the two batting giants became known as the 'M&M boys,' lethal to pitchers. Maris, who was selected as the league's Most Valuable Player in 1960 and 1961, smashed a record-shattering 61 homers in 1961. A farm boy from North Dakota at heart, Roger Maris never enjoyed the limelight, and played the last two years of his 12-year career with the St Louis Cardinals.

Right: On 4 July 1957 Yogi Berra belted a home run, the 250th of his career, to score Tony Kubek and Mickey Mantle. Berra finished the day with eight runs batted in as the Yanks swamped the Red Sox, 10 to 0.

The Pirates came up in the bottom of the ninth with Bill Mazeroski leading off. Although not considered a dangerous hitter, the second baseman connected with a high fast ball that sailed over the left-field fence, to clinch the game and the Series for Pittsburgh. In the locker room following the game Mickey Mantle sat down and cried. It was a tough Series for the Yankees to lose, and soon heads began to roll.

Five days after the final game Casey Stengel announced that he had been fired because of his age. 'I'll never make the mistake of being 70 years old again,' said the disgruntled Stengel. The decision to fire him was called 'cold blooded' by the press. Columnist Arthur Daley in *The New York Times* wrote: 'Casey imparted warmth to a cold organization and gave it an appeal that couldn't be bought for a million dollars. He was priceless. From a public relations standpoint the Yankees have done great damage to themselves.... It's a shabby way to treat a man who has not only brought them glory but also has given their dynasty firmer footing than it ever had. So long, Case, you gave us 12 unforgettable years.'

General Manager George Weiss also lost his job that November. He was the other person most responsible for putting together the teams that had won so many pennants and championships. Happily, he and Stengel were soon reunited in their old capacities in the New York expansion franchise, the Mets. In another shake-up, managers Jimmy Dykes of the Tigers and the Indians' Joe Gordon switched jobs in the league's first managers' trade.

entire American League produced only 439, so that Babe's 60 accounted for some 14 percent of all the home runs in the entire league. In 1961 the American League yielded a record of 1,534, making Maris's clout a mortal four percent. Maris's beatification did occur, though, and he shares the official record, albeit with an asterisk next to his name.

Meanwhile, the Yankees devoured their opponents in 1961, winning the pennant under manager Ralph Houk. New York hit a record 240 home runs, with Bill Skowron, Yogi Berra, Elston Howard and Johnny Blanchard joining Mantle and Maris in hitting over 20 each. Even so, the Yankees did not lead the league in runs; the second-place Tigers scored 841 to the Yankees' 827.

New York's pennant victory was the second straight. The club enjoyed pitching support from Whitey Ford, whose reliable right arm produced a 25-4 season. Ford was clearly worth his $50,000 salary. Other clubs demonstrated powerful hitting during the 1961 season. Third in batting were Minnesota's Harmon Killebrew and Baltimore's Jim Gentile, both hitting 46 homers. Rocky Colavito bashed 45, while Norm Cash, his Detroit teammate, powered 41 over the fence. In his most sensational season, Cash won the league's batting title, the first in his 17-year league career.

In the 1961 World Series contest between the Yankees and Reds, Whitey Ford put to rest Babe Ruth's most cherished record of pitching 29 and two-thirds consecutive scoreless innings in World Series play. Shutting out Cincinnati in the opening game, 2-0, Ford extended his streak of scoreless pitching to 27 innings. Pitching again in the fourth Series game, Ford went five scoreless innings before his ankle gave out, thereby setting a record of 32. The Yankees won the Series in five games.

The Yankees brought aboard their first black player in 1955 when they signed Elston Howard. The big man played outfielder, then catcher for them until 1967, ending his career the following year in Boston. He played 10 World Series during his 14-year career.

The 'M&M' batting fusillade nearly eclipsed Yogi Berra's yeoman records. By now he had played in 14 World Series, including 75 games, with 259 times at bat. He would make the World Series record books with runs scored (41), total bases (117), hits (71), doubles (10), home runs (12), runs batted in (39), and walks (32).

President John F Kennedy threw out the first ball of 1962 as the Senators opened in their new $24 million stadium built at the taxpayers' expense. A throng of 44,383 watched the home squad inaugurate their magnificent palace by beating Detroit, 4-1. Kennedy stayed for the whole game, leaving Laotian Ambassador Tiao Khampan back at the White House meditating on the inscrutability of American presidents.

The ebbs and flows of the 1962 season may have differed from the previous year but the Yankees again rose to the top. The batting hurricane of the previous year was tempered, with Maris dropping to 33 and Mantle to 30 home runs for the year. Harmon Killebrew surged to 48, thereby winning the second of the six home run titles he would garner. The greatest surprise of the season was the ferocity of the two new clubs, the Minnesota Twins and the Los Angeles Angels. Like nimble sharks, they gashed the league leader until the final two weeks of the season, when New York burst to the surface. The Angels were the most surprising club in the game. General manager Fred Haney netted some astounding deals to keep his team in the water.

In the 1962 Series, the Yankees faced the Giants, who forced them to play seven games before they could wring out a victory. Whitey Ford's record-breaking pitching streak was stopped in the second inning of the first game. Ford had little trouble winning, 6-2, but the game ended his scoreless Series total at 33 and two thirds consecutive innings. But the most memorable episode in the 1962 Series came in the seventh game, in the bottom of the ninth, with the Yankees leading only 1-0 and the Giants at bat. The Giants got two men on, one on second, the other at third, with two out, when Willie McCovey came to bat. Ralph Terry was pitching – the very Ralph Terry who two years before had delivered up the fateful pitch to Bill Mazeroski. McCovey was a far more powerful hitter than Mazeroski, and sure enough, he got hold of Terry's third pitch and sent a line drive rocketing toward right center field. But this time Yankee second baseman Bobby Richardson snared it – and the Yankees had done it again.

Early Wynn might have been the most tragic figure of the 1962 season. At the year's end he stood one game short of the cherished goal of winning his 300th lifetime victory. The White Sox released him at the end of the season, then allowed him to join spring training in 1963 and attempt to win a berth. Failing to do so, he nonetheless stayed in shape, hoping for another opportunity. Finally the Cleveland Indians offered him a contract. Years before Wynn had pitched his best games with Cleveland; he had taken more than 20 scalps in four great seasons. Now, aching with gouty arms, legs and feet, his dream eluded him his first four times out. He used painkillers to ease the suffering. In July, in his fifth try, he crossed the line, capturing the big gold watch in a game against Kansas City. In the last victory of his major league career he led the Indians to a 7-4 triumph over the Athletics. Wynn became the fourteenth major league pitcher to win 300 games and the first in the American League since Lefty Grove went over the top in 1941.

Within weeks of the opening of the 1963 season, the league witnessed another record-shattering performance by the explosive Minnesota Twins. Playing in a doubleheader against Washington, they slugged eight home runs in the first contest and four in the second. The 1939 Yankees had been the only other American League team to hit eight homers in a single contest. Harmon Killebrew and Vic Power (true to his name) hit a pair each and Bob Allison, Jimmie Hall,

Below left: Hall of Famer Harmon 'Killer' Killebrew led the league in homers six times during his 22-year career.

Below: Pitcher Camilo Pascual won 20 and 21 games for the Twins in 1962 and 1963.

Bernie Allen and Rich Rolling connected for one each.

All this was chickenfeed to the Yankees, who gobbled up the pennant despite injuries to Mickey Mantle, and Roger Maris's bad back. Mantle was badly hurt when he crashed into the center-field fence while chasing a Brooks Robinson home run. He played in only 65 games and Maris appeared in 90. Nonetheless the team did have something to crow about. They finished 10 and a half games in front, their largest margin since 1947. New York then went on to lose four straight against the cocky Los Angeles Dodgers. They lost two to Sandy Koufax, and one each to Don

Drysdale and Johnny Podres. New York was held to four runs, 22 hits and a team batting average of .171. Yogi Berra made his last active appearance as a Yankee player in game three, when he lined out while pinchhitting for Jim Bouton.

Berra came back in a Yankee uniform as manager and Houk replaced Roy Hamley as the club's general manager. 'My big problem as manager will be to see if I can manage,' commented Yogi from his new vantage point. Before his selection he had closely eyed every one of Houk's moves in anticipation of the moves by the front office.

Opposite top: In 1962 right-hander Ralph Terry led the league in wins with 23 and in innings pitched with 298.2. He helped the Yankees to a Series victory that year by winning two of the three games he pitched.

Opposite bottom: On the last day of the 1961 season, Roger Maris blasted his 61st homer to break Babe Ruth's landmark record.

The 1964 season opened as usual in Washington. President Lyndon B Johnson took obvious delight in being the tenth Commander-in-Chief to throw out the first game ball. (Johnson confided to the Senators' manager Gil Hodges that before entering politics he played first base back in Texas.) The Senators lost to the Angels, 4-0, with pitcher Claude Osteen making the only hit, a double. During the fourth inning the stadium's loudspeakers blared the announcement that there was a quorum call on the floor of the Senate over the Civil Rights Bill. Several Senators – politicians, not players – raced out of Johnson's box and to the exits.

Right: The big right-hander Dean Chance, who pitched for Los Angeles from 1961 to 1964, had a phenomenal season in 1964, turning in 20 wins and only 9 losses, with a 1.65 ERA and 11 shutouts.

Right: Outfielder Tony Oliva played for the Minnesota Twins for his entire 15-year career, during which time he won the batting title three times. In 1964 he was selected as Rookie of the Year, leading the league in hits with 217, in doubles with 43 and in runs scored with 109. He retired from active play in 1976 with a .304 lifetime batting average.

The loudest bat in the early season belonged to Minnesota's Tony Oliva. The left-handed rookie right-fielder clobbered pitchers daily. He had been briefly used during the 1963 season, making four hits in nine tries; now that he was playing full-time there didn't seem to be any way of getting him out. He went on to win the batting title with a .323 average, 217 hits and 32 home runs.

In Boston and elsewhere in the league a new crop of talent put on some outstanding performances. Nineteen-year-old outfielder Tony Conigliaro and Dick Radatz, an outstanding relief pitcher, were stirring up the crowds in Boston's Fenway Park. Conigliaro played furious ball until he was hit by a pitch that broke his arm late in July; he returned late in the season, showering a total of 24 home runs and achieving a .290 batting average. Radatz, known as 'The Monster,' came in almost every other day to shut down batters in late innings of play. A workhorse, he appeared in 79 games – only two shy of the American League record of 81 appearances on the mound. Radatz, in fact, appeared in 29 more innings than John Wyatt, the record-holder, and earned an astounding 16 wins in games he did not start.

A fine defensive player, Jim Fregosi played shortstop for the California Angels from 1965 to 1971, when he was traded to the Mets in exchange for Nolan Ryan. Fregosi finished his 18-year career in the National League with Pittsburgh, in 1978.

Below: The big power-hitter Boog Powell played outfield and first base for the Baltimore Orioles from 1961 to 1974, finishing his 17-year career with the Indians and the Dodgers. During the five seasons he went to the league championships with the Orioles, he averaged 23 home runs and 85 RBI's each year.

Meanwhile Baltimore fans were having a love affair with John 'Boog' Powell, who walloped 39 homers. A large man, left-hander Powell had trouble keeping his weight under 225 pounds. His season's batting average was a respectable .290. Angels fans were singing the praises of Jim Fregosi at shortstop and Dean Chance on the mound. Luis Tiant, a fine Cleveland pitcher, and Bert Campaneris, a Kansas City infielder, were also part of the crop of new young players who had earned respect during the season.

Early in 1964, Charles O Finley, the owner of the Kansas City team, tried to raise a storm about the lay-out of Yankee Stadium. According to Finley, New York gained an unfair advantage because the Stadium favored left-handed pull hitters. To prove his point he raised a replica of the barrier at Yankee Stadium in his park, calling it the 'pennant porch.' League officials ordered the contraption dismantled and the matter was soon forgotten. Gabe Paul, general manager of the Cleveland Indians, summed things up when he said, 'We have more important things to worry about than that. The Yankees have won several pennants not because of the dimensions of their park but because of their great talent.'

The Yankees were indeed the subject of the '64 season question.' Could the New York club reinflate again after being so badly stomped by the Dodgers? After all, only the 1940 Cincinnati Reds had recovered from such a rout to take the pennant again. The Yankees somehow won the American League title instinctively, as if their chromosomes were programmed to play the cycle of World Series fall after fall. Through most of the summer they played sluggish baseball, and it seemed as if Yogi Berra, who had taken over as manager, couldn't maintain control. A headline-making scuffle over Phil Linz's harmonica seemed to knock the team out of its stupor and they started a serious race for the pennant. Rookie pitcher Mel Stottlemyre came up from the minors in August and played a key role by supplementing the pitching of Whitey Ford and Jim Bouton. Yogi Berra had had Stottlemyre brought up from Richmond farm club out of desperation. Whitey Ford had developed a bad hip and the Yankees had sunk to third place. In his debut, Stottlemyre went the distance, defeating Chicago, 7-3. His overhand sinker had helpless batters swinging at

the ground. Soon veterans Mickey Mantle, Roger Maris, Elston Howard and Joe Pepitone put their shoulders to the wheel in order to power the Yankee drive. The Yankees got back on track, grabbing the pennant on their way to the World Series against the St Louis Cardinals.

Whitey Ford's contribution to New York's 29th league championship deserves special comment. In 13 seasons he had won 216 games while losing only 84 for a .720 percentage. This surpassed Spud Chandler's old mark of .717. It was the highest win ratio in major league history for any pitcher who had won more than 200 games.

Once again the Yankees entered the contest burdened by injuries. A bad leg left Mantle limping and Tony Kubek couldn't play in the classic because of a sprained wrist. Ace Whitey Ford opened for the Bombers against Ray Sadecki. Ford let in five runs before being relieved by Al Downing, then Rollie Sheldon and Pete Mikkelsen. The Cardinals won 9-5. The Series then seesawed, with the Yankees winning the second and third games, and St Louis winning the

Yankee Elston Gene 'Ellie' Howard batted .274 for his 14-year career. In 1964 he helped hit his team to the Series, with a .313 batting average and 84 RBI's. In the Series itself he went 7 for 24 as the Yanks lost a close contest to St Louis, four games to three.

fourth and fifth games. Consecutive homers by Maris and Mantle, and Joe Pepitone's grand slam in the eighth inning clinched a Yankee victory in the sixth game, tying the Series at three games each. For the decisive seventh game, Berra picked Stottlemyre to pitch against Bob Gibson. The Cards scored three times in the fourth and three times in the fifth to run up a 6-0 lead. Mantle then belted a three-run homer, putting the Yankees back in the race, but St Louis scored again in the seventh inning. New York went down fighting as Clete Boyer and Phil Linz hit solo home runs in the ninth before Gibson tied up a 7-5 victory for the Cards. The day after the Series ended, the front office fired Berra, while Johnny Keane quit as manager of the Cardinals; both decisions had been reached during the midsummer doldrums. Ironically, the Yankees later recruited Keane to manage the team.

In 1965, the New York Yankees couldn't get going. Age and injuries had humbled baseball's premier club into the mire of sixth place. It was their lowest finish since 1925. Now a rainbow of possibilities awaited the other American League clubs, and the Minnesota Twins won the championship for the first time ever. For decades they had played as the lowly Washington Senators before moving to the far north in 1961. Managed by modest Sam Mele, the Twins gained their

laurels by hitting the long ball. Harmon Killebrew, Bob Allison, Don Mincher and Jimmie Hall swung heavy-duty bats, while Tony Oliva won the league's Most Valuable Player award with his solid hitting and play at shortstop. Ace 21-game winner Jim 'Mudcat' Grant and the other Minnesota pitchers were buoyed by such hitting prowess.

The Series opened in Minnesota on Yom Kippur, a Jewish High Holy day, which prevented Sandy Koufax from pitching for the Dodgers. To the horror of Los Angeles fans their starting pitcher, Don Drysdale, was swept from the mound in the top of the third and the Twins won, 8-2. Koufax took the mound the next day and again the Dodgers were stunned as their ace was tagged for two in the sixth and pulled for a pitch hitter; the Twins went on to win, 5-2. Gloom hung over Los Angeles like smog as the teams approached game three. Dodger pitcher Claude Osteen, who had an unimpressive 15-15 record, turned the Series around by papering the Twins, 4-0. Drysdale then triumphed in game four as the Dodgers plastered their opponents, 7-2. The next day Koufax shut down Minnesota, 7-0. The Twins' Mudcat Grant then beat Osteen on the mound and hit a three-run homer to win the game 5-1, bringing the Series race down to the wire. Sandy, with two days rest, faced Jim Kaat going for the Twins. The two southpaws staged a thrilling

James Timothy 'Mudcat' Grant pitched for Cleveland for six years, turning in an unimpressive 64 wins and 59 losses. He moved to Minnesota in 1964, however, and in 1965 won 21 games, losing only seven, to help his team to the World Series.

In 1966 the Orioles went all the way, helped by such outstanding talent as pitcher Dave McNally (above), who had a .684 winning percentage that year, the future Hall of Famer at third base, Brooks Robinson (opposite top), and outfielder Frank Robinson (opposite bottom), who won the batting title that year.

duel, which could have gone either way. Kaat was then replaced by a string of relievers as Koufax, who kept a slight edge by allowing only three hits, sealed the Series with a 2-0 victory.

In 1966 the American League pennant belonged to the Baltimore Orioles. They ran off a 13-game lead by the end of July and sashayed to their first pennant since rising from the ashes of the 1954 St Louis Browns. Frank Robinson, an outfielder obtained the previous winter from Cincinnati, fired up the club. An

outstanding hitter, Robinson set out to burn every opposing American League pitcher while he ignited his teammates into action. Slugging first baseman Boog Powell, and clutch hitter and third base wizard Brooks Robinson grilled mounds of determined pitchers. Fielding stars Luis Aparicio and Paul Blair joined a well-balanced pitching staff to close the lid on the teams that found themselves on the Baltimore skillet.

Both Robinsons, Frank and Brooks, had been outstanding ballplayers for a decade before Baltimore made it to the Series. Yet they were hardly what one could call household names. Frank came into the majors with the Cincinnati Reds in 1956 and was voted Rookie of the Year. He earned the Most Valuable Player of the Year Award in the National League in 1961, but his triumphs were overshadowed by the Mantle and Maris performance that year. The Reds inexplicably gave Baltimore a wonderful gift by trading Robinson while he was still in his prime. Robinson promptly earned the American League Triple Crown and was named the league's Most Valuable Player in 1966, thereby becoming the only person to garner that title in both leagues. He eventually became the first black to manage a major league team.

Brooks Robinson's talent had also been overlooked for years by fans and sports commentators. He finally gained the reputation of being the finest third baseman of his time and possibly in history. Upon retiring after 20 years with Baltimore he held just about every fielding record a third baseman could hold. Even old-timers had begun comparing him with vintage heroes Pie Traynor and Billy Cox.

While Baltimore blazed, the Yankees fell from their sixth place purgatory to the bottom. This was only the third time in the club's 64-year history that they had sunk so low. Keene was dropped as manager, and Houk left the front office to resume his old position. In mid-September Don Topping sold his shares of the club to CBS; Mike Burke, a network vice-president and former University of Pennsylvania football player, was named the club's president. A month later Lee MacPhail, son of the old baseball magnate, joined the front office as general manager. Other developments in the American League in 1966 included the unveiling of the California Angels' new park in Anaheim. The triple-decker structure was built in less than two years at a cost of $24 million.

The 1966 Series looked like it was going to be a test of Baltimore's hitting power against Los Angeles' pitching. The Orioles began blasting early in the

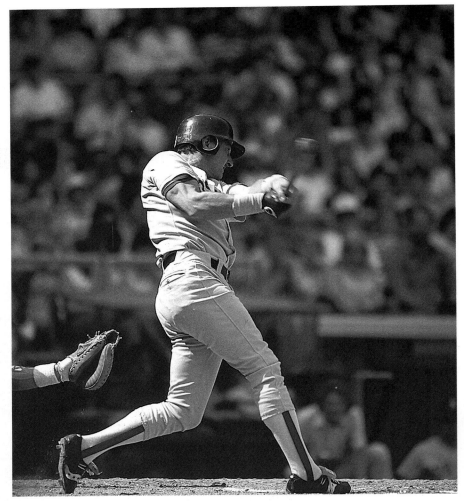

Left fielder Carl Yastrzemski whacks a long line drive. Yaz played his entire 23-year career with the Boston Red Sox, powering the team to the World Series in 1967. He won the Triple Crown and was selected as league MVP that year, with 44 home runs, 112 runs scored and 121 RBI's. The Sox won the pennant on the last day of the season as Yaz went 4 for 4 against Minnesota. Then, despite Yaz's three homers, his team lost a close Series to St Louis, four games to three.

Right: Dave Boswell pitched for Minnesota from 1964 to 1970, ending his career in 1971 with the Tigers and Orioles. His best season was 1969, when he turned in 20 wins and his team won the division.

Far right: The big right-hander Jim Lonborg pitched for Boston from 1965 to 1971, striking out a league-leading 246 batters in 1967 to win 22 games and the Cy Young Award. Lonborg won two of the three games he pitched in the '67 Series, including a one-hit shutout.

ever.' The starting nine players averaged only 24 years of age, but were fast on their feet. A number of pundits predicted a secure last-place finish for the club, and any suggestion that they would win the pennant would be have been met with charges of lunacy. Boston seemed as allergic to the pennant title as some people are to goldenrod.

The new-found Boston strength developed in part through the promotion of a group of capable rookies from the Red Sox's Toronto farm club. In 1967, Toronto manager Dick Williams had been moved to Boston to harness the calves he had nourished down on the farm. Williams was a strict disciplinarian who was not afraid to crack the whip during training and in the regular season, on or off the field. In the past, Red Sox players had been protected from harsh criticism by Tom 'Papa' Yawkey, the club's owner. Dick Williams and a bit of luck changed all that.

Billy Rohr pitched in Boston's first contest against the Yankees. The youngster had spent a sleepless night the evening before, thinking about his first major league start. He won the game, pitching a one-hitter, and then found himself on the Ed Sullivan show being touted as the best in the league. Boston sportswriters were rhapsodic and fans began celebrating in the first weeks of the season, only to be disappointed when the club became sloppy and started losing

opener against pitcher Don Drysdale. In the first inning with one man on base, Frank Robinson tagged the Dodgers for a home run. Then even before many of the fans had found their seats, Brooks Robinson, the next batter, hit another homer. Each team picked up a run in the second and the Dodgers one more in the third – their last run in the entire Series! Paralyzed, they suffered through an excruciating 33 consecutive scoreless innings – the most of any team in championship history. Los Angeles made six errors in one game, three of them in one inning. The Orioles responded by playing errorless ball throughout the Series, with Jim Palmer, Wally Bunker and Dave McNally pitching consecutive shutouts. They gave Baltimore its first World Series victory as well as the first pennant since the old National League Baltimore Orioles of 1896.

The Boston Red Sox, only one step away from the basement in 1966, fought their way to the top in 1967. Under the leadership of Carl Yastrzemski, a modern-day Samson, they muscled their way up to take the pennant on the final day of the season. 'Yaz,' a moody leftfielder, won the Triple Crown with more pith than even Frank Robinson. Yastrzemski seemed to win games daily with his home runs as he tied the Twins' Harmon Killebrew with 44, and led with 121 RBI's and a .326 batting average. Boston came out on top of a furious four-team contest, which included Minnesota, Detroit and Chicago.

Just how Boston won the pennant has been the subject of a great deal of ironic commentary. Some of the team showed up at spring training overweight, and it seemed unlikely that they would climb higher than ninth or tenth place. Yet by the start of the season manager Dick Williams' coaches were boasting that their squad was in 'the best physical shape games. As smiles turned to frowns, the manager and players started calling each other names. Williams scolded pitcher Jim Lonborg for 'throwing the ball right down the pipe' on a two-strike count with bases loaded. He questioned George Scott's brain power for swinging at a pitch when he had been given the 'take' sign. Williams himself muddled things up by moving outfielder Reggie Smith to second base, and playing first baseman George Scott in the outfield. After everyone tired of name-calling and Scott and Smith regained their positions, the team started winning again. Yastrzemski and Tony Conigliaro blasted balls out of everyone's reach, and Williams reserved his name-calling for umpires and league officials.

By the end of April, Boston was tied with New York for first place. Fans were ecstatic, and the players' dreams of glory pulled the team together. Williams imposed a jailhouse routine, insisting that every member of the club, star or not, had to attend morning practice and obey strict curfews, complete with bed checks. Every time the players grew restive, the rebellion was smothered by a string of victories.

Yaz experienced ups and downs as did other team members. He was benched for a while in the midst of a slump. Russ Gibson, the promising catcher, never caught fire, and Reggie Smith struck out 13 times in 25 visits to the plate. To make matters worse, Rico

Right: Red Sox outfielder Tony Conigliaro became the youngest player ever to hit 100 home runs. In his rookie season (1964) he belted 24 homers, then led the league the following year with 32. With 104 homers under his belt at age 22, in August 1967 a fastball hit him in the face, sidelining him for the rest of the season and curtailing his rise to greatness.

Below: Outfielder Al Kaline played for the Detroit Tigers for his entire 22-year career (1953-74). His outstanding hitting won him acclaim early on, as he won the batting title in 1955 with a .340 average. In 1967 he batted .308 with 25 homers as his team finished the season tied with the Twins for second place, one game behind the Red Sox.

Petrocelli suffered acute tendonitis and catcher Bob Tillman accidentally beaned his teammate, pitcher John Wyatt.

Then in a game against Boston's archrival, the Yankees, Red Sox infielder Joe Foy hit a bases-loaded home run which seemed to turn the tide, starting Boston's rise into orbit. Some have claimed that criticism only served to kindle the Boston fire. White Sox manager Eddie Stanky remarked of Carl Yastrzemski: 'Maybe an all-star ball player, but only from the neck down.' Outraged fans showered Stanky and his team with beer cans, paper cups and an array of garbage when they next visited Fenway Park. Perhaps it was the trade that brought the Red Sox catcher Elston Howard that catalyzed the pennant. Howard, briefly heartbroken by the deal, soon was coaxing winning games out of Boston's often shaky pitching staff.

Opponents argued that it took more than Howard's catching experience to boost the Boston pitching staff. Joe Pepitone of the Yankees bluntly stated, 'John Wyatt has so much Vaseline on him that if he should ever overslide second base he'd keep on going to the fence.' The Boston team faced constant complaints about Wyatt's Vaseline ball and other teammates' spitballs. One day umpire Hank Soar asked to examine the ball but found it wiped clean; he threw it back – but not before indicating that he knew very well what Wyatt was pitching by first spitting on it himself.

Playing with grit and sheer determination, Boston stayed in the 1967 race despite the fact that Tony Conigliaro, who had hit 20 homers and knocked in 67 runs, was tragically hit in the face by a pitch in August that would end his season and ruin his exceptional career. He would play for four more years after sitting out the 1968 season, but would never regain his former level of brilliance. On 7 September four clubs were virtually tied at the top: Chicago and Minnesota shared first, while Boston and Detroit shared second, only one percentage point behind. Chicago was the first to drop out, only two games before the season's finish. Detroit and Minnesota held on tenaciously until the last day. Boston defeated Minnesota twice and then had to wait for the outcome of the

Right-hander Denny McLain hurled his way to 31 wins in 1968, winning the Cy Young Award and helping the Tigers become world champs.

Tigers' doubleheader against California. The Tigers took the opener, but the Angels then turned Detroit's pennant dream into a nightmare by taking the second game. Boston had done the impossible.

The 1967 World Series lasted seven games. Cardinal pitcher Bob Gibson struck out 10 as St Louis won a close first game 2-1. Although the Red Sox, fired by two Yaz homers and Lonberg's superb pitching, stomped the Cardinals 5-0 in game two, Boston's hopes began to fade as St Louis racked up impressive victories in the next two games, shutting down the Sox 6-0 in game four. They now led the Sox by three games to one, but Boston kept alive with a 3-1 victory in game five, then switched on their power for game six. Three fourth-inning home runs by Yastrzemski, Smith and Petrocelli set a World Series record, as eight St Louis pitchers tried to douse the Boston fire. With an 8-4 win, the Red Sox tied the Series at three games each. But in the decisive seventh game, Gibson again struck out 10 for the Cardinals, winning the game and Series for St Louis.

Although Yaz batted .400 for the Series with 10 hits, including two doubles and three homers, Cardinals Roger Maris, Lou Brock (who hit .414 and stole a record seven bases) and Bob Gibson (who won three games, striking out 26 and giving up only 14 hits) proved unbeatable.

Thwarted in 1967, the Tigers devoured their opponents in the 1968 season, smoothly running to a 12-game lead by the finish of the pennant race. Their pitching ace Denny McLain was the first 30-game winner since Dizzy Dean in 1934. Winning 31 games and losing only six, McLain was voted the league's

Left-hander Mickey Lolich's superb pitching complemented McLain's, as he worked his magic for the Tigers as well. In the '68 Series Lolich hit a home run and won all three of the games he pitched. After 13 years with Detroit, Lolich pitched for the Mets and Padres, ending his career in 1979 with a lifetime won-lost record of 217-191.

Most Valuable Player and the winner of the Cy Young award. Denny enjoyed tremendous batting power to back him up: Al Kaline, Norm Cash, Dick McAuliffe, Jim Northrup, Willie Horton, Mickey Stanley, Gates Brown and Bill Freehan were all capable of getting runs across the plate. In addition, the Tigers had another pitching ace in Mickey Lolich, a pleasant and paunchy southpaw who, though overshadowed by McLain, could throw a fast ball as close to the speed of sound as any Denny propelled.

The year's batting records were the inverse of the ones in pitching. The combined batting average for both leagues amounted to a mere .236, the lowest ever recorded. Only one American League player batted better than .300: Carl Yastrzemski passed a hair's breadth over that mark by taking the batting title with an average of .3005, the lowest league-leading average in the history of the majors. Mickey Mantle had a moment in the sun during the 1968 season. His 18 home runs moved him past Ted Williams' 521 and Jimmie Foxx's 534 into third in the all-time home run contest with 536. Another notable event of the year was the move of the Kansas City

Athletics to Oakland, where some future greats – including Reggie Jackson, Bert Campaneris, Jim 'Catfish' Hunter and Joe Rudi – would work toward making history.

The Tigers won the World Series in seven games. Affable Mickey Lolich pulled the contest out from under the seemingly unbeatable Cardinals. St Louis' Brock and Gibson tormented their opponents on offense and from the mound. Brock hit .464 with two home runs, and stole seven bases. Gibson shut out the Tigers in the opener with a record 17-strikeout performance. Denny McLain, who faced Gibson in the opener, had trouble controlling the ball and left after five innings.

Lolich pitched a six-hitter in game number two, winning 8-1. He surprised everyone, himself included, by hitting the first home run in his six-year major league career. The Cardinals went on to win the next two games, first behind Ray Washburn and then as Gibson fanned 10 batters to take his seventh straight World Series victory, 10-1. Again McLain was the loser, and the Cards were ahead, three games to one.

Lolich came back to win the fifth contest for the

Tigers, 5-3. The Tigers then exploded in the sixth game, including a ten-run inning; McLain was the winning pitcher as the Tigers roared to a 13-1 victory. In the final match Lolich faced Gibson. The score was 0-0 with two outs in the seventh inning when Gibson gave up singles to Tigers Norm Cash and Willie Horton. Next Jim Northrup hit a line drive that center fielder Curt Flood misjudged and it flew over his head for a triple. Northrup then scored on a Bill Freehan double. Each team scored once in the ninth and when the game ended at 4-1, Detroit catcher Bill Freehan ran out to the mound and hugged Lolich, lifting him off his feet.

The 1969 season saw the expansion of both the major leagues to 12 teams each, adding the Montreal Expos and the San Diego Padres to the National League, and the Kansas City Royals and the Seattle Pilots to the American. The leagues were then split

The outstanding Tiger outfielder Al Kaline demonstrates his swing. Kaline put his swing to good use in the '68 Series, going 11 for 29 and popping two homers. Al Kaline finished up his career in 1974 with 3007 hits, and was elected to the Hall of Fame in 1980.

Below: As part of Detroit's unstoppable team, Tiger outfielder Willie Horton smashed 36 homers in 1968, then batted .304, with one round-tripper, in the World Series.

into two streamlined divisions, each with six teams, playing a 162-game schedule. Under the new system the league championships were decided in favor of the team that passed a new hurdle, a best-of-five play-off. The American League Eastern Division was comprised of New York, Boston, Baltimore, Detroit, Washington and Cleveland; the Western included Oakland, Minnesota, California (as Los Angeles renamed itself), Chicago, Seattle and Kansas City.

In addition to these changes, new rules were devised to help batters in their confrontations with pitchers. Pitching in both leagues had become so dominant that too few runs were being scored to keep fans watching television or coming to the stadiums. Batting averages were slipping as games seemed to creep along with all the action of a cricket match. In order to rectify this situation, the pitching mound was lowered five inches and the strike zone reduced in size: instead of being from the top of the shoulder to the bottom of the knee, it was contracted to the area between the armpit and the top of the knee. These measures provided an aid to batters while making even greater demands on pitchers.

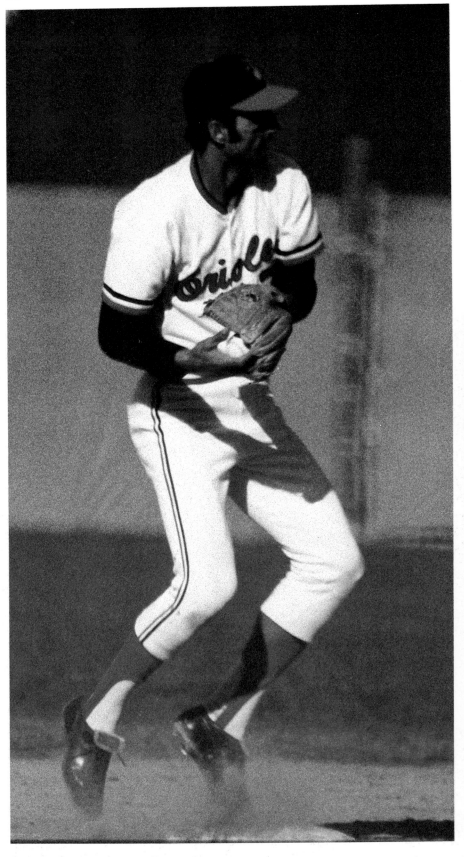

Baltimore shortstop Mark Belanger makes a double play. Belanger played for the Orioles for 17 years, ending his career in 1982 after one season with the Dodgers. Belanger went to the play-offs six times and the Series four times with the Orioles. His .977 fielding average rates him an all-time second place.

The Orioles, under skipper Earl Weaver, won the American League Eastern Division pennant in 1969 with a solid 109 victories. They left defending champions Detroit 19 games behind in second place. Baltimore allowed their opponents an average of only 2.38 runs per game all year. Their distinguished pitching staff included Mike Cuellar (23-11) as well as Dave McNally (20-7) and Jim Palmer (16-4). Palmer pitched a no-hitter, while the other two came close by not allowing men on before the final inning of nearly perfect games. Six Orioles batted .280 or better with 'Boog' Powell and Frank Robinson most successful at

the plate. In addition, the club enjoyed the best defense in the league. Shortstop Mark Belanger handled a glove with the finesse of Luis Aparicio. Second base belonged to Dave Johnson, while Paul Blair controlled center field. It seemed all a Baltimore pitcher had to do was let the opponents hit the ball and his colleagues make the out.

The Minnesota Twins won the Western Division title after a season-long fight against the Oakland A's. The heated contest left the managers of both teams without jobs. Hank Bauer lost his because the Athletics failed to win, while victorious Billy Martin was kicked out because of frequent conflicts with the Twins' front office. Harmon Killebrew's 49 home runs and 140 RBI's led the Minnesota offense, and teammate Rod Carew's .322 batting average foreshadowed his future achievements. Other outstanding performers included Oakland's Reggie Jackson, who hit 47 home runs, and Washington's Frank Howard, who sent 48 balls over the fence. Pitcher Denny McLain came through with an impressive 24-9 season for Detroit, but it proved to be his last winning season.

Baltimore won three straight in the American League's first play-offs, shutting out Minnesota for the pennant. The first two games went into extra innings, the Orioles winning the first 4-3 in 12 innings, and the second 1-0 in 11. The final game was a romp, ending at 11-2.

Baltimore was clearly the favorite going into the 1969 World Series. They faced the New York Mets, a relatively inexperienced club that stood eighth in National League batting at .241. Despite their low overall batting, some on the squad managed to pull off a game-winning hit with almost daily regularity. Their strong pitching staff was led by Tom Seaver, a 25-game winner, and Jerry Koosman, who finished with 17-9. They were rich in depth and spirit and led by the rarest of managers, Gil Hodges, the former Brooklyn first baseman.

The Orioles won the first game, 4-1, as Mike Cuellar

Left: Second baseman Davy Johnson played for Baltimore from 1965 to 1972, turning in a respectable .280 batting average in 1969.

Below: Left-handed hurler Mike Cuellar pitched his best years for Baltimore, beginning in 1969 when he tied Denny McLain for the Cy Young Award. For half of his eight years with the Orioles, Cuellar won at least 20 games, helping bring his team to five league play-offs and three Series.

beat Tom Seaver. New York won the second game, 2-1, on Jerry Koosman's two-hit pitching. From then on the Mets didn't stop winning until the Series was over. They took the third game behind the pitching of Gary Gentry, 5-0. Tommie Agee, the Mets' center fielder, put on an incredible one-man show that game. He blasted a homer in the first; then in the fourth, with two Baltimore runners on base and two out, he sprinted to the 396-foot marker and made an unbelievable back-handed, finger-tip catch against the wall. In the seventh inning, with two out and the bases loaded, Baltimore's Paul Blair smacked a line drive to right center that seemed a certain triple until Agee snared it with a diving catch. Both plays ranked with the most sensational in Series history. Agee by himself saved six runs, and Gary Gentry, the rookie pitcher, was credited with the 5-0 win. Seaver came through in the fourth game by pitching a six-hit game, winning 2-1 in the tenth inning. Then the Mets took the final game 5-3, despite the fact that Baltimore clobbered Koosman for two home runs and three runs in the third. Regaining his cool, he pitched score-

less ball for the rest of the game.

The sixties were closing with Ted Williams' return to the sport. The last .400 hitter ended nine years of self-imposed exile by accepting the position of manager of the Washington Senators in 1969. The team offered him a $1 million stock deal and a partnership with owner Robert Short. Williams went on to lead the Senators to their first winning season in 17 years and was voted the American League Manager of the Year. In this way the torch of tradition was handed on to the seventies.

Opposite: The Orioles' pitching phenomenon, Jim Palmer won 16 games – including a no-hitter – and lost only four in 1969, giving him a league-leading .800 winning percentage.

Above: Baltimore outfielder from 1964 to 1976, Paul Blair hit 26 homers and scored 102 runs in 1969.

CHAPTER SEVEN

The Seditious Seventies

"I only regret that I didn't sell more of them. I hope to wake the stupid owners to the facts of reality."

– Charles O Finley, owner of the Oakland A's, reacting to the beginning of the free-agent era in 1976.

Any decade of major league baseball is apt to combine some changes with stability, some innovations along with traditions, but by any measure the seventies must stand out as one of the most revolutionary in the history of baseball. As so often since it first challenged the senior National League at the outset of the twentieth century, the American League seemed to take the lead in assaulting tradition. There was nothing much new about the various shifts of American League franchises to different cities, but its expansion to 14 teams was a novelty that the National League chose not to adopt. Far more upsetting to many students of the game was the American League's adoption of the designated hitter in 1973, a change that continues to divide fans of both leagues.

However, it must be admitted that the most radical of all changes in the 1970s did not start within the American League. It began with Curt Flood of the St

Louis Cardinals when he challenged the reserve clause in 1970, for although Flood's case would be rejected by the nation's courts, it led the way for the eventual dislodging of what had come to be accepted as the keystone of organized baseball's great superstructure. Baseball, of course, survived the blow, but there is no denying that the relationships of players to their clubs, cities and fans would never again be quite the same – not to mention the impact it would have on the economics of organized baseball.

The reserve clause that had become so crucial was never formally promulgated as such at one single moment. What had become known as 'the reserve clause,' in fact, was a group of clauses or terms that had become part of the standard contract of virtually every player in professional baseball since the early twentieth century. Originally the newborn American League had challenged the concept of total ownership of a player and had successfully raided the estab-

The Red Sox left fielder Carl Yastrzemski entered the seventies with a bang, batting .329 with 40 home runs, 102 RBI's and a league-leading 125 runs scored.

Opposite: Jim Palmer would win the Cy Young Award three times, in 1973, 1975 and 1976, turning in eight 20-game seasons for the Orioles during the decade.

lished National League. But as soon as it was accepted as a second major league, the American League's club owners were only too willing to accept and enforce these terms. And under the terms that became known as 'the reserve clause,' each player was legally bound to his original contracting team until he was sold or traded to another team, which then retained total control of the player. There was, to be sure, the possibility that a club might release a player, who would then be free to sign on with another team – but in practice a club was not apt to release a player until he was either too old or inept to be of interest to other teams. If a player, for whatever reason, didn't want to play with a team that held him under contract, essentially his only option was to retire from professional baseball. By their absolute adherence to these conditions, the major league club owners effectively owned the players.

If it was not exactly a form of slavery – to the extent that the players had entered into these contracts of their own free will – it seemed suspiciously like a monopoly and restraint of trade of the kind that the American legislatures had been trying to eliminate during the twentieth century. But the Supreme Court, although it had never actually ruled on the reserve clause as such, had, since 1922, in a series of decisions, ruled that organized baseball was exempt from the antitrust laws that applied to the rest of the businesses of America. Ironically, this exemption was a tribute to the special standing of baseball in American society, because the Supreme Court ruled that other organized sports – boxing, hockey and professional football – did have to comply with the antitrust laws. But irony was of little consolation to players who saw their salaries and careers, almost their entire lives while active professionals, controlled by the owners. Meanwhile, the owners had long convinced many that the reserve clause was necessary to keep the richest clubs from buying up all the better players and thus tearing apart the network that had allowed so many teams to remain competitive for so many years.

Then, on 16 January 1970, Curt Flood filed a suit against organized baseball's sacred cow, the reserve clause, and in so doing began what might be called the seditious seventies. Flood was a 32-year-old outfielder who had just finished his 12th year with the St Louis Cardinals. Regarded as one of the better players in the majors, he had just been paid $90,000 for the 1969 season – at that time, one of the highest salaries in either league. When the 1969 season ended, however, the Cardinals decided to trade Flood to the Philadelphia Phillies. This type of deal had been occurring in organized baseball for decades, but Curt Flood now charged that the reserve clause was 'a contract for perpetual service' and he refused to be treated as 'property . . . a chattel . . . a slave for a team against his will.' Backed by the Major League Baseball Players Association, Flood brought a suit for $3 million against organized baseball club owners in the United States District Court in New York City. The District Court quickly ruled that it could not go against the decisions of the Supreme Court; after the US Circuit Court of Appeals also turned down Flood's suit, he appealed to the Supreme Court. It was 1972 before the Supreme Court ruled that the reserve clause was binding since organized baseball had always been treated as exempt from antitrust laws; but the majority of opinion did call this exemption an 'aberration' and suggested that Congress reconsider this situation.

Above: New York's renovated Yankee Stadium in the Bronx has a seating capacity of 57,545 and a depth from home plate to the center field wall of 417 feet.

Right: Comiskey Park, home of Chicago's White Sox, seats up to 44,492 fans and measures a depth of 445 feet. The park was originally built in 1910 by Charles Comiskey.

But Flood had definitely forced a shift in the way players regarded their contracts and in this sense he had led the charge for the seditious seventies, paving the way for an arbitrator's ruling in 1975 that would achieve what all the players and lawyers of the previous 70 years had failed to do. Whether it was because of Flood's bold charge or because of the 'temper of the times,' baseball players of the seventies would become increasingly more outspoken and individualistic. This was prefigured by a book published in 1970, *Ball Four*, by Jim Bouton, a former Yankee pitcher. Bouton revealed what might be called 'the locker-room dimension' of major league baseball, and although no one who knew much about professional baseball had too many illusions about the players, certain boundaries had been respected so that they could serve as models. Now Bouton told it all – and in four-letter words that everyone could understand. But Bouton's book was more a sympton than a cause of the new spirit that exploded in the 1970s, as increasing numbers of players began to speak out, as club uniforms became more gaudy, as players and managers went public with their quarrels, as long hair and moustaches began to flourish. Even in that most staid of all clubs, the New York Yankees, the Board of Directors took to carrying on like a circus. Major league baseball in the 1970s, it might be said, had caught up with America of the 1960s.

The 1970 season itself did not produce any revolutionary surprises. Indeed, in the American League it was an exact repeat of the 1969 season, with the Orioles again winning the Eastern Division and the Twins again winning the Western Division. The Orioles achieved this with essentially the same team as in 1969, managed by the same feisty Earl Weaver. With such superb players as Boog Powell and Brooks Robinson, and three 20-game winners – Mike Cuellar, Dave McNally and Jim Palmer – the Orioles won 108 games and left the Yankees in second place, 15 games behind (even though the Yankees had the league's Rookie of the Year in Thurman Munson and the Manager of the Year in Ralph Houk). In the Western Division, the Twins left the Oakland A's nine games behind, thanks to such achievements as Jim Perry's 24 victories and Harmon Killebrew's 41 homers, and despite the fact that a knee injury kept Rod Carew out for much of the season.

As in 1969, the Orioles wiped out the Twins in the play-offs in three straight (10-6, 11-3, 6-1), scoring their 27 runs on 36 hits. This year, though, the Orioles went into the Series not against 'The Amazing Mets' but against 'The Big Red Machine' from Cincinnati. But the machine had some mechanical problems – specifically, its pitchers were suffering from injuries, and the Orioles swept the first three games. It looked like it would be a clean sweep in the ninth game when in the eighth inning, with two Reds already out, Lee May hit a three-run homer and the Reds won, 6-5. But

the Orioles took the fifth game, 9-3, and their Brooks Robinson not only was named the Series Most Valuable Player, the glove that he wore in making several spectacular catches was acquired by the Baseball Hall of Fame.

Another American Leaguer who had a stand-out year was Luis Aparacio, shortstop for the Chicago White Sox, who set a league record of 2219 games at his position (on his way to his all-time career record of 2581 games as shortstop). But one player who would probably prefer to forget the 1970 season was Denny McLain of the Detroit Tigers. After his spectacular 31 wins in 1968, McLain had never quite been able to live up to his image, but throughout 1970 he was constantly being suspended for everything from investing in a bookmaking operation to tossing water on sportswriters to carrying a gun. When the season ended, the Tigers traded McLain to the Washington Senators, but it was all downhill for McLain from this point on. 1970 was the year, too, that the Seattle Pilots, after one disastrous season in that city, moved to Milwaukee where they became the Brewers.

The next season, 1971, saw another American League team go through its own time of troubles. The Washington Senators – not the original Senators, which had gone to Minnesota as the Twins in 1961 –

had been steadily losing support, despite all the rhetoric about the nation's capital needing a major league team. In 1971, the Senators became most notable for having the controversial Curt Flood and Denny McLain on their roster. Flood left the team after the first three weeks to avoid the publicity that had surrounded him ever since his suit challenging the reserve clause. Denny McLain would stay to pitch for the Senators, but he ended up losing 22 games. After the season ended, the Senators left town, reappearing in Texas as the Rangers in 1972, but the complaints that the nation's capital required a major league team would continue in the years ahead.

In the 1971 pennant race, the Baltimore Orioles won the Eastern Division of the American League for the third straight year, this time leaving the Tigers 12 games behind. Once more, too, the Orioles relied heavily on their strong pitching, as this year Pat Dobson (20-8) joined Cuellar (20-9), McNally (21-5), and Palmer (20-9) to give Baltimore only the second team in major league history (the White Sox of 1920 was the first) with four 20-game winners. In the Western Division, 1971 was the year that the Oakland A's finally broke through the pack, with Kansas City 16 games behind in second place. The A's had several stars, including Reggie Jackson with his 32 home runs

Left-hander Vida Blue pitched for Oakland from 1969 to 1977, ending up with a won-lost record for those years of 124-86. Blue, who had pitched a no-hitter at the end of 1970, went on in 1971 to win 24 games and lose only eight, with a 1.82 ERA, and walked away with both the Cy Young Award and the league's Most Valuable Player designation.

and 'Catfish' Hunter with his 21 wins and Rollie Fingers and his numerous saves in relief. But much of the excitement was generated by their 22-year-old left-handed fastball pitcher, Vida Blue, who, after losing his season's opener, went on to win 10 straight. He ended up with a 24-8 record, and such other impressive stats as 24 complete games, eight shut-outs, 301 strikeouts and an ERA of only 1.82. Blue not only took the American League's Cy Young Award – as the youngest pitcher to ever achieve such an honor – but also claimed its Most Valuable Player Award. Everyone agreed, though, that Manager Dick Williams

(formerly of the Red Sox) deserved a lot of the credit for disciplining a group of often unruly individualists into a true team.

In the play-offs, however, Baltimore's experience proved too much and the A's were defeated in three straight. The Orioles' sweep of the play-off completed their fourth pennant in six years. The Orioles then went on to the Series heavily favored over the Pittsburgh Pirates, who despite such solid players as Roberto Clemente and Willie Stargell lacked a strong pitching staff. The Orioles won the first two in Baltimore, but the Pirates took the next three in Pittsburgh

– including the fourth game, the first night game in World Series history. Back in Baltimore, the Orioles won the sixth game, 3-2, on Brooks Robinson's sacrifice fly in the 10th inning, but Steve Blass held the Orioles to four hits in the seventh and deciding game, and the Pirates won 2-1 to become the champions.

The 1972 season began in a way that prefigured an increasingly – some would say depressingly – familiar phenomenon within the major leagues: a strike – the first general strike by players in organized baseball. The issue was one of pension and medical benefits. Refusing to play all their spring training exhibition games, by the time the strike was settled on 13 April, the players had missed 86 regular season games as well. These games were never made up, the result being that different teams played different totals of games. Further signs of the growing unrest and temerity among the players was Vida Blue's temporary 'retirement' from baseball in order to see if he could obtain a better salary after his previous spectacular season. He ended up returning for far less than he wanted and having a losing season (6-10) as well. This was also the year that the Supreme Court upheld the lower courts in preserving the reserve clause, and suggested that Congress reconsider allowing organized baseball to remain exempt from antitrust legislation.

In the 1972 pennant race, the Oakland A's repeated in the Western Division, beating out Chicago by 5 and a half games. The A's claimed a formidable team, with such as Reggie Jackson, Bert Campaneris, Joe Rudi, Sal Bando and Gene Tenace to back the pitching of Catfish Hunter and Rollie Fingers. On the other hand, the A's seemed to have a 'fifth wheel' in the person of their owner, Charles O Finley, an irascible and often irritating millionaire from Chicago. The only real contest in the majors in 1972 was in the American League's Eastern Division, where even as late as Labor Day four

Above: Hall of Fame third baseman Brooks Robinson relaxes between innings in the Baltimore dugout. Although Robinson sacrificed in the winning run in game six of the 1971 World Series, the Orioles lost the final, deciding game by one run.

Left: Sal Bando takes a big cut. A solid third baseman, Salvatore Leonard Bando played for the Oakland A's from 1968 to 1976. He played the last five seasons of his 16-year career with Milwaukee.

Above: The Detroit Tigers' left-hander Mickey Lolich turned in two superb seasons in 1971 and 1972, winning 25 and 22 games. Lolich's career won-lost record is 217-191.

Right: Shortstop Bert 'Campy' Campaneris played for the Oakland A's from 1968 to 1976, averaging 44 stolen bases per season during that time. In the 1973 World Series he went 7 for 21, smashing a homer in the seventh game to help his team clinch the title.

average of .913. Other American League players who enjoyed a banner season in 1972 included the Cleveland Indians' Gaylord Perry (obtained from the San Francisco Giants) who had a 24-16 season, and Richie Allen (obtained from the Los Angeles Dodgers) who played for the White Sox and led the league in home runs (37) and RBI's (113).

The 1973 season will always remain in the history of baseball as the year that the American League adopted the rule allowing a designated hitter for the pitcher. Originally it was to be merely a three-year trial, but after this first year when the statistics showed that the American League teams had higher team batting averages, scored more runs and drew more crowds, the rule was adopted permanently. The National League refused to go along even with the trial year – and National League fans would never let American League supporters forget that they regarded this as 'kid stuff' from the junior league. (Almost everyone would forget that the founder of the American League, Ban Johnson, had earlier in the century said the same thing about pinch-hitters.)

As it happened, despite all the predictions that the designated hitter would wipe out pitchers' records, the 1973 season turned out to be 'the year of the pitcher' for the American League. Twelve of the league's pitchers won 20 or more games, and there were five no-hit games in the league. The most remarkable records were those compiled by Nolan Ryan, acquired by the California Angels in a trade with the New York Mets. His win-loss record was a respectable 21-16, but this included two no-hitters and two one-hitters, plus an ERA of 2.87. Going into his final game of the season, Ryan needed 15 strikeouts to tie Sandy Koufax's all-time one-season (1965) record of 382 strikeouts – and although he needed 11 innings

teams – Boston, Baltimore, Detroit and New York – were separated by only half a game. With only five days to go, Baltimore was finally eliminated; with four days to go, New York was eliminated and with three days to go, the Red Sox led the Tigers by half a game. In the final series of the season, Detroit took the first two games so that even though Boston won the final game, the Tigers squeaked by with its half-game lead.

With spunky manager Billy Martin and with such hot pitchers as Mickey Lolich and Joe Coleman, the Tigers felt they had a solid chance of deposing the A's, but in five hard-fought games Oakland ended up winning the last and deciding game. Once again, though, the exuberant A's found themselves facing a disciplined and experienced team, the Big Red Machine of Cincinnati. Yet the A's took the first two games of the Series, with Oakland's Gene Tenace making Series history by hitting homers his first two times at bat. The Reds won the third by a close 1-0, but the A's came back and took the fourth by a slim 3-2 victory, scoring two of their three runs in the ninth inning. When the Reds rebounded to win the fifth and sixth and tie up the Series at three games each, it seemed that experience would win out. But in the seventh game, played in Cincinnati, the A's came through with a 3-2 victory and the World Championship – their first since 1930, when the franchise was in Philadelphia. For most of the players on both teams, it was a lean Series: six games were decided by only one run, while the A's team batting average was .207 and the Red's was .208. The notable exception was the amazing performance of the A's Gene Tenace, who hit four homers (having hit only five all season), batted in nine of the A's 16 runs, and ended up with a slugging to get them, Ryan ended up with 16, thus taking over the major league record with 383 strikeouts.

In the end, though, this didn't help the Angels in their Western Division, won again by the Oakland A's for the third consecutive year. The A's had 20-game winners in Catfish Hunter, Vida Blue, and Ken Holtz-mann, backed by Rollie Fingers in relief; they also had the solid hitting of Bert Campaneris and Gene Tenace and the superlative hitting of Reggie Jackson, whose 32 home runs and 117 runs batted in were enough to make him the Most Valuable Player in the league (although Rod Carew of the Twins had the highest

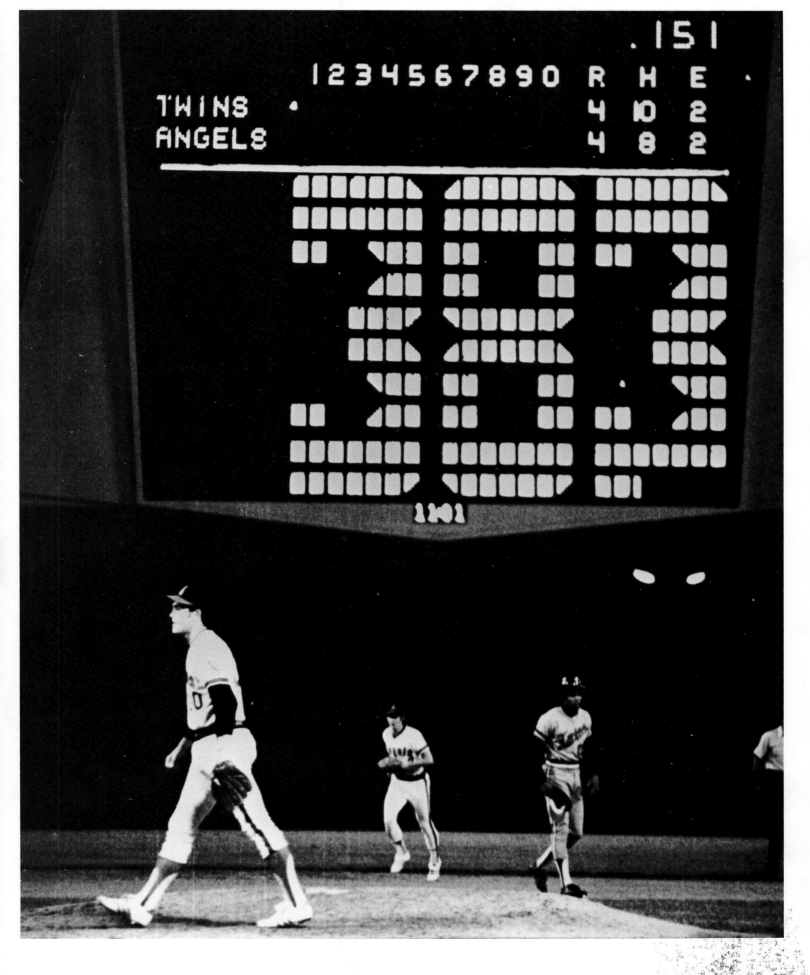

Nolan Ryan, after his record-setting 383rd strikeout on 27 September, 1973.

Right: Rollie Fingers pitched for the Oakland A's from 1968 to 1976, helping them to five consecutive league play-offs and three Series during that time. In his last Series for the A's in 1974, Fingers turned in a 1.93 ERA. Fingers moved to San Diego in 1977, then to Milwaukee in 1981.

Below: A young Rod Carew waits on deck. Voted Rookie of the Year in 1967, Carew quickly lived up to his promise by winning the batting title seven times during his 12 years with the Minnesota Twins (1967-78).

batting average with his .350). In the Eastern Division, the Baltimore Orioles returned to the top spot, eight games over the Boston Red Sox, thanks in large part to their stellar pitching trio, Palmer, Cuellar and McNally. But in the play-offs, Oakland beat the Orioles, although it took them all five games to do so.

The World Series again required all seven games to produce a winner. The National League's team was the New York Mets, who had surprised everyone by winning their division on the last day of the season. Inevitably, many fans began to think that the 'Miracle Mets' were going to pull a replay of their 1969 season. But although it took all seven games and Oakland had to win the last two of these, the A's did again win the Series. The most extraordinary episode of the Series was in the second game, which had gone into 12 innings with the teams tied 6-6. The Mets came up in the top of the inning and scored four runs, three of them due to two errors by the A's substitute second baseman, Mike Andrews. When the A's could only

pick up one run in the bottom of the inning, that meant the game. The A's owner Charles Finley, excitable in the best of circumstances, announced after the game that second baseman Andrews had a 'sore shoulder' and was being put on the disabled list – so that the A's could activate another player – but Andrews almost immediately revealed that Finley had pressured him into signing the statement about his 'injury.' Baseball fans and the Oakland players protested Finley's blatant effort to punish Andrews, and Commissioner Bowie Kuhn ordered that Andrews be reinstated – and fined Finley $5000. As this was just one of many instances of Finley's interference, little wonder that Dick Williams quit as manager of the A's, despite leading them to the World Series championship for the second year in a row.

For the 1974 season, Oakland was managed by Alvin Dark – although Finley was literally on the phone much of the time trying to call plays – and the A's continued their winning ways, despite all the headlines about the flamboyancy and fights. With their especially strong pitching staff of Hunter, Blue, Holtzmann and Fingers, they beat out the Texas Rangers by five games to take the Western Division title again. The Baltimore Orioles also repeated in the Eastern Division, winning 27 of their last 33 games to beat out the Yankees by two games. In the league play-offs, however, the Orioles were no match for the A's, losing three games to one. Oakland's superb pitching staff held the Orioles to only one run in the final 27 innings of the four-game series.

In the 1974 World Series, the A's found themselves facing a rival from down the coast, the Los Angeles Dodgers, and although the A's sometimes seemed like escapees from a situation comedy, when it came to the crunch, 'They play the game the way it should be played.' That was how the Dodgers' manager Walter Alston put it after the Series, and he should know, for the A's took the Series four games to one. Not that it was a breeze for the A's as four of the five games were decided by 3-2 scores. The heroes for the A's were Rollie Fingers, who came on in relief in all four of the A's wins, and Joe Rudi, whose homer won the last game.

The 1974 season was marked by a number of record-breaking performances – the most notable, of course, being Hank Aaron's breaking of Babe Ruth's lifetime home run record. Nolan Ryan pitched his third no-hitter while compiling a 22-16 record; he set a record by striking out 19 in a nine-inning game and struck out 367 for the season (with his fastball timed at 100.9 mph). Gaylord Perry of the Cleveland Indians pitched 15 consecutive wins – and then lost six in a row; Al Kaline of the Tigers became the 12th player in modern major league history to get 3000 hits and Rod Carew of the Twins took his third straight American League batting championship with .364. Catfish Hunter of the A's won over 20 games for his fourth straight season. Declared a free agent at the end of the season, he was signed by the Yankees (for over $3 million on a five-year contract). Hank Aaron, after his record-breaking season, also left his team. Dissatisfied with the Braves' refusal to appoint him as manager, he got himself traded to the Milwaukee Brewers (thus reversing the route taken by Babe Ruth, who after setting his records in the American League went on to end his career in the National League).

Had Aaron been appointed manager of the Atlanta Braves he would have been the first black to manage a major league team and it would have complemented the National League's pioneering appointment of Jackie Robinson as the first black player. Instead, the honor of the first black manager came to the Cleveland Indians, who signed on Frank Robinson from the California Angels at the end of the 1974 season. Robinson had experience as manager of the Santurce team of the Puerto Rican Winter League, and the Indians' front office gave him a one-year contract for 1975. At the end of the season the Indians had won almost half their games (.497 to be precise), which was only good enough for fourth place in the Eastern Division, but Robinson would be offered a second year's contract. The last major barrier to blacks in major league baseball had come down.

Cleveland Indian manager Frank Robinson argues with the home plate umpire. Hall of Famer Frank Robinson was the first black manager in the major leagues. After a 21-year playing career he managed Cleveland from 1975 to 1977, when he moved to San Francisco.

Although an injury kept him out of post-season play, Red Sox outfielder Jim Rice sparked the team to a league championship in his rookie year (1975), batting .309 with 22 homers and 104 RBI's. Selected as the league's Most Valuable Player in 1978, Rice took over left field from Carl Yastrzemski to carry on a tradition of greatness that began over three decades earlier with Ted Williams.

But the 1975 season in the American League belonged to another club, the Boston Red Sox. On paper, the Orioles appeared to be a much stronger team; the Red Sox, starting with their manager, Darrell Johnson, were largely unknowns. The exception was Carl Yastrzemski, but he was more a Boston favorite than an American League power. And there was the now-aging pitcher, Luis Tiant. But after that came some relative unknowns such as Dwight Evans and Carlton Fisk and a couple of rookies named Fred Lynn and Jim Rice. These rookies were soon to become household names, as Rice hit .309 with 22 homers and 102 RBI's, while Lynn hit .331 with 21 homers and 105 RBI's – earning Lynn not only the league's Rookie of the Year

Award but also the Most Valuable Player title, the first man in major league history to win both in the same year. Baltimore did well, with Jim Palmer and Mike Torrez winning over 20 games each, but Boston did even better and took the division by four and a half games over the Orioles. In the Western Division, it was the A's once again, this time by seven games over the Kansas City Royals. But in the pennant play-offs, whether it was because they missed Catfish Hunter or not, the A's went down three straight to the Red Sox.

Certainly the Red Sox were hardly a team top-heavy with pitchers, despite the solid efforts of Tiant, Rick Wise and Bill Lee. On the other hand, their opponent in the World Series, the Cincinnati Reds, wasn't

Left: Red Sox right fielder Dwight 'Dewey' Evans stands ready at the plate. Dewey joined the Sox in 1972, and became a perennial Golden Glover with his sure glove and his rifle arm. In the 1975 World Series, Evans batted .292 with five RBI's.

Below left: Luis Tiant pitched for the Red Sox from 1971 to 1978, turning in three 20-game seasons during that time. In 1975 he won 18 games, then won one playoff game and two Series games. Win or lose, Tiant always entertained the fans with his variety of colorful pitching motions.

Below: Centerfielder Fred Lynn joined the Red Sox in 1974. The following year he helped carry the team to the Series with outstanding performances at the plate and in the field, becoming the only player ever to win both Rookie of the Year and Most Valuable Player awards in the same season. He went on to have five more good years with Boston and was then traded to the California Angels.

Above: Catcher Carlton 'Pudge' Fisk joined the Red Sox in 1972, and was selected Rookie of the Year. He played for Boston through 1980, then was lost to free agency through a front office error, to the chagrin of hometown fans. The most memorable hit of his career is perhaps the game-winning twelfth-inning home run that sent the 1975 World Series into a seventh game.

Opposite: George Brett entered the major leagues in 1974 and quickly warmed up to American League pitchers. In his first three years he accrued 539 hits, twice led the league in hits and triples, and won the batting title in 1976 with a .333 average. A skilled third baseman, Brett has played his whole career for the Kansas City Royals.

that Jim 'Catfish' Hunter was a free agent because the Oakland A's owner Charles Finley had broken his contract. Then in 1975 pitcher Andy Messersmith played the full season for the Los Angeles Dodgers without any contract while Dave McNally played only part of the season for the Montreal Expos, also without a contract. When the season ended, both pitchers claimed they were free agents because they had played out their option. Needless to say, the owners recognized this as yet another assault on the reserve clause, but unlike Curt Flood, who had made a frontal assault, McNally and Messersmith came around from behind by treating their claim as one for arbitration rather than for the courts. And on 23 December 1975 Seitz ruled that players, after completing their contracts, were free to sign with any club. It was, in effect, the end of the reserve clause.

The impact was both immediate and long-term. Two federal courts would uphold the arbitrator's ruling. Meanwhile, with the expiration of the club owners' overall contract with the Major League Baseball Players Association, the owners and players failed to reach an agreement on how to handle this new development, so the owners refused to open the spring training camps on 1 March. By 17 March, the players indicated they would be willing to negotiate certain points, so Commissioner Kuhn ordered the camps to open while negotiations proceeded. Agreement on a four-year contract incorporating the new phenomenon of free agents was finally reached on 12 July, the very eve of the 1976 All-Star Game. The terms attempted some compromise between total freedom and the old reserve clause: after five years in the major leagues, a player could ask to be traded (and could veto up to six clubs); if he was not traded, he became a free agent. After six years in the majors, a player became a free agent, although he could only negotiate with 13 clubs, including his latest owner, that participated in a draft.

Although the owners signed this agreement, they were not alone in predicting that it would mean the end of organized baseball, as it seemed that the richer clubs would buy up all the star players. But the results in the first year were somewhat mixed. It was November 1976 before the first free-agent draft was held, and it was true that many of the 24 players who participated were able to get contracts for much more money than they had been earning, but they did not all go to the so-called rich clubs. Meanwhile, fearing that they might lose good players once they became free agents, clubs began to offer present players multi-year contracts at much better salaries. Not unexpectedly, though, the most extreme response came from Charles Finley, owner of the Oakland A's. Even before the agreement of July, he began to dismantle his team before his star players could become free agents. He traded Reggie Jackson and Ken Holtzman to the Baltimore Orioles in April. Then in June he tried to sell Vida Blue to the Yankees and Rollie Fingers and Joe Rudi to the Red Sox, but Commissioner Kuhn immediately voided the sale of these three on the grounds that it was 'inconsistent with the best interests of baseball.' Finley sued Kuhn, but Kuhn was upheld by the courts.

After such a start to the season, the amazing thing was that the Oakland A's did as well as they did. They played hard-driving ball, stealing a record-setting team total of 341 bases, and they made a late-season charge against the leaders, the Kansas City Royals. But the Royals – led by George Brett and his league high .333 batting average – came out ahead by two

especially strong in pitching either. But what the Reds did have was power and experience – embodied in such players as Pete Rose, Johnny Bench, Joe Morgan and Tony Perez. In what many fans would long remember as one of the most exciting Series, Boston extended the Reds to every last inning and it took Joe Morgan's single in the ninth inning of the seventh game to sneak the Reds by with a 4-3 victory and the World Championship. This was the Series with a controversial incident in the third game: the Reds Ed Armbrister bunted to sacrifice a teammate to second and then didn't move fast enough as Boston's Carlton Fisk leaped forward to pick up the ball. As Fisk collided with Armbrister, then threw wildly to second, the upshot left Reds safe on second and third and led to a game-winning single by Joe Morgan.

There were several more positive moments in the 1975 season. Rod Carew won his fourth consecutive batting title with a .359 average, while Nolan Ryan pitched his fourth no-hitter (tying Sandy Koufax). On 28 September, four Oakland A's pitchers pooled their talents to win a no-hitter against the Angels – the first time that more than two pitchers had won a no-hitter.

But all of this action on the diamond was overshadowed by a ruling made at the end of the 1975 season, a ruling that was to have a major impact on major league baseball. It had really begun in 1974 with the owners' agreement to submit various issues regarding salary and contracts to binding arbitration. At the end of 1974 arbitrator Peter M Seitz had ruled

and a half games in the Western Division. Over in the Eastern Division, the teams found themselves confronting, of all things, the new Yankees. Billy Martin had taken over as manager in the middle of the 1975 season, and the team was back in a renovated Yankee Stadium, after playing in New York's Shea Stadium for two years. The Yankees' prime owner, George Steinbrenner, had assembled the team with a fair amount of cash, including such outstanding players as Thurman Munson, Mickey Rivers and Chris Chambliss, as well as the two recently acquired former Oakland A's, Catfish Hunter and Ken Holtzman. Inspired by Billy Martin's aggressive style, the Yankees ended up in first place, 10 and a half games ahead of the Orioles (even though at one point the Orioles enjoyed a 20-game winning streak).

The 1976 league play-offs between the Yankees and the Royals went the full five games, with the Yankees winning the fifth and decisive game on Chambliss's ninth-inning homer. (Chambliss hit .524 in the five games.) Having won their first pennant since 1964, however, the Yankees lost the World Series to the Cincinnati Reds in four straight games. About the only point the fans had to argue over, it being such a swift and decisive Series, was that the second game was played on a Sunday evening, instead of the traditional Sunday afternoon, to satisfy the preferences of the television audience. Since the temperature fell to 40 degrees, the ballpark fans – and players – really felt they had been shut out in the cold. One image that warmed the cockles of all baseball fans' hearts during the 1976 season, though, after all the legal and financial squabbles, was the performance of the Detroit Tigers' rookie right-hander, Mark Fidrych. It was not only his fine record of 19-9, nor his leading ERA of 2.34, it was his spontaneous and high-spirited antics on the mound that reminded everyone that baseball was still a game for the young at heart.

The American League took another step on its own away from the National League when in 1977 it expanded to 14 teams; the Mariners were established in Seattle and the Blue Jays set up in Toronto. Not unexpectedly, the Blue Jays came in last in their Eastern Division, but the Mariners came in only next to last in the Western Division – a half game ahead of the

Oakland A's. Whether the A's precipitous decline was due to the behavior of the free agents or Charles Finley himself would be debated by students of baseball, but in fact it was still far too early to say whether the movement of free agents was having much effect on any baseball statistics other than individual player's salaries.

But the big story, if not scandal, of the 1977 season was provided by the Yankees, which seemed to have taken on not only some of the Oakland A's players – including now Reggie Jackson – but also the A's unruly manners. George Steinbrenner, thanks to the emergence of free agents and his own checkbook, had assembled what was dubbed 'the best team that money could buy,' and he had put them under the feisty Billy Martin. What resulted was an often incredible spectacle of arguments, confrontations and actual fights involving principally Martin, Reggie Jackson and Steinbrenner, but drawing several other players into the maelstrom. Yet just as the Oakland A's had managed to play ball when it counted, so now these bickering Yankees managed to come through. As late as 7 August, the Yankees were five games out of first place, but they won 13 of the next 14 games and 38 of their last 51 – ending up two and a half games ahead of both the Red Sox and the Orioles in the Eastern Division. The Red Sox had 213 home runs, the fourth highest team total in American League history, but they lacked the pitching of the kind that Ron Guidry, Catfish Hunter and Don Gullet provided for the Yankees.

Opposite: Golden Glove second baseman Frank White turns a double play. White has played an important role in Kansas City's winning tradition since joining the team in 1973.

Left: After seven successful years with the Oakland A's, in 1974 Catfish Hunter became one of the first players to enter the open market as a free agent. George Steinbrenner won the bidding war, signing Hunter to a $3-plus million contract. The investment paid off as Hunter won 23 games, pitching 328 innings and completing 30 games in 1975. In 1976 he aided a Yankee run to the World Series.

Below: Left-hander Ron Guidry – 'Louisiana Lightning' – won 16 games in his first full season with the Yankees in 1977, and the following year won the Cy Young Award with his league-leading 25 wins and 1.74 ERA.

Outfielder Bobby Bonds played for the California Angles in 1976 and 1977, batting in 115 runs in the latter year.

(for Babe Ruth's three homers in two different Series games, 1926 and 1928, involved more pitches). The Yankees won the Series, four games to two, with Jackson taking the honors as Most Valuable Player.

But for the regular season of 1977, the most impressive batting performance was that of Rod Carew, who won his sixth American League batting title with his average of .388 – the highest since Ted Williams' .388 in 1957 – and a total of 239 hits, the most since Bill Terry's 254 in 1930. Another remarkable performance was given by Dennis Eckersley of the Cleveland Indians, who pitched a total of 22 and a third consecutive hitless innings over three games.

In the 1978 season the same four teams won the league's four divisions as had the year before, and 1978 featured the same Yankee turmoil as well. Gone were the austere, pinstriped Yankees of former years, the team that seemed so superior to the ordinary sweating ballplayers that it was dubbed 'the Board of Directors.' Once again, most of the controversy revolved around Martin, Steinbrenner and Jackson, three of a kind in a territory where there was probably room for only one (and a need for none). Aside from the verbal brickbats, Jackson and Martin almost came to blows. Their showdown came on 17 July, when Martin signaled Jackson to hit at three successive pitches but Jackson tried (unsuccessfully) to bunt each time. Jackson was then suspended for five days. But instead of letting it go at that, Martin made a crack

In the Western Division the Kansas City Royals repeated their victory of the previous year, beating out the Texas Rangers by eight games. Considering that the Oakland A's had been effectively dismantled, their last-place finish was not totally unexpected. More surprising was the fifth-place finish – 28 games out – of the California Angels, but it was at least partially explained by the injuries suffered by Joe Rudi and Bobby Grich and by the fact that Nolan Ryan somewhat canceled out his 341 strikeouts with 204 walks, thus ending up with a respectable but not overly-impressive 19-16 record.

The American League play-offs were a re-run of 1976, pitting the Yankees against the Royals again and also going into a fifth and deciding game. Once again, too, the Yankees took that fifth game, this time with three runs in the ninth inning. The Yankees thus found themselves back in the World Series for a second successive year, this time facing the Los Angeles Dodgers. With four 30-home run hitters, the Dodgers were top-heavy with hitters, but it was Yankee home runs that beat them, particularly Reggie Jackson's five home runs, including three consecutive homers on only three pitches – both Series records

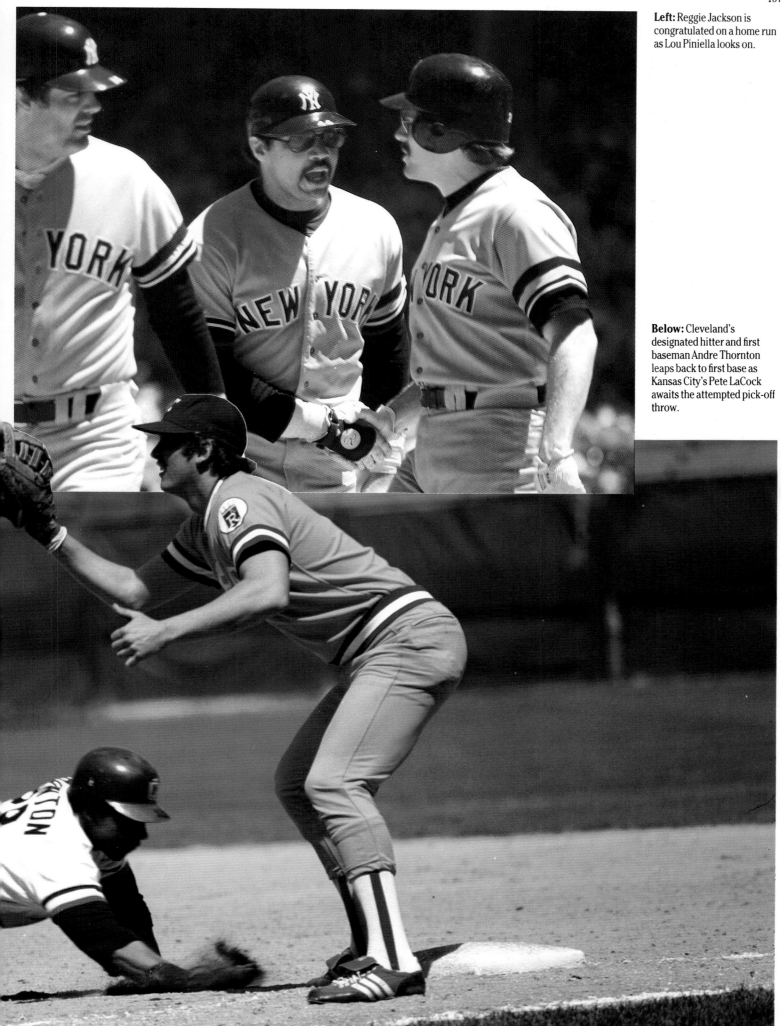

Left: Reggie Jackson is congratulated on a home run as Lou Piniella looks on.

Below: Cleveland's designated hitter and first baseman Andre Thornton leaps back to first base as Kansas City's Pete LaCock awaits the attempted pick-off throw.

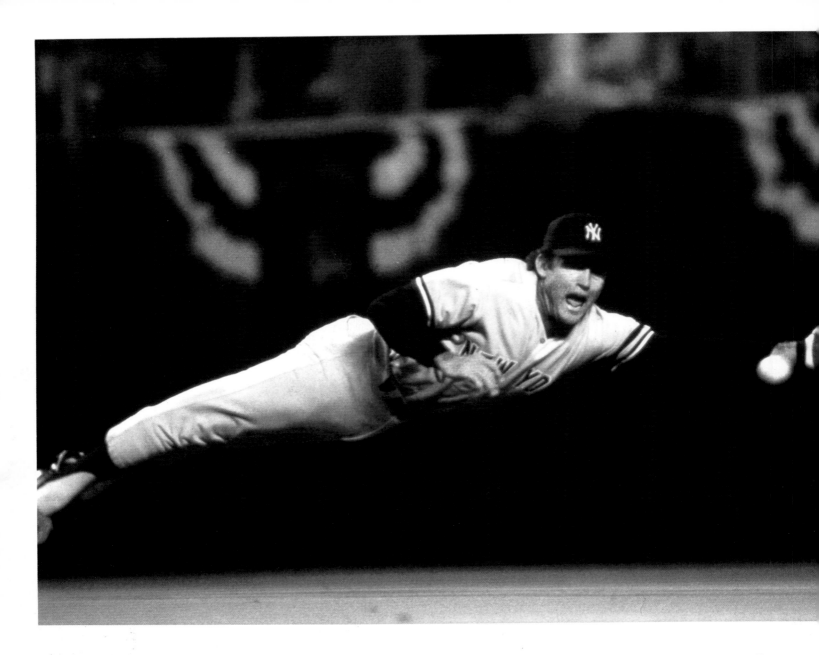

Above: The Yankee whiz at third base Graig Nettles leaps for a low line drive. Nettles worked his magic for the Yankees from 1973 to 1983, when he joined the Padres. He helped his team win the division and the pennant in 1978, smashing 27 homers during the season and batting .333 in the play-offs.
Opposite top: Red Sox right-hander Mike Torrez fires a fastball. Torrez came from the Yankees in 1978 as a free agent. That same year he started and lost the memorable one-game play-off in Boston that sent the Yankees to an eventual World championship.
Opposite bottom: Don Baylor, designated hitter and outfielder for the California Angels from 1977 to 1982, waits in the on-deck circle. Baylor was named the league's Most Valuable Player in 1979, when he powered 36 homers, batted in 139 runs and scored 120. In 1983 he moved to the Yankees.

to sports reporters on 23 July about Jackson and Steinbrenner: 'One's a born liar, the other's convicted.' (This last a reference to the fact that Steinbrenner had pleaded no contest to federal charges of making illegal political contributions.) By the next day, Martin was reading a resignation statement: 'I owe it to my health and my mental well-being to resign.' Bob Lemon took over as manager for the rest of the season – although to thoroughly confound everyone, on 29 July, the Yankees announced that Martin would return as manager in 1980.

By the time Lemon took over, the Yankees were 10 and a half games behind the division-leading Red Sox, who looked unbeatable with their combination of hitting and pitching. But now the Yankees seemed to want to play ball instead of games, and led by such pitchers as Ron Guidry, Ed Figueroa, Rich Gossage and Sparky Lyle, the Yankees began to win. Then in September the Red Sox lost 14 out of 17 games and the Yankees took over the lead. When the Red Sox won their last eight games, however, they pulled even with the Yankees, and both teams ended the regular season with 99-63 records. A tie-breaker game was necessary, and the Yankees put in Ron Guidry, whose season record was already 24-3, the highest win percentage for a 20-plus game winner in major league history. Helped by Bucky Dent's three-run homer and Reggie Jackson's game-winning home run, Guidry raised that percentage to an astounding .893 and the

Yankees had the championship of the Eastern Division.

In the Western Division it was the Kansas City Royals for the third consecutive year; with strong pitching from Dennis Leonard, Paul Splittorff, Larry Gura and Rich Gale, and with the powerful bat of George Brett, the Royals left the California Angels five games behind. In the play-offs, however, despite Brett's three homers, the Yankees beat the Royals three games to one. The World Series also turned out to be a rematch between the Yankees and the Dodgers, with the Dodgers slightly favored. And when the Dodgers took the first two games, it seemed that the Yankees were doomed, but with the strong bats of Reggie Jackson, Lou Piniella, Bucky Dent and Thurmon Munson, and some superb fielding by third baseman Graig Nettles, the Yankees rebounded to take the next four games and the World Series – the first team to lose the opening two games and then end up winning the Series in six games.

Ron Guidry's record-breaking win percentage of .893 was one of the personal highlights of the 1978 season. Another was Rod Carew's seventh American League batting title with a .333. This seventh title tied him with Rogers Hornsby and Stan Musial, with only Ty Cobb's 12 and Honus Wagner's 8 holding the lead. The Red Sox's Jim Rice also had an extraordinary year, with 46 home runs and 139 RBI's, giving him the league's lead in each category.

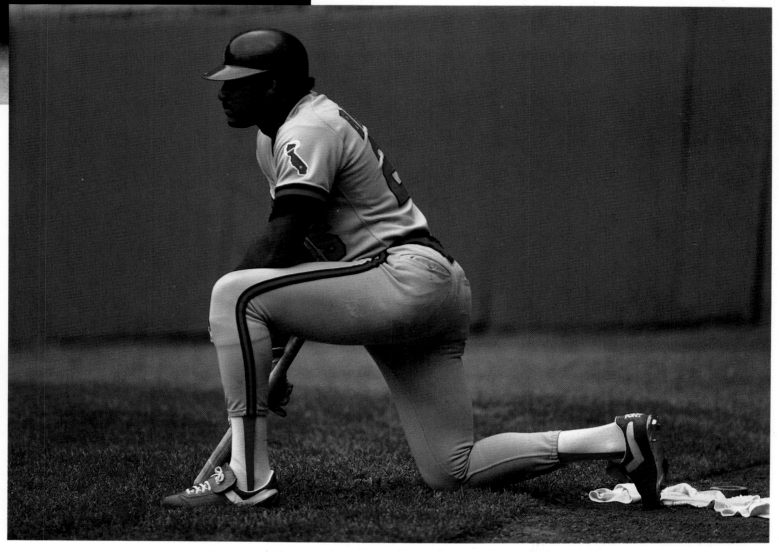

Right: The California Angels'
great Rod Carew holds a
career batting average of .330.

Below: Don Baylor looks on
imploringly after umpire
Durwood Merrill called him out.

The 1979 season was one of those 'turnover' years.
Just when it seemed that a few teams were settling
down as permanent dynasties, new teams took over
first place in all four divisions. In the case of the
American League's Eastern Division, the Yankees fell
from first place, 13 games down into fourth place. It

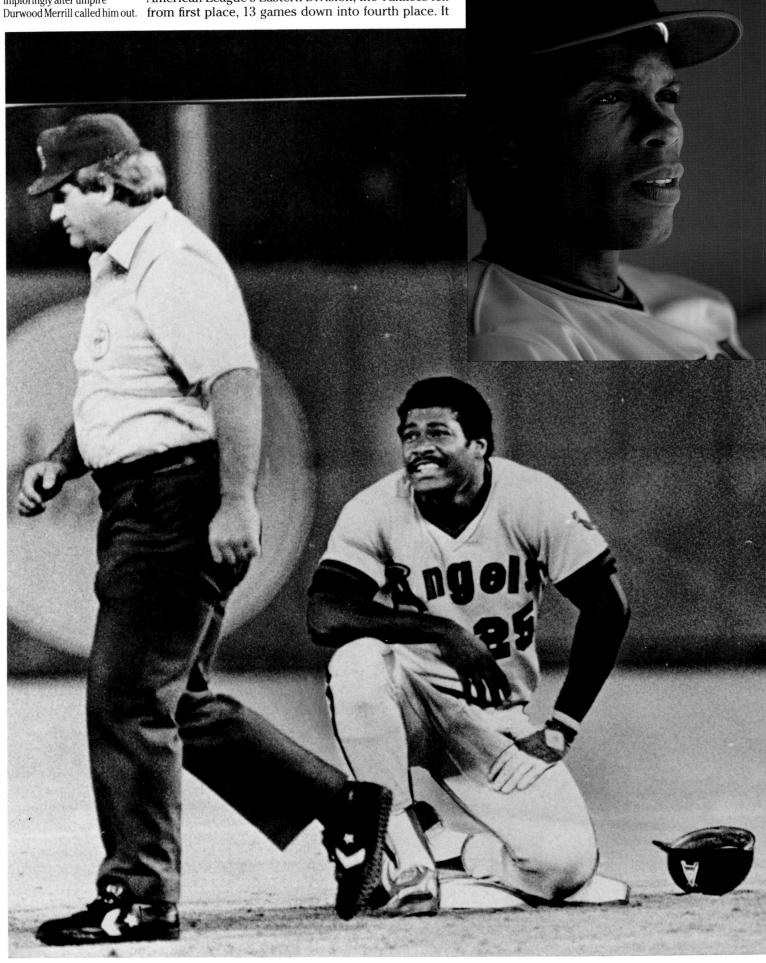

seemed that all the headlines finally caught up to them. The trouble began in April when Rich Gossage, the relief pitcher, got into a fight in the shower with catcher Cliff Johnson. Gossage tore a ligament in his right hand and was out of the lineup for three months. (Johnson was traded to the Cleveland Indians.) Then in June, with the team going nowhere, Bob Lemon was fired as manager – only to be replaced by none other than Billy Martin. In August, the Yankee catcher, captain and sparkplug Thurman Munson died in the crash of a jet plane he owned and was piloting. Finally, in October, Billy Martin was fired after he was caught covering up his involvement in a barroom brawl.

But by then it was too late for the Yankees to do anything with the 1979 season. The Baltimore Orioles had won 102 games and beat out two hard-hitting challengers, the Milwaukee Brewers (by eight) and the Boston Red Sox (by 11 and a half) to give manager Earl Weaver his sixth division title win in 11 years. The Orioles themselves, with such as Ken Singleton and Eddie Murray, were no slouches at bat and had a team total of 181 homers, and when Jim Palmer injured his elbow and was out for two months, Mike Flanagan came through with a 23-9 record. But if Baltimore's being in first place was no great surprise, the California Angels in first place in the Western Division was: they had been finishing an average of 23 and a half games down for the previous 18 seasons! With the old cowboy star Gene Autry as owner and Jim Fregosi as manager, the Angels were able to field

an impressive if not overpowering team, including Don Baylor, Dan Ford, Brian Downing and Bobby Grich. They also could boast of Nolan Ryan, who struck out 223 batters that year; and although they had acquired Rod Carew from the Twins and he hit a respectable .318, he was out for much of the season due to a finger injury.

In the league's play-offs, however, the Angels were beaten out by the Orioles, three games to one. The Orioles then found themselves in what was billed as a 'railroad series' because the National League's winner was the Pirates of nearby Pittsburgh. And it was a good thing that the teams didn't have to fly because the foul weather might have grounded them. As it was, the rain and cold affected several key plays. But it was as bad for one team as the other, and when the Orioles took three of the first four games, they were sure that the pot of gold was just the other side of the gray clouds. Instead, the Pirates took the last three games – as remarkable as it seems, as only three other teams had previously done this – and became the World Champions.

But if such upsets are hard for the losers, they are good for the game. Attendance figures for 1979 broke the record for the fourth straight year, with the total for the major leagues being 43,548,450 – up 46 percent from 1975 – and observers agreed that this was at least in part due to the new winners. Whatever the reasons, the American League, designated hitters and all, was ready to take on the 1980s.

Oriole Ken Singleton cracks a rightfield hit in the 1979 World Series against Pittsburgh. Despite Singleton's 10 for 28, Baltimore lost the Series four games to three.

A multiple exposure shows the Royals' relief pitcher Dan Quisenberry's characteristic sidearm motion.

CHAPTER EIGHT

The Unsettled Eighties and Into the Nineties

"My goal is to take the club to arbitration when I'm 50 – and win."

Jerry Koosman, 42-year-old pitcher

Below: Outfielder Steve Kemp joined the Tigers in 1977 and quickly rose to stardom. The Tigers, wary of his impending free agent status, traded him to the White Sox in 1981. The following year he left the White Sox as a free agent and signed with the Yankees. After two years of mediocre performances, Kemp was traded to the Pirates along with Tim Foli and $400,000 for Dale Berra and a minor league pitcher.

Opposite: Yankee outfielder Dave Winfield begins a powerful swing. Winfield played for San Diego for eight years before he signed a 10-year, $15-plus million contract with the Yankees in 1981. In his first four years with New York he racked up 390 RBI's, and won three Golden Glove Awards.

As the American League entered the 1980s, most longtime observers of the major leagues would probably agree that organized baseball would continue to change. True, there had been all kinds of changes in the sport even since the first professional teams had agreed on the rules and operations in the last quarter of the ninteenth century. But in the 1970s, a different kind of change seemed to be occurring, some fundamental shift in the relations among all the participants, including the fans. The striking down of the reserve clause in the 1970s undoubtedly was the major and most tangible blow to the old arrangements, but the role of television was arguably even more influential.

Television, after all, disconnected organized baseball from the simple financial link between ballpark attendees and available income. Television brought in a whole new source of money – and lots of it. Given the spirit of the country in the 1960s, with many formerly consenting groups demanding to renegotiate their contracts with society at large, it should be no surprise that baseball players insisted on renegotiating theirs, too, so that they could get what they considered their fair share of the new and large sums of money. Thus followed the free agents, the drafts, the arbitration, the agents, the million-dollar contracts – and the strikes.

Between 1978 and 1981, 43 players negotiated contracts worth over $1 million each; the peak would be reached by outfielder Dave Winfield when in November 1980 the New York Yankees signed him to a 10-year contract worth at least $13 million (and a cost-of-living clause that made it worth a possible $20 million). All players were riding the coattails of the major free agents and superstars, too, and the average salary of all major-league players went from $50,000 in 1976, when the reserve clause was still in effect, to $200,000 by 1981. Inevitably, the owners of the major league clubs decided that they should obtain some advantage from the free-agent inflation. When the owners' agreement with the players expired on 31 December 1979, the owners demanded a new condition: any club that lost a player when a free agent moved must be allowed to obtain a player from the club that signed the free agent.

The players immediately recognized that this would put a brake on the free agent system and they refused to accept this condition. During the final week of spring training in 1980, the players staged a walk-out and threatened to go on strike on 23 May if there was no agreement with the owners. Minutes before the deadline, the club owners and the Players Association agreed to set up a committee – formed of two player representatives and two general managers – that would study the whole issue of free agents; if they

could not come up with a solution that received the endorsement of all parties by 31 January 1981, each side could take whatever action it chose to. So the conflict between the owners and players was set aside and the 1980 season was played out. The American League fans did not seem too upset about the squabbles over terms and money, for a record-breaking 22 million turned out for just this league's games during 1980.

In the American League's Eastern Division, an exciting and hard-fought battle developed between 1979's winner, the Orioles, and 1978's winner, the Yankees. The Orioles could not count on their old pitching trio of Cuellar, Palmer and McNally, but they came up with two 20-game winners in Steve Stone and Scott McGregor. The Yankees had three equally strong pitchers in Tommy John, Ron Guidry and Rudy May, along with relievers Rich Gossage and Ron Davis. And where the Orioles could take to the attack with Ken Singleton and Eddie Murray, the Yankees could counter with Reggie Jackson and Dave Winfield. (Jackson's 41 homers tied him with the Brewers' Ben Oglivie for the league's lead.) The Brewers also remained a threat – as a team, they hit 203 home runs – but in the end the Yankees prevailed.

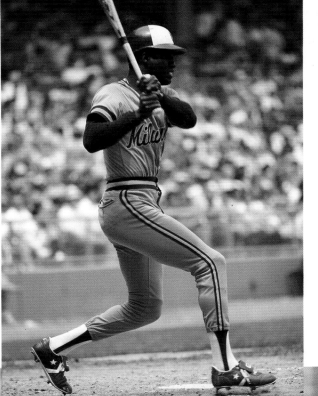

Opposite: Yankee ace Tommy John winds up. John helped his team to the division title in 1980, winning 22 games and losing only nine.
Opposite (inset): The Texas Rangers' third baseman Buddy Bell batted .329 in 1980, with 83 RBI's. Bell joined the Rangers in 1979 after seven years with the Indians.
Left: Ben Oglivie takes a cut. The power-hitting outfielder joined the Milwaukee Brewers in 1978 and led the league the following year in homers, with 41. In 1982 his 102 RBI's helped bring his team the pennant.
Below: The Oriole first baseman Eddie Murray fields a ball. Murray, who joined Baltimore in 1977 and was named Rookie of the Year, wields a heavy bat and is known for his excellent defensive play as well.

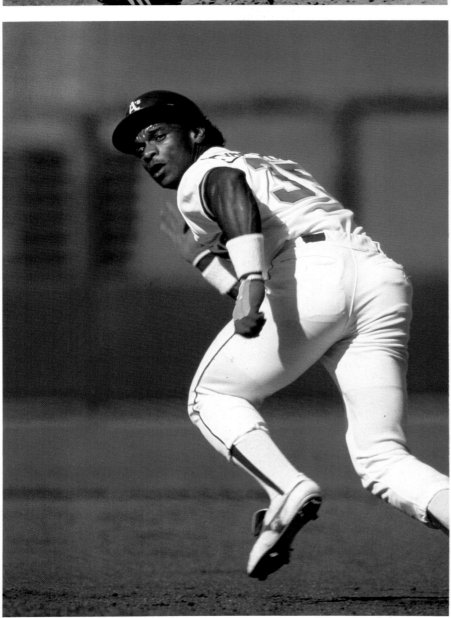

In the Western Division in 1980, however, it was hardly a contest, as the Kansas City Royals left the Oakland A's 14 games behind in second place. The Royals were paced by two truly hot players, George Brett and Willie Wilson. Brett looked like he might end up with a .400 batting average but had to settle for .390 (still the highest since Ted Williams' .406 in 1941), a .664 slugging average and 118 RBI's, while Wilson got 230 hits on his way to a .326 batting average. But one Oakland A was positively sizzling: Rickey Henderson broke Ty Cobb's 1915 league record of 96 stolen bases when he ran off with 100.

In the league play-offs, the Royals met the Yankees for the fourth time in five years; the Yankees had won three of these, but 1980 was the Royals' turn. The Royals, in fact, beat the Yankees three straight, with one of those storybook confrontations coming in the third game. In the seventh inning with the Yankees ahead, 2-1, George Brett with his .390 average came to bat against Rich 'Goose' Gossage with his 100-mph pitches. Brett hit a homer with two on and this assured the Royals their victory. In the World Series, though, the Royals fell to the Phillies, four games to two.

All of which was quite cut-and-dried compared to what happened in the 1981 season – which may or may not go down as a major watershed year in the history of organized baseball. The January 1981 deadline proposed in the May 1980 agreement had come and gone without the owners and players coming to terms over the issue of compensating teams that lost free agents. The players maintained their position that any form of compensation would undermine the value of a free agent. The owners' final offer as the 1981 season got underway was that for every 'premium' player who left a club as a free agent, that club was to get a replacement choice from a select roster of players from the club that signed the free

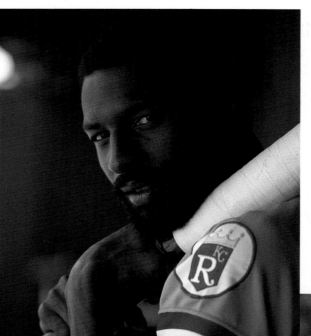

Opposite top: Ace relief pitcher Goose Gossage fires a fastball. Gossage led the league in saves twice during his six years with the Yankees.
Opposite bottom: During the years speedster Rickey Henderson played for Oakland, he led the league in stolen bases five times.
Left: Outfielder Willie Wilson joined the Royals in 1976, led the league in stolen bases in 1979, and won the batting title in 1982.
Below: George Brett readies himself to tag out the runner. Brett's defensive skills and astounding .390 average earned him the batting title and MVP honors in 1980.

agent. (A 'premium' player was defined by a complex formula involving his statistics in relation to other players at his position.) Although rejecting this compromise, the players began the season but made it clear they would strike if some progress wasn't made in negotiations.

So the 1981 season got underway on schedule, and also as if on schedule, the Yankees and the Orioles came rolling into mid-June in first and second place, respectively, in the Eastern Division. In the Western Division, Oakland was once again leading, with the Texas Rangers one and a half games behind them on 11 June. And then, just as they had threatened to do, all players in both major leagues went on strike, starting on 12 June. Day after day it went on, and soon Americans accepted that there was not going to be any major league baseball in the immediate future. Minor league and other teams found themselves with unexpectedly large crowds, and countless words were written about the role of baseball in American life. All the major league players went unpaid, of course, while the owners lost all the profits for those days. Seven hundred and fourteen games were eventually cancelled during the 49 days the strike lasted –

the longest strike in the history of organized sports – but finally, on 31 July, the club owners and the players arrived at a compromise. Teams that lost a 'premium' free agent could be compensated by drawing on a pool of players formed by players contributed from all the clubs, not just the signing club; the teams that lost players through this pool system would be compensated from a fund supported by all the clubs; the net effect was to disperse the impact and cost so that owners would not lose the incentive to bid large sums for the premium free agents.

This, at least, was the essence of the compromise and when it was announced that the players would report for a 10-day summer 'training session' before resuming play, fans were ready to forgive and forget. 'Let's play ball!' was the cry. Then came the outcry when it was learned that the owners had decided to 'split' the season: namely, first-place teams in each division at the end of the first half would play the first-place teams at the end of the second half to settle division winners. If the same team happened to win both halves, it would play the runner-up from the second half only to determine the winner. That did not occur, but something else that was predicted

Opposite: Willie Randolph readies himself at the plate. Since joining the Yankees in 1976, the second baseman has played in four league play-offs and three World Series.

Below: Minnesota's third baseman John Castino dashes in for a bloop hit.

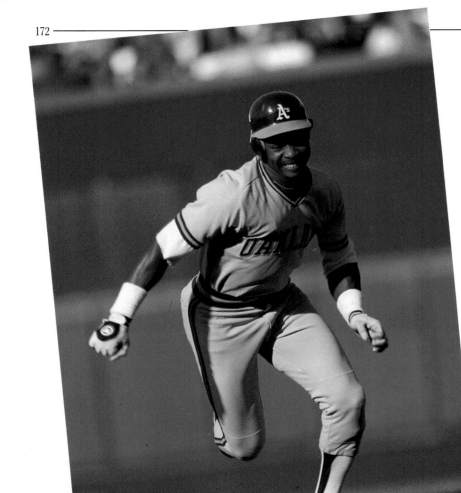

might happen did occur: the two National League teams that had the best overall records, the Cincinnati Reds and the St Louis Cardinals, both came in second for each 'season' and thus did not get a chance at a play-off slot.

With a certain amount of grumbling from various sides, then, 1981's second season got underway on 10 August. This time, the Milwaukee Brewers won in the Eastern Division, beating out the Red Sox by only one and a half games and then only by winning 11 of their last 17 games. In the Western Division, the Kansas City Royals edged out the Oakland A's by only one game. But by the irony of the system, Oakland, as winner of the first half, came right back and defeated the Royals in three straight to win the Western Division play-offs. In the Eastern Division play-offs, the Yankees beat the Brewers, three games to two. After all this, the pennant race was still not over, and for the American League, this saw the Yankees facing the A's – with Oakland now managed by Billy Martin, late of the Yankees. If Martin was supposed to jinx the Yankees, it didn't work as New York beat the A's in three straight games. Actually, Yankee Graig Nettles almost singlehandedly beat the A's, with his nine RBI's – three of them coming off his double in the ninth inning of the final game.

In the World Series the Yankees came up against their archrivals, the Dodgers, for the 11th time. Although the Yankees had taken eight of these Series, this was not to be the year for the ninth. The Dodgers lost the first two, then came back and won the next four (only the second team to achieve this, the first being the Yankees, who did exactly the same thing to the Dodgers in 1978). All in all, 1981 had been a topsy-turvy season. Because the teams had played only about two-thirds of their games, the records for the season included such feats as Eddie Murray's 78 RBI's. But one player who would never complain of the 1981 season being too short was Len Barker of the Cleveland Indians, who on 15 May pitched a perfect game against the Toronto Blue Jays – only the 11th perfect game in major league history.

For the 1982 season, the strike seemed to have been totally forgotten and baseball was back to normal – which by now meant a fair amount of intramural fighting among the Yankees. George Steinbrenner, it might have been thought, got rid of one of his sparring partners when he let Reggie Jackson, once more a free agent, sign with the California Angels for 1982. (Jackson immediately announced he had no intention of becoming the 'team leader' – but he did end up with 39 homers, the sweetest of which was certainly the one he hit in his first game against the Yankees. Steinbrenner, meanwhile, tried to get even by accusing the Angels at one point of using 'illegal bats'). Stein-

Above: Reggie Jackson cracks a long ball. Jackson led the league in home runs and in strikeouts in 1982, his first year with the Angels.

Left: Sal Bando waits in the on-deck circle. Bando played third base for Milwaukee from 1977 until his retirement in 1981.

Opposite top: Dwayne Murphy rounds second base. Outfielder Murphy joined the A's in 1978. In the Western Division play-offs in the 1981 strike season, Murphy went 6 for 11.

Opposite bottom: Manager Billy Martin signals from the dugout. Martin managed the A's from 1980 to 1982.

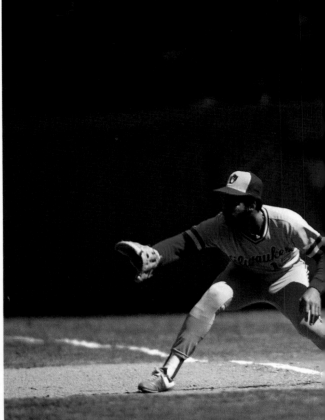

brenner displayed his insensitivity to the players when he wrote a letter urging them to come to spring training three weeks early and then he tried to cut pitcher Tommy John's salary for failure to produce enough wins. When he announced that the Yankees were considering playing their first home games in Denver, Colorado – because Yankee Stadium's renovations might not be ready – he drew the wrath of all New Yorkers. Kicking a process server out of his office one day did not enhance Steinbrenner's image as a cool executive, either.

And since the Yankees also went through three managers during the 1982 season, it is no wonder that they didn't finish in first place in their division. (The Yankees began with Bob Lemon; on 25 April, Gene Michael took over, and on 3 August Clyde King got the nod.) But two teams did produce an old-fashioned race in the Eastern Division – the Brewers and the Orioles. The Brewers had an imposing array of power players in Paul Molitor, Cecil Cooper, Robin Yount, Ben Oglivie, Gorman Thomas and Ted Simmons, and had several respectable pitchers, while the Orioles had a more seasoned and balanced team playing under their longtime manager Earl Weaver. As occasionally happens with the chance of scheduling, the Orioles and Brewers found themselves in a four-game series in the final days of the regular season, but the Brewers had a three-game lead and looked virtually safe. Then the Orioles took the first three games, drew up to a tie, and turned it into a one-game season. The Brewers had acquired Don Sutton near the end of the season for just such a crisis, and in the final game he came through and the Brewers took over first place by winning 10-2.

In the Western Division, the California Angels took first place, but not without a struggle with the ever-threatening Kansas City Royals. Even with the likes of Willie Wilson and George Brett the Royals weren't able to overcome the Angels' power-packed lineup that included Reggie Jackson, Don Baylor, Fred Lynn

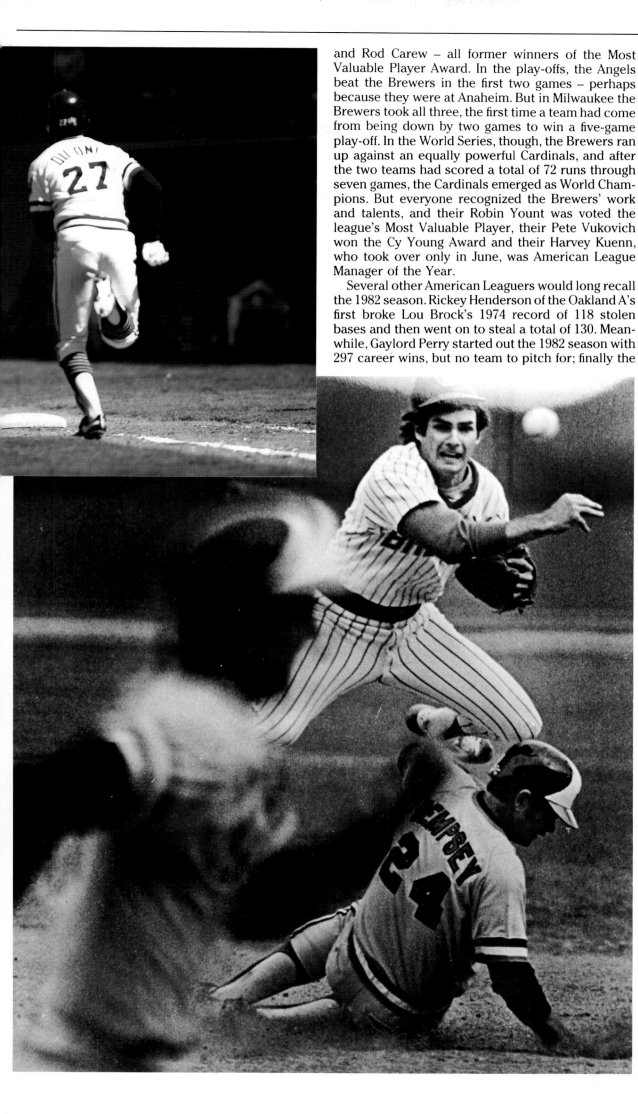

and Rod Carew – all former winners of the Most Valuable Player Award. In the play-offs, the Angels beat the Brewers in the first two games – perhaps because they were at Anaheim. But in Milwaukee the Brewers took all three, the first time a team had come from being down by two games to win a five-game play-off. In the World Series, though, the Brewers ran up against an equally powerful Cardinals, and after the two teams had scored a total of 72 runs through seven games, the Cardinals emerged as World Champions. But everyone recognized the Brewers' work and talents, and their Robin Yount was voted the league's Most Valuable Player, their Pete Vukovich won the Cy Young Award and their Harvey Kuenn, who took over only in June, was American League Manager of the Year.

Several other American Leaguers would long recall the 1982 season. Rickey Henderson of the Oakland A's first broke Lou Brock's 1974 record of 118 stolen bases and then went on to steal a total of 130. Meanwhile, Gaylord Perry started out the 1982 season with 297 career wins, but no team to pitch for; finally the

Opposite top: Outfielder Gorman Thomas contributed to the Brewers' power line-up. Thomas' league-leading 39 home runs in 1982 helped bring Milwaukee the pennant that year.

Opposite bottom: Milwaukee's shortstop Robin Yount was selected as the league's Most Valuable Player in 1982, the year he cracked 210 hits and 46 doubles for a league-leading .578 slugging percentage. Despite Yount's becoming the first player in World Series history to have two four-hit games, Milwaukee lost the Series in seven games to St Louis.

Left: First baseman Cecil Cooper stretches for the throw. Cooper joined Milwaukee in 1977 after six years with Boston. The big power-hitter led the league twice in RBI's and twice in doubles for the Brewers, maintaining a solid .305 batting average.

Left: Paul Molitor turns a double play. Molitor joined the Brewers in 1978, playing mainly second and third base. In 1982 he scored a league-leading 136 runs, and popped two homers in the league playoffs.

Below: Yankee phenomenon Dave Winfield pumps his way around the bases for a stand-up triple.

Seattle Mariners signed him on and on 6 May Perry got his 300th win, only the 15th major league pitcher to achieve this. And just in case anyone feared that baseball was running out of traditions to maintain, the Oakland A's fired Billy Martin when the season was over – and the Yankees would take him on to manage for 1983.

Every so often, major league baseball has one of those seasons where all kinds of sideshows seem to overshadow the main events at center ring – and 1983 was such a season. There was the ongoing saga of the decline and fall of Bowie Kuhn, Commissioner of Baseball for the previous 15 years. Kuhn had failed to satisfy some of the club owners and in November 1982 they had managed to get enough votes to oust him. However, they asked him to stay in office until his successor could be found, and throughout 1983 Kuhn openly lobbied in every way possible to see if he couldn't get the owners to re-appoint him. (He would hang on through 1983 – but would ultimately fail.) Ironically, one of the charges against Kuhn was that he didn't exercise sound financial judgment – i.e. the owners wanted to make more money. This charge came at a time when two of the television networks, NBC and ABC, signed a new contract for televising baseball games that guaranteed the teams some $1,100,000,000 over the next six years.

Speaking of television, a poll of active players showed that most of them opposed the use of television's instant replay to resolve disputes over controversial calls by umpires – a proposal that often surfaces. A more disconcerting development was the increasing number of players who were being charged with using drugs – cocaine in particular. Four members of the Kansas City Royals alone were found guilty of cocaine use in 1983, and there were several others already serving prison sentences for drug cases. A somewhat lighter moment came on 4 August when Dave Winfield of the Yankees was arrested in Toronto for 'cruelty to animals': he had thrown a baseball at one of the numerous seagulls that hover over the Blue Jays' home field – and killed the bird. (Winfield would explain that he had intended only to frighten it away and the charge was dropped.)

There had been a close race within the Eastern Division well into July, with the Yankees, Tigers and Orioles all in contention, while in the Western Division the Kansas City Royals were giving the division-leading Chicago White Sox a run for their money. Although the Yankees were having yet another of their tempestuous seasons under Billy Martin, they were on the verge of taking first place away from the Orioles. As for the White Sox, everyone was aware that it was not the first time the team had been on a hot streak, only to collapse. So when the Yankees met the Kansas City Royals at Yankee Stadium on 24 July, each team was needing every win it could get. It was the top of the ninth with the Yankees leading 4-3 and two Royals out when George Brett stepped up and hit a homer off reliever Rich Gossage that gave the Royals two runs and a 5-4 lead. At that point, Billy Martin stepped out of the dugout and pointed out to the umpire that Brett had used a bat with more than the 18 inches of pine tar allowed by the rules. Once the umpire was convinced, he ruled that Brett's homer didn't count, that he was out – and the Yankees thus won the game. (What was not generally known at the time was that Gaylord Perry, on the Kansas City team, tried to sneak the bat away during all the commotion at the plate, but the umpire chased him all the way into the runway between the dugout and the locker room and retrieved the bat.) The Royals naturally protested the umpire's ruling, and four days later Lee MacPhail, president of the American League,

Tiger right-hander Dan Petry hurls a pitch. Petry joined Detroit in 1979, turning in 19 wins for them in 1983 and 18 wins (with a .692 winning percentage) the following year to help bring the Tigers to the Series.

Main picture: Oakland catcher Mike Heath goes into the stands for a foul ball.
Inset: A catcher's profile.

Opposite: The Orioles' shortstop Cal Ripken fires a throw to first base. Ripken was named Rookie of the Year in 1982, and the following year was selected as the league's Most Valuable Player as his team went all the way to win the World Series.

Above right: The Angels' outfielder Fred Lynn perches in the California dugout. In the 1982 league play-offs Lynn batted 11 for 18, and the following year he gained acclaim with his All-Star grand slam.

Below: Lou Whitaker fields a grounder. As Detroit's second baseman, 'Sweet Lou' was named Rookie of the Year in 1978. His solid play has contributed to the Tigers' rise to the top.

overruled the umpire: 'Games should be won and lost on the playing field – not through technicalities of the rules.' The game was to be replayed from the moment after Brett's homer. On 18 August, before 1245 fans, one more Royal came up, then the final three for the Yankees – and the game ended in 9 minutes and 41 seconds with Kansas City on top, 5-4.

But by then, the damage had been done. The Yankees had been tied for first place with the Orioles on 28 July, but they had gone into a slump after the disputed game and by the time the final innings were played, the Yankees were in fifth place. The Orioles then went on to hold off the Detroit Tigers and take first place in the Eastern Division. In the Western Division, the White Sox finally held on to a lead and for the first time since 1959 qualified for post-season play. In the playoffs, the Orioles beat the White Sox in three straight, taking the third game on Tito Landrum's homer. The World Series was billed as another 'railroad series,' since it pitted the Orioles against their neighbors up the line, the Philadelphia Phillies. The Phillies seemed loaded with talent with the likes of Mike Schmidt, Joe Morgan, Pete Rose and Steve Carlton, but the Orioles had their own talents such as Eddie Murray and Cal Ripken, Jr. (What they couldn't count on, though, was their star designated hitter, Ken Singleton, since this was an odd year, and thus the Series didn't allow for the DH.) Although the Phillies took the first game, the Orioles went on to sweep the next four and take the Series.

So all in all, 1983 turned out to be a successful year for most of the members of the American League. After more losses in the All-Star Game than anyone could remember, the American League won the 50th anniversary game, 13-3, with Fred Lynn hitting the first grand slam home run in the history of All-Star games. The Texas Rangers set a record of sorts in 1983, too, when they got 12 runs in an extra inning, the most ever in major league history. And in the same season the Brewers played the White Sox for four hours 11 minutes, the longest game in American

Padres – which Goose Gossage had already left the Yankees to join. Meanwhile, Dave Righetti, considered one of the hottest pitchers around, was assigned to be a relief pitcher for the Yankees. And in one of the more surprising moves, the Yankees signed up the oldest active player in the major leagues, 44-year-old Phil Niekro, the famed knuckleballer who had worked for the Braves, first in Milwaukee and then in Atlanta, for 19 years.

One of the more astounding developments of the 1984 season was when Tom Seaver, long a National League ace pitcher, suddenly appeared on the roster of the Chicago White Sox. This came about through a simple error on the part of the Mets' front office, which neglected to put Seaver's name on their list of 'protected' players – those not eligible for the pool

Opposite: After 17 years in the National League, pitching great Tom Seaver was lost to the Chicago White Sox, in 1984. 'Tom Terrific' won 15 games for the Sox that year. His career ERA stands at about 2.80.

Left: The Royals' ace reliever Dan Quisenberry helped them clinch the 1985 World championship title with his steady performances.

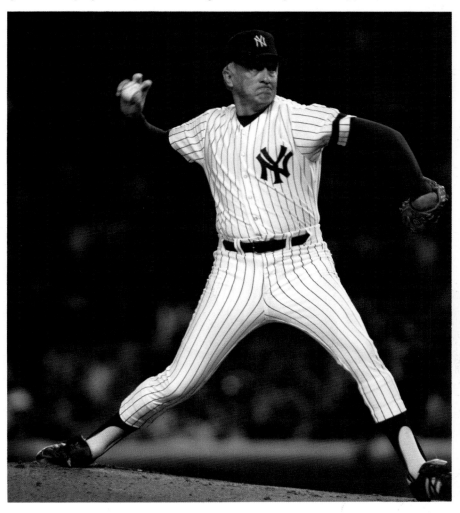

League history. (The Brewers won, 12-9.) Dan Quisenberry set a major league record when he posted 39 saves for the Kansas City Royals; Dave Righetti pitched a no-hitter for the Yankees (over the Red Sox, 4-0), the first for the team in 27 years and Carl Yastrzemski of the Red Sox set a new American League record of 3058 appearances, and then retired on 1 October. Lee MacPhail also retired as president of the American League at the end of 1983 – and Billy Martin was fired by the Yankees again.

The Yankees started out the 1984 season, in fact, with numerous changes. Aside from having Yogi Berra as manager, Steinbrenner decided to shake up a team he felt wasn't producing what he expected for his money. This left several players fed up, and when Graig Nettles publicly criticized Steinbrenner's changes, he was promptly traded to the San Diego

draft. The alert White Sox noticed this and immediately claimed Seaver; at first Seaver threatened to retire rather than go, but he realized that he was more interested in his career than his location, so in February he settled with the White Sox.

Another major personnel change for major league baseball came about in March 1984 when the club owners finally agreed on a successor to Bowie Kuhn as Commissioner of Baseball. Their choice was Peter Ueberroth, president of the Los Angeles Olympic Organizing Committee who, even before the Olympics were held, was recognized for his mastery of its financial and organizational complexities. It would be 1 October 1984, however, before he would actually take over as commissioner for a five-year term.

But the really exciting news of 1984 was made on the playing field. In the Eastern Division, the Yankees were a threat as usual, but although Dave Winfield and Don Mattingly raced each other down to the last

Above: Knuckleballer Phil Niekro throws a pitch. After 20 years in the National League, Niekro signed with the Yankees in 1984, winning 16 games for them and losing eight.

Left: First baseman Don Mattingly, who joined the Yankees in 1982, won the batting title in 1984 with a .343 average.

day for the individual batting title – with Mattingly just sneaking into the lead with his .343 – the team couldn't get it all together. The World Champion Orioles were also picked as a good prospect to repeat but they also didn't make it. Instead, the Detroit Tigers opened the season with a win, like 12 other major league teams; but unlike the other 12, Detroit just went on winning and winning, setting a record by winning 35 out of their first 40 games. At one point they also won 17 straight games on the road, and Tiger Jack Morris pitched a no-hitter on 7 April. By 18 September, the Tigers had clinched first place in the Eastern Division, and their manager, Sparky Anderson, would end the season as the first manager to lead two different clubs with 100-plus victories.

In the Western Division the Chicago White Sox seemed like the top prospect when the season began, but instead it was the Kansas City Royals, with the Twins in second. It hardly made any difference to the Tigers, since they took the playoffs in three straight. And the story in the World Series was not much different, although the Padres did manage to win the second game. Detroit took the Series, four games to one, with the same well-balanced team that had been winning all season – including such as Kirk Gibson, Alan Trammell and Willie Hernandez (who ended up winning both the Cy Young Award and the Most Valuable Player Award). The only thing that marred Detroit's spectacular season was the riotous celebration that occurred in Detroit after their Series clincher – and which left one innocent bystander dead.

With a season such as that, it might be assumed that Detroit was picked to be an easy winner for 1985, but the experts thought better. They decided that Detroit simply couldn't maintain the pace – and that another team was due to get hot. The team they picked for the Eastern Division was the Toronto Blue Jays, and indeed the Blue Jays got off to a good start

Opposite: White Sox catcher Carlton Fisk slams a home run. Fisk, who joined the Sox in 1981, hit 37 home runs in 1985.

Above: Shortstop Alan Tramell joined the Tigers in 1977. In 1984 Tramell's .314 batting average helped the Tigers' unstoppable run to the Series, and his pair of two-run homers in game four of the Series helped Detroit take the championship.

Left: The World Champions in 1984 – the Detroit Tigers.

Right: George Brett handles a smash down the third base line with ease. Brett's sparkling 1985 post-season performance helped the Royals take it all.

Far right: In 1986 Boston Red Sox pitcher Roger Clemens led his team to the pennant with his 24-6 performance. Clemens, whose 20 strikeouts in one game set a new major-league record on 29 April 1986, won the Cy Young Award and was voted American League MVP.

Below: Red Sox third baseman Wade Boggs won the batting title in 1985 with his .368 batting average.

and by mid-season were in first place, two and a half games ahead of the Yankees. The Yankees started out the season under Yogi Berra but were doing so poorly that in May he was replaced – by Billy Martin! The Yankees now had, in addition to such hitters as Mattingly, Winfield, and Don Baylor, none other than Rickey Henderson, newly signed from the Oakland A's to a generous five-year contract. The Red Sox had high hopes at the outset, with such players as Jim Rice, Wade Boggs, Dwight Evans, and Bob Stanley, but with a shortage of pitching talent the team couldn't get the wins. The Baltimore Orioles also looked good, having just acquired Fred Lynn to go with an already strong lineup, but by June the Orioles were doing so poorly that Earl Weaver came out of retirement to manage them again.

Over in the Western Division, the Kansas City Royals had been picked to repeat, but at mid-season they were seven and a half games down in third place, with the Angels in first, six games ahead of the A's. The Brewers, incidentally, had decided to try a new tactic and signed on a star pitcher from Japan, Yutaka Enatsu, but he never really felt at home with American baseball and was soon dropped.

Two players who were at home with American baseball and who had been exiled for some years were Mickey Mantle and Willie Mays; both had taken jobs as public relations 'greeters' for gambling casinos, and Commissioner Bowie Kuhn had thus

Above: The Royals' pitching ace Bret Saberhagen, who joined the team the year before, hurled his way to a victory in game seven of the 1985 World Series.

owners. The players insisted that the owners were making profits and should share more of these profits with the players. The owners insisted that many of the clubs were losing large sums. And so as the weeks passed and threat of a strike drew nearer, finally 6 August was set by the players as the absolute deadline for an agreement.

The players did strike, but for barely a day and a half; by 8 August the players were back on the fields, and all missed games were made up during the rest of the season. The differences that caused the strike were resolved by compromise and the strike was quickly forgotten as the annual race for the pennant moved into the final laps. In the American League, the Toronto Blue Jays won the Eastern Division, in an excitingly close race with the Yankees, who ended up two games behind. In the Western Division the first-place Kansas City Royals came in one game ahead of the California Angels. The Royals won the playoffs in seven games and went on to meet the St Louis Cardinals in the 1985 World Series, which the Royals won, repeating their playoff feat by coming from behind 3 games to 1 to win 4 to 3.

As the 1986 season began to emerge from hibernation, the conventional wisdom was that the Kansas City Royals would repeat – at least to take the Western Division if not go all the way. In the Eastern Division, the Yankees seemed to come out on top in most of the predictions, with the California Angels projected at about third place and the Red Sox even farther down by these same measures. While these predictions proved, of course, to be wildly off-base, few other changes would come about in the league. Lou Piniella replaced Billy Martin as manager of the Yankees, and when Dick Williams left the San Diego Padres in the National League he soon showed up as manager of the Seattle Mariners in the American League West. Kirk Gibson, the Tigers' star, threatened to move on if he didn't get a better salary offer, but in the end he signed on – the fact was that no teams were showing any interest in high-salaried free agents – as did Carlton Fisk with the White Sox and Don Mattingly with the Yankees. One crucial swap during the season occurred when Don Baylor of the Yankees went over to the Red Sox in return for Mike Easler; both were to serve as their teams' designated hitters, and Baylor would turn out to be his team's sparkplug as well. And Phil Niekro, at 46 the oldest active pitcher, hoped to play the season with his brother Joe on the Yankees, but he was soon let go and signed on with the Cleveland Indians.

At first it looked as though Phil Niekro had made a lucky move as the Indians took an early lead (after leading the American League in losses in 1985). Then the spotlight suddenly shifted to the Red Sox on 29 April as a hitherto not widely acclaimed young pitcher, Roger Clemens, astonished baseball fans by setting a new modern major-league record of 20 strikeouts in a nine-inning game against the Mariners. And in case it seemed that this was one of those flash-in-the-pan performances, Clemens continued to win and win and win – his first 14 games, in fact. Not an all-time record but good enough to help the Red Sox take over first place in the Eastern Division by 15 May.

By the mid-season All-Star game (which the American League won, 3-2), there were the Red Sox, still in the first, with a solid seven-game lead over the favored Yankees. (Making some wags swallow that old chestnut about 'June is the month when both the basketball and baseball seasons end in Boston.') And in the Western Division, instead of the highly-touted

banished them from any association with major league baseball. The new commissioner Peter Ueberroth reinstated Mantle and Mays and won the instant approval of most baseball fans. But Ueberroth did not gain the approval of all active players when he also called for mandatory urine tests by everyone connected with major league baseball, as an attempt to end the ongoing drug use by players.

In the end, all of the controversies over drugs and salaries were swept away by the threatened strike by all major league players due to their inability to negotiate a new basic agreement with the club

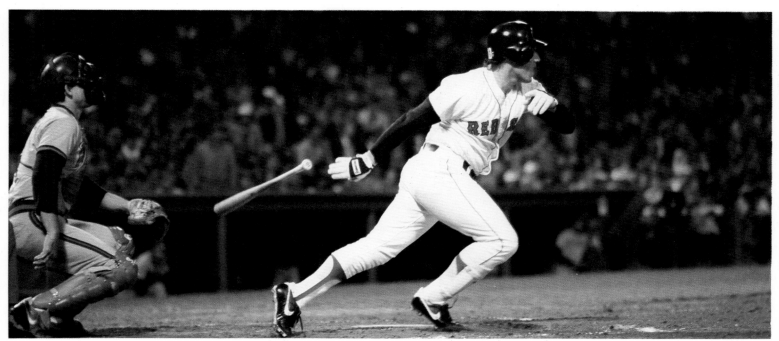

Royals, there were the California Angels – with only a one-and-a-half-game lead, but still not bad for a team of senior citizens. Two of the latter had done quite well. On 14 May, Reggie Jackson hit his five hundred thirty-seventh home run, taking over sixth place from Mickey Mantle among career home run hitters; and on 18 June, Don Sutton won his three hundredth game.

During the second half of the season, the Red Sox found themselves challenged at various times – by the Yankees, the Orioles, the Tigers and the Blue Jays – while the Angels had to hold off the Texas Rangers. But despite all the predictions, the Red Sox and the Angels ended up on top of their divisions. Going into the playoffs, it seemed the two teams were fairly evenly matched. Boston finally had what it had lacked for so many years – pitchers to support their hitters. Not only did Clemens come through with the best record in the majors (24-6), but there was Bruce Hurst and Oil Can Boyd. (Tom Seaver, who had come over to the Red Sox from the White Sox during the season, didn't figure that much in the team's victory, and injuries kept him out of the playoffs.) For hitting, the Red Sox could count on Wade Boggs (who had taken the league's batting championship with his .357), Jim Rice, Dwight Evans, Rich Gedman and Don Baylor. The Angels, meanwhile, could point to Mike Witt, Kirk McCaskill, John Candelaria and Don Sutton as pitching aces, while at bat they relied on Doug DeCinces, Bobby Grich, Brian Downing and the rookie sensation, Wally Joyner (although injury also kept him out of the playoffs).

The Angels took the first game of the playoffs, collapsed in the second and came back to take the third. In the fourth game the Red Sox took a 3-0 lead into the ninth inning, blew it, and then lost in the eleventh – it seemed that the Angels were unstoppable. The Red Sox went into the fifth game, down 3-1 in games, and sure enough, when the ninth inning came round, the Angels had a 5-2 lead. Buckner got on first and Don Baylor ripped a home run, but this still left the score 5-4 and soon there were two outs. Then Gedman got hit by a pitch and went to first, and up came one Dave Henderson, a Red Sox only since being acquired from the Mariners in August and hardly a known quantity to even many Boston fans. Henderson soon had two strikes on him and in the Angels' clubhouse the champagne was one pitch from

being poured – when Henderson hit a home run, giving the Red Sox a 6-5 lead. The Angels tied it up in the bottom of the ninth, but Boston went on to take the game in the eleventh inning, 7-6. After that, anything might seem anticlimactic, but the Red Sox went on to win the sixth and seventh games – depriving the Angels' manager, Gene Mauch, of yet another pennant (in his 25 years as a manager, he had never won one) but providing baseball fans with a tale to recount over many a winter.

Now on to the World Series, where the Red Sox – in their first since 1975 – found themselves facing the New York Mets, generally conceded to be the strongest team of 1986, with the winningest record (108 victories). Few would give Boston much chance in the first two games at Shea Stadium, but the Red Sox took them both. Then just to prove how baseball continually defies the statistics, the Mets went up to Fenway Park and took the first two there. The Red Sox won the fifth game, though, and the teams returned to Shea Stadium with the Red Sox holding a 3-2 lead in games. In the sixth game, the Red Sox went into the ninth inning with a 2-0 lead and it looked like they were finally going to take their first Series since 1918. But the Mets managed to get two runs and send the game into extra innings; again, the Red Sox came through, first on a homer by Henderson and then on some hits that gave them an insurance run. The Mets came back in the bottom of the tenth with three runs and won 5-4, tying the Series at three a piece. In the seventh, deciding game Boston took an early 3-0 lead, but the Mets caught up, went ahead on a homer by Ray Knight, and won the game 8-5. But the Red Sox had more than exceeded expectations, and true baseball fans agreed it was a season to be proud of and one that proved yet again just what an intricate and unpredictable game baseball truly is.

The American League began the 1987 season with no particular shakeups or scandals: The road was clear for a classic season of old-fashioned baseball. True, there were those free agents – Rich Gedman and company – who held out, found no takers and ended up rejoining their teams in May. This was part of the larger issue of alleged collusion among the team owners to cease bidding for free agents: It was 21 September when an arbitrator ruled that there had been collusion at least since 1985, but no one knew quite

Red Sox catcher Rich Gedman rips a line drive in the 1986 American League playoffs against the California Angels.

Right: Hard-hitting Kirby Puckett, who joined the Twins in 1984, was one of the factors that led the team to the World Championship in 1987.

Below: Ace hurler Willie Hernandez was in his tenth year with the Tigers in 1987.

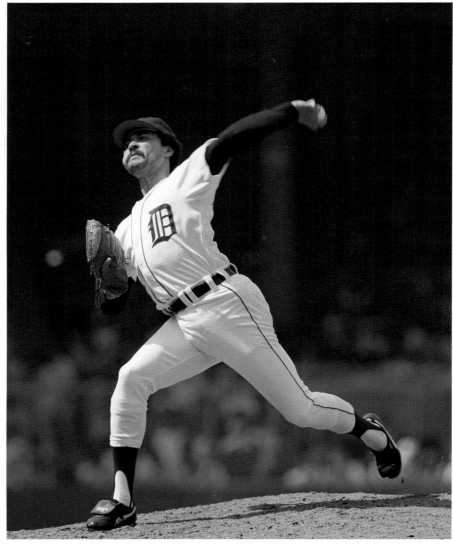

what to do with that conclusion. Likewise, the issue of racism that emerged during the celebration of the 40th anniversary of Jackie Robinson's breaking down the color barrier in the major leagues: It was quite clear that blacks and Hispanics were still being denied any significant role in management or administrative positions – a few coaches, a couple of front-office slots, and that was about it. Although it was a profoundly serious issue and was going to have to be resolved before too many more seasons, it did not seem to affect the play on the field during 1987.

When the season began, some students of the game thought that Cleveland was going to take the American League's Eastern Division, although others predicted that the Yankees were going to claim the crown. One thing all agreed on: The Red Sox could not repeat. In the Western Division some thought the Texas Rangers were due, some picked the Angels again, some the Kansas City Royals and still others the Oakland As. One thing they all agreed on: The Minnesota Twins didn't have a chance.

In the event, Cleveland never even made a serious bid. The Brewers set a major-league record by winning their first 13 games, but by mid-July the Yankees had taken over first place in the East. And they did have a lot going for them – Don Mattingly was having an especially good year – but they also had George Steinbrenner as owner, and he ended up keeping the team and its manager, Lou Piniella, in almost constant turmoil. Meanwhile, Rickey Henderson, from whom so much was expected, never got over a series of physical and 'social' afflictions (and by the end of the season was talking of moving on). The result was that the Yankees were constantly being pressed by both the Tigers and the Blue Jays. By mid-August the Blue Jays had taken over the lead. Then, in one of those coincidences of scheduling, the Blue Jays found them-

Above: Frank Viola (seen here), along with teammate Bert Blyleven, was one of the Twins' regular starters in 1987.

Left: A pulled hamstring kept daunting Yankee baserunner Rickey Henderson from having one of his better seasons.

selves coming into the last days of the season with two series against the Tigers – seven games altogether. In the first set, at Toronto, the Blue Jays took the first three and lost the fourth, leaving them with a 2½ game lead over the Tigers. During the week, however, the Blue Jays proceeded to drop three more games to Milwaukee, so when they came up against the Tigers on the final weekend in Detroit their lead had been reduced to one game. The Tigers won that first game and were tied for first; they won the second and took a one-game lead; then they won the third and clinched the Eastern Division title.

Over in the Western Division things went a bit differently. Outfoxing the experts, the Twins gained first place relatively early on, but they were constantly pressed by Oakland, the Angels and the Royals. By mid-September only 3½ games separated the fourth-place Royals from the first-place Twins. But the Twins fooled everyone and stayed on top. Much credit was given to their new manager, Tom Kelly, at 37 the youngest in the majors, but it was nevertheless a true team effort. The Twins had no superstar pitching, but Frank Viola and Bert Blyleven came through, and the Twins had acquired Jeff Reardon and Juan Berenguer who delivered in relief. Kirby Puckett had a good year, and non-headline-grabbers such as Kent Hrbek, Tom Brunansky, Gary Gaetti and Dan Gladden came through when needed.

Right: In 1987 the Brewers' Paul Molitor had a 39-game hitting streak.

Above: The Twins scored two firsts in the 1987 Series. They won all their home games, and they brought the Championship home to Minnesota.

had done in the 31 times a World Series has gone into seven games – win all of their home games. True, the unusual environment of the Metrodome – its distracting lighting and the ear-splitting noise level – played some part, but the fact is that all the Twins came through, while the Cardinals never quite found their level. Thus, against all predictions, the Minnesota Twins won their first World Series.

So the 1987 season ended – nothing spectacular, but baseball as it is supposed to be: defying the odds, statistics and predictions. Several American League players had a season they would not soon forget. Paul Molitor made one of the most successful assaults on Joe DiMaggio's 56-game hitting streak, but he finally stopped at 39. Don Mattingly, however, set a new major league record with six grand-slam homers for the season, and he homered in eight consecutive games, tying Dale Long's 1956 record. Bob Boone took over a major-league record long held by Al Lopez, the most games caught in a career. And Don Baylor took over a record of dubious achievement: awarded first base the most times (255) by being hit. (Most observers agree that Baylor generously helped himself to this record.) The MVP award, after being debated all season as due either George Bell of the Blue Jays or Alan Trammell of the Tigers, went to George Bell, while the Cy Young award went to Roger Clemens. Rookie of the year went to Mark McGwire of the Oakland As, who not only broke the major-league record of most homers for a rookie but went on to win the league's home run record with his 49. With rookies like that, the future of the American League seemed more than secure.

The 1988 season in the American League began with one of those major league records teams prefer not to set: the Baltimore Orioles lost their first 21 games. Little wonder the Orioles finished last in their division, with a 52-107 record. But the rest of the Eastern Division more than made up for this with one of the classic surprises in recent major league history. The Yankees had been predicted to go all the way, but by the All-Star Game (which the American League won, 2-1)

The Tigers, meanwhile, had many of their veterans from the spectacular 1984 season – Alan Trammell, Lou Whitaker, Kirk Gibson and Darrell Evans – and under veteran manager Sparky Anderson they were generally conceded to have the advantage over the Twins. But in the playoffs the Twins' pitching pretty much shut down the Tigers' hitters, while the Twins came through with the runs when they needed them. With some ace relieving by Reardon and Berenguer, the Twins managed to defeat the Tigers by an impressive four games to one.

So the Twins went into the World Series with their first pennant since 1965 to meet the St Louis Cardinals. Once more, the smart pickers seemed to favor the seasoned Cardinals, although they had two injured stars, Jack Clark and Terry Pendleton. When the Twins took the first two games in the Metrodome, the smart ones began to wonder, but when the Cardinals swept the three games in St Louis they began to relax. But the Twins went on to do something no other team

Detroit was in the lead, with the Yankees and Brewers close behind. The Red Sox were 8½ out, but no one except a few diehard Red Sox fans thought of them as a contender. Indeed, things were so bad in Boston that John McNamara was fired during the mid-way break and an obscure third-base coach, Joe Morgan, was named manager of the Red Sox in what looked like a mere holding operation. Instead, the Sox began to win game after game – 24 consecutive wins at Fenway Park – and by Labor Day were in first place, ending up with a one-game lead over Detroit even though they lost 7 out of their last 10 games.

In the Western Division, it was another story, with the Oakland A's quickly moving into first place and never being seriously threatened; with the aid of Jose Canseco's 42 homers and 40 stolen bases (the first such 40/40 man in major league history) and the likes of Dave Henderson and Mark McGwire, they cruised to a 13-game lead over the Twins. No wonder, then, that this Oakland team crushed the Red Sox four straight in the playoffs. No wonder, either, that the A's were generally picked as favorites in the World Series. But the surprises that make baseball the game it is came around – surprises named Kirk Gibson and Orel Hershiser – and the Los Angeles Dodgers won the Series, four games to one.

The year 1988 was notable for several other events off the field. Most notably, the major leagues decided

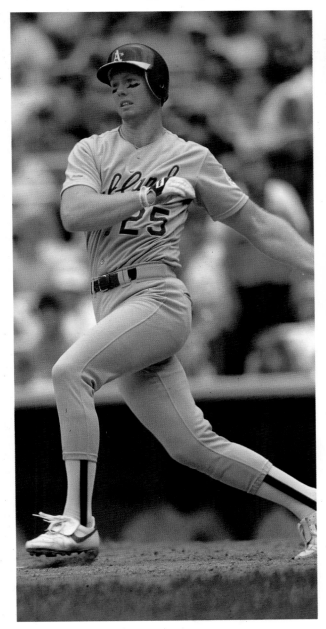

to enforce the balk rule – instructing umpires to watch closely that pitchers paused at the 'set' position before proceeding to throw. This led to a record number of balk calls throughout the season. Although many complained that this new stringency would distort the game, the balk rule did not seem that crucial in subsequent seasons as pitchers made sure they came to a halt.

The 1989 season seemed to be one of those in which events off the field at times overshadowed the game itself – specifically the scandal over charges that Red manager Pete Rose had gambled on baseball games, and the tragic death of baseball's recently appointed commissioner, A. Bartlett Giamatti. On a more positive note, Jim Abbott, the young one-handed pitcher from Michigan and a hero of the 1988 Olympics, joined the California Angels and ended up with an ERA of 3.92 to go with his 12-12 record. Meanwhile, another hard-to-match event took place when Ken Griffey, Sr., and

Above: With 42 homers and 40 stolen bases in 1988, Oakland's Jose Canseco became major league baseball's first 40/40 man.

Left: Homer-hitting Mark McGwire of Oakland was a clear choice for 1987 Rookie of the Year.

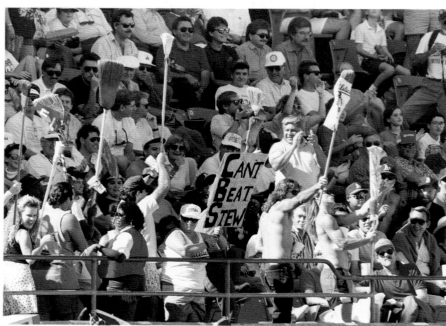

nickname of the late 'Bart' Giamatti (to whom the Series was dedicated) and the Bay Area's Rapid Transit system – but the Series became memorable for another reason. The A's won the first two games in their ballpark, then on October 17, as game three was about to begin at Candlestick Park, an earthquake hit the Bay Area. Not only did the Series halt, there was even some suggestion that it should be canceled, but the Series did resume on October 27, and the A's two aces – Dave Stewart and Mike Moore – supported by the team's heavy hitters, completed their sweep.

As the 1990 season began, the accepted wisdom was that the Oakland A's were now a full-fledged dynasty, and indeed they did dominate the Western Division again, beating out the Chicago White Sox by nine games. The A's were greatly aided by Rickey Henderson's MVP performance. In the Eastern Division, Toronto once again looked like it was going to meet the A's at the showdown; with eight games to play, Toronto led the second-place Red Sox by one and a half games. Then the Blue Jays lost six of their last eight games, while the Red Sox managed to win most of theirs and ended up in first place, two games ahead of Toronto. The exciting Jays could be partially consoled by having an all-time record with over four million fans in their Skydome.

In the playoffs, Oakland repeated its 1988 sweep of Boston, but the tables were turned when the A's came

Top: Seattle Mariners Ken Griffey, Sr. and Ken Griffey, Jr., played together in 1989.

Above: A's fans hold brooms to signify their hopes for a sweep of Boston during the fourth game of the 1990 ALCS. **Right:** Oakland's Dave Stewart turned in his third straight 20-win season in 1989. In 1990 he was one of nine pitchers who threw a no-hitter.

Ken Griffey, Jr., both played for the same team, the Seattle Mariners.

Meanwhile, the Oakland A's were picked to win the Western Division and with the aid of Dave Stewart's third straight 20-win season – and after Jose Canseco came back from an injured wrist – the A's did indeed pull away, beating the Kansas City Royals by seven games. In the Eastern Division, Toronto inaugurated its new Skydome in July and with record-breaking crowds cheering them on, the Blue Jays caught up to the amazingly rejuvenated Baltimore Orioles and squeaked into first place with a two-game lead.

In the playoffs, although the Blue Jays were the sentimental favorites, they couldn't compete with the likes of Canseco, McGwire, and now Rickey as well as Dave Henderson, and the A's took the league crown four games to one. Because the A's were to play their neighbors, the San Francisco Giants, the World Series was soon dubbed the 'BART' Series – a pun on the up against the Cincinnati Reds, and in one of the biggest upsets in recent World Series, the A's fell in four straight games.

Off the field, 1990 was the year that the controversial George Steinbrenner was forced to give up his post as the chief owner and managing partner of the New York Yankees for 'the best interest of baseball.' Among the player standouts were Cecil Fielder – just back in the American majors after a season in Japan – who hit 51 homers for Detroit. Chicago White Sox reliever Bobby Thigpen set a new major league record by making 77 appearances, during which he pitched 88 innings and had an 1.83 ERA. Veteran reliever Dennis Eckersley of the A's had 48 saves (second all-time) with his astounding 0.61 ERA.

The 1991 season began with the A's once more perceived as the team to beat in the American League, but plagued by injuries, Oakland never got off the ground; instead virtually every team in the division took turns at first place until finally the race settled down to one between the Twins and Chicago. Gradually the Twins pulled away, taking first place by eight games – the first time a team had come from last place to first place in one year. In the Eastern Division, many people picked the Red Sox, what with Roger Clemens and a pack of strong hitters. And they did start strong, with an 18-9 record, but by 7 August the Red Sox were 11½ games behind the Blue Jays. Then the Bosox took four games from Toronto, and went on to win 31 of 41 games so that by 22 September they were only a half game out – only to collapse again by losing 10 of their last 13 games. By the end, the best the Red Sox could do was to salvage a tie for second place with Detroit, both seven games down from the Blue Jays, who had shaken their reputation for 'choking.' Many attributed the Jays' rise to the top to their new acquisitions, such as Joe Carter, Roberto Alomar, Devon White, Tom Candiotti, and Candy Maldonado.

In the playoffs, there was no single dominating favorite. Although it was pointed out that the Twins had never lost a postseason game in their Metrodome, there's always a first time in baseball, and after losing

the opener, the Blue Jays did beat the Twins in the Metrodome. But in the next three games, the Twins proved too strong and took the division crown, four games to one. In the World Series, the Twins came up against the Atlanta Braves, thus setting up a historic confrontation between two teams that had come from last place the year before. The Twins were generally favored – among other reasons because they had never lost a World Series game in their home field, and they had the advantage of playing the first two and the last two there. Indeed, the Twins did take the first two from the Braves, but the games were close, and when the Series moved to Atlanta, the Braves astonished all but their most dedicated tomahawk-wielding fans by sweeping the three games there. Two were tight games, but the third was a 14-5 blowout, and when the teams headed back to the Twin Cities with the

Left: In game four, Oakland players celebrate the ninth-inning double play that sealed their 1990 ALCS victory.

Left: Minnesota's 1991 World Series MVP Jack Morris waves his hat after pitching the 10-inning seventh game over the Braves.
Below: The Blue Jays' Roberto Alomar helped Toronto win their division in 1991, as the Jays drew a record four million fans.

journeymen Braves leading the old-masters Twins, three games to two, fans sensed that this could be one of those great Series in which nothing was decided until a final pitch. In the sixth game, the teams matched each other run for run through the ninth inning, and it took Kirby Puckett's homer in the bottom of the twelfth to give the Twins a win. It was a record-breaking third Series game decided by a final pitch. And so the season came down to a World Series seventh game between two evenly matched teams. And that's the way the finale went, inning by inning with scattered hits and brilliant fielding, as each team went scoreless until the bottom of the tenth, when the Twins got one run across and became the 1991 World Champions. Minnesota's Jack Morris, who pitched all 10 innings for his second win, was chosen Series MVP. The Twins players were the first to agree that the Braves had nothing to apologize for, that this was one of those World Series in which the teams were so evenly matched it was hard to call one team losers.

The American League's 1991 season was especially memorable for seeing Rickey Henderson's inevitable takeover of the all-time major league career stolen base record, Nolan Ryan's seventh no-hitter, and Cal Ripken, Jr.'s pursuit of Lou Gehrig's record of consecutive games played. With records like this, the American League seemed certain to continue to provide many more thrills in the years to come.

So, too, in the final decade of the American League's first century of existence, the 25-year difference between the two major leagues came to seem less and less significant. And if major league baseball faced some serious problems – from drug abuse to financial crises – it was only because baseball is inseparable from the fabric of American life. With its new generation of players and fans, the American League is assured of moving into the 21st century as a leading player in the national pastime.

Above: The Rangers' Nolan Ryan pitched an unprecedented seventh no-hitter in 1991, at age 44.
Right: Minnesota's Gene Larkin and Chuck Knoblauch celebrate the thrill of victory after Larkin knocked in the winning run in the seventh game of the 1991 World Series.

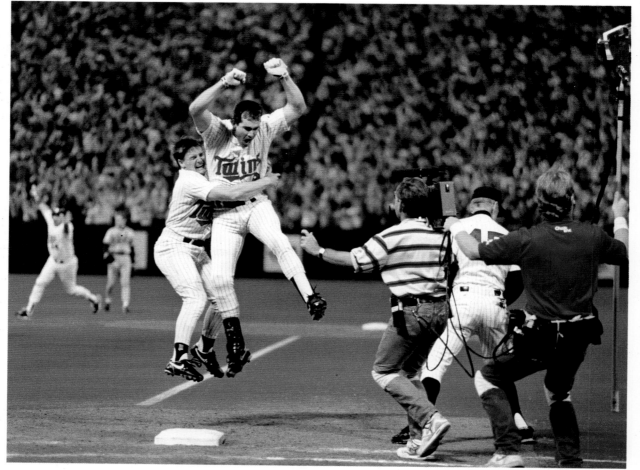

INDEX

Aaron, Hank 107, 149
Abbott, Jim 193
Agee, Tommie 134, 135
Alexander, Dale 55
Alexander, Grover C 24, 44
All-Star Game (50th) 180
Allen, Johnny *54*, 55
Allen, Richie 146
Alomar, Roberto 195, *195*
American Association (Players) 9, 11
American League: attendance 30, 31, 40, 54, 67, 99, 167; formation 8-11; franchises 11, 12, 13 (moving 95, 114; expansion 138, 155 *See also* baseball leagues); players switch to 11; profitability 13, 171, 176; recognition of 13
Anderson, Sparky 185
Aparicio, Luis 101, *103*, 124, 143
Appling, Luke *60*
Atlanta Braves 149, 195, 196
Auker, Eldon 58
Averill, Earl 61
Avila, Bobby 96

Bagby, Jim 33
Baker, 'Frank' *20*, 20, 23
balls: cork-centered 20; lively 30, 31, 33, 52
Baltimore Orioles 12-13, 95, 124-26, 132, 133, 141, 143-45, 148, 149, 150, 155, 161, 167, 171, 174, 180, 185, 192, 194
Bando, Sal *145, 173*
Barker, Len 173
Barrow, Edward 34
Barry, Jack *19*, 20, 23
baseball: attendance 52, 58, 74, 79, 83, 97, 161; early *6*; longest game 180; night games 70; as power game 30, 32, 52, 54; Presidential opening/ involvement 30, 37, 41-2, 56, *95*, 95, 100, *112*, 117, 119; public image 8, 13, 70, 140; rule changes 31, 32, 193 (*See also* designated hitter)
baseball leagues:competition 12; franchise expansions 97, 114, 131, 155; and National agreements 9-10, 12, 37; and St Nicholas peace pact 13, 14, 15
baseball managers 88, 116, 125, 135, 174; black players as 149; strategy 54-5, 58, 60, 65, 70, 84-5, 89-90, 102-04, 121, 126
baseball players 8; accidents/ injuries/illness/deaths 22, 30-31, 33, 42, 44, 64-5, 80, 106, 122, 129, 161; contracts/options 9, 12, and antitrust laws 139, 145, and arbitration/negotiation 145, 152, 164, 188 (*See also* reserve clause); drug taking by 176, 188, 196; as free agents 152, 169; in military *68*, 73-4, 75-7, *77*, 93; organizations/ unions 10, 11, 139, 152; purchase prices of 47, 57, 60, 114; raiding 11, 12, 79; safety 31; salaries 11, 24, 26, 37, 117, 139,

152, 164; strikes/walkouts 145, 164-67, 171; World Series shares 14, 18. *See also* black players
Bauer, Hank 85, *95* 132
Baylor, Don *159, 160*, 174, 188
Beardon, Gene 82, *83*
Bedient, Hugh 21
Belanger, Mark *132*, 132
Bell, Buddy *166*
Bender, 'Chief' *15*, 15, 20, 23
Berenguer, Juan 191, *192*
Berra, Yogi 98, 100, 104, 108-10, *109, 116-17*, 117, 119, 121, 183, 186
Bevens, Bill 80-1
Bird, Harry 98
black players 70, 78-9, 81, 94, 111
Black Sox *See* Chicago White Sox, scandal
Blair, Paul *180-01*, 124, 132, 135
Blanchard, Johnny 117
Blue, Vida *144*, 144, 145, 148, 152
Blyleven, Bert 191
Blyska, Mike 98
Boggs, Wade *186*, 189
Bonds, Bobby *156*
Bonham, Ernie 74
Boone, Bob 193
Boone, Ray *102*
Boston Braves 23
Boston Red Sox 12, 14, 21, 22, 23, *24*, 24, 34, 58, 66, 73, 79, 83, 85, 88, 102, 111, 125-28, 129, 146, 150-51, 155, 188-9, 190, 193, 195
Boswell, Dave *126-27*
Boudreau, Lou 82, *82*, 83
Bouton, Jim 122, 140
Brett, George *153*, 158, 168, *168-69*, 169, 177, *186*
Bridges, Tommy 57
Brooklyn Dodgers 33, 73, 80, 85, 90-1, 94, 98-9, 102, 104-5. *See also* Los Angeles
Brown, Bobby 93
Brown, Gates 130
Brown, Willard 70
Brunansky, Tom 191
Brush, John 9, 12, 13, 14, 15
Bunker, Wally 126
Burdette, Lew 107-08, 111
Bush, Joe 34, 38, 39

California Angels 114, 118, 156, 161, 173, 174-75, 189, 193
Campaneris, Bert 121, 145, *146*, 147
Candiotti, Tom 195
Canseco, Jose *193*, 193, *194*
Carew, Rod 132, *148*, 149, 152, 156, 158, *160*, 161, 174
Carrigan, Bill *19*
Case, George *75*
Casey, Hugh 73
Cash, Norm 117, 130
catchers 38, 41, 52, *71, 101*, 128, *178-79*
Chambliss, Chris 155
Chance, Dean *120*, 121
Chance, Frank 18
Chandler, Albert 78, 79, 80, 88
Chandler, Spud *63*, 65, 70, 75-6, 122
Chapman, Ben *60*
Chapman, Ray 33
Chapman, Sam *73*
Chicago Cubs 18-19
Chicago White Sox 12, 15, 18,

24-5, *26*, 33-4, 101-02, *103*, 111, 180, 185; scandal 25-7
Cicotte, Eddie 25, 26
Cincinnati Reds 9, 146, 150, 152, 195
Clemens, Roger *187*, 188, 189, 195
Cleveland Indians 18, 33, 70, 81-2, 95-7, *97*, 102, 105-06, 111, 119, *157-58*, 190
Cobb, Ty *4-5*, 15-16, *16*, 17-18, 20, *21*, 22, 23, *24*, 33, 36, 37, *46*, 46
Cochrane, Mickey *48*, 48, 49, 57, 58, 63
Colavito, Rocky 102, *105*, 110, 117
Coleman, Jerry 85, 93
Collins, Eddie 17, 20, 25, *46*, 72
Collins, Jimmy *11*, 11, 14, 23, 25
Combs, Earle 43, 52, 55
Comiskey, Charles 8, 8-9, 26
Comiskey Park *140-41*
Conigliaro, Tony 120, *128*, 129
Continental League 114
Coombs, Jack 20, 23
Cooper, Cecil 174, *174-75*
Cooper, Mort 75
Cooper, Walt *77*
Coveleski, Stanley *30*, 30, 42
Covington, West 107
Cramer, Doc 66
Crawford, Sam 20, *24*
Cronin, Joe 55, *58*, 66, 73, 110, *110*, 114
Crosetti, Frankie 63, 90
Crowder, Alvin 55, 58
Cuellar, Mike 132, *132-33*, 141, 148

Davis, Harry 20
Davis, Ron 167
Delahanty, Jim 19
Del Guercio, Ted 98
Dent, Bucky 158
designated hitter 138, 146, 180
Detroit Tigers 17-18, 19, 37, 56-7, 58, 63, 70, 77, 117, 129-31, 145-46, *185*, 185, 190, 191, 193, 195
Dickey, Bill 52, *53*, 61, 64, 65, 90
Dickson, Murray 79-80
DiMaggio, Dom 79
DiMaggio, Joe 58-60, *59*, 63, 65, *66*, 70, 71-2, 81, 88-9, 91, *92*, 93, *136*
Dinneen, William *14*
Ditmar, Art *115*
Dobson, Pat 143
Doby, Larry 70, *81*, 81, 102
Doerr, Bobby 66, 72, *79*, 79
Donald, Atley 65
Donovan, Wild Bill 18, *23*
Drysdale, Don 123, 126
Dugan, Joe 34, 43
Durocher, Leo 80
Dykes, Jimmy 49, 52

Earnshaw, George *47*, 47
Eckersley, Dennis 156, 195
Ehmke, Howard *48*, 49
Erskine, Carl 49
Evans, Darrell 193
Evans, Dwight 150, *151*, 156

farm systems 47, 55, 63, 65, 74, 88, 89-90, 98, 122, 126
Federal League 22, 24
Feller, Bob *61*, 61-3, 70, 73, *77*, 79, 82, 96
Felsch, Oscar 25, *27*
Fenway Park 20

Ferrell, Wesley *52*
Fidrych, Mark 155
Fingers, Rollie 144, 145, *148*, 148, 152
Finley, Charles 121, 148, 152
Fisk, Carlton 150, *152, 184*
Flanagan, Mike 161
Flood, Curt 138, 139, 140, 143
Forbes Field 114
Ford, Whitey *88*, 89, 93, 98, *99*, 114, 117, 122
Foster, George *24*
Fox, Nellie 102, *103*
Fox, Pete 57, 58
Foxx, Jimmie 48, 49, 52, 54, 55, 56, 63, 66, *67*
Frazee, Harry 34
Freehan, Bill 130
Fregosi, Jim *121*
Frick, Ford C 88, *110*
Fridley, Jim 98

Gaedel, Eddie 90
Gaetti, Gary 191
Gandil, Arnold 25
Garcia, Mike 96, *97*
Gedman, Rich *189*
Gehrig, Lou *31*, 43-4, *44*, 45, 46, *50*, 52, 53, 55, 61, 63, 64-5, 196
Gehringer, Charlie 37, *53*, 57, 58, 63, 70
Gentile, Jim 117
Gentry, Gary 135
Giamatti, A Bartlett 193
Gibson, Bob 129
Gibson, Kirk 185, 188, 193
Gionfriddo, Al 81
Gladden, Dan 191
Gomez, Lefty 52, 53, 55, 58, 63, 65
Gordon, Joe 63, *65*, 65, 74, *84*
Goslin, Goose 37, *41*, 41, 56
Gossage, Rich 161, 167, *168*, 169
Gowdy, Hank 23
Grant, 'Mudcat' *122*, 123
Gray, Pete 78
Greenberg, Hank, *57*, 57, 58, 63, 70, 71, 77, 79
Griffey, Ken Sr and Jr 193-94, *194*
Griffith, Clark 9, 11, 12, *21, 23*, 95
Grim, Bob 90
Groh, Heinie *32-3*
Grove, 'Lefty' *47*, 47, 52, 55, 56, 66
Guidry, Ron *155*, 155, 158, 167

Haas, Mule 49
Harridge, Will 54, 90, 110
Harris, 'Bucky' *40*, 41, 42, 84
Hart, Jim 9, 10
Heilmann, Harry 33, *37*, 37, 45
Heinrich, Tommy *62*, 63, 65, 73
Hemsley, Rollie *71*
Henderson, Dave, 193, 194
Henderson, Rickey *168*, 168, 175, *176*, 186, 190, 194, 196
Hermann, August 13
Hernandez, Willie 185
Hershiser, Orel 193
Higgins, 'Pinky' *62*
hitting records 15, 17, 23, 31, 32-3, 36-7, 43, 46, 55, 56, 57, 58-60, 61, 64, 65, 73, 102, 119, 146, 149, 156, 158, 195
Hodges, Gil 134
Holtzman, Ken 148, 152, 155
home run records 20, 25, 32, 33, 34-5, 37, 38, 40, 44, 45, 48, 53, 63, 101, 106, 110, 114, 119, 126,

130, 149, 156
Hooper, Harry 23, *36*
Horton, Willie 130, *131*
Houk, Ralph 90, 117, 125, 141
Howard, Elston 94, 105, 110, *117*, 117, *123*, 128
Howard, Frank 132
Hoyt, Waite *34*, 34, 37, 39, 45, 46, 49
Hrbek, Kent 191
Hubbell, Carl 90
Hughson, Tex *76*
Hunter, Billy 98
Hunter, 'Catfish' 144, 145, 148, 149, 152, *155*, 155
Huston, T L 38

International League 55

Jackson, Joe 20, 22, *24*, 25, 26, *27*, 27
Jackson, Reggie *1*, 132, *143*, 145, 147, 152, 156, *157*, 158, 167, *173*, 173, 174, 189
Jamieson, Charles *40*
John, Tommy *166*, 167
Johnson, B Banford *8*, 8-9, 10-11, 12, 13, 15, 20, 42, 46, 146
Johnson, Cliff 161
Johnson, Darrell 98, 150
Johnson, Davy 132, *133*
Johnson, Walter 17, *18*, 20, 22, 23, 34, *40*, 41-2, 43, 46
Jones, Sam 34, 39
Jones, Tom 19
Joss, Addie *18*, 18

Kaline, Al 101, *128*, 130, *131*, 149
Kansas City Athletics 95, 97. *See also* Oakland
Kansas City Royals 131, 152, 155, 156, *156-57*, 158, 168-69, 172, 174, 177-80, 186, 190, 194
Keller, Charlie *65*, 65, 74
Kelly, Tom 191
Keltner, Ken *75*
Kemp, Steve *164*
Killebrew, Harmon 117, 118, *119*, 132, 141
Killian, Ed 18, 123
King, Clyde 174
Knoblauch, Chuck *196*
Koenig, Mark 43
Koosman, Jerry 133
Korean War 93
Koufax, Sandy 123
Kryhoski, Dick 98
Kubek, Tony 90, 107, *108*, 122
Kucks, Johnny 105
Kuhn, Bowie 148, 152, 176

LaCock, Pete *156-57*
Lajoie, Nap *11*, 11, 12, *19*, 19, *21*
Landis, K M *26*, 27, 30, 37, *46*, 47, 58, 78
Lardner, Ring 31
Larsen, Don 98, 102, *103*, 104, 110-11
Lary, Frank 110
Lavagetto, Cookie 81
Lazzeri, Tony 43, 44, *45*, 55, 61, 63
Lemon, Bob 82, 96, *98*, 158, 161, 174
Leonard, 'Dutch' *24*
Leppert, Don 98
Lewis, George 'Duffy' 21
Lolich, Mickey *130*, 130-31, *146*

Lollar, Sherman 102
Lombardi, Ernie *66*
Lonborg, Jim *127*
Lopat, Ed 90, *91*
Lopez, Al 96
Los Angeles Dodgers 119, 123, 125, 148, 156, 158, 172, 189, 193
Lynn, Fred 150, *151*, 174, *180, 186*
Lyons, Ted 74, *75*

McAuliffe, Dick 130
McBride, John *50*
McCarthy, Joe 53, 54, 65, 87
McCosky, Barney 70-1
McDonald, Jim 98
McDougald, Gil 90, 92-3, 106, 110, *111*
McGinnity, Joe 11
McGraw, John G 11, 12, 14, *15*, 95
McGregor, Scott 167
McGwire, Mark *192*, 193, 194
McInnis, 'Stuffy' *33*
McLain, Denny *129*, 129-30, 132-33, 143
McMullin, Fred 25
McNally, Dave *124*, 126, 132, 141, 148, 150
McNamara, John 193
MacPhail, Lee 125, 183
McQuinn, George *77*
Mack, Connie 13, *21*, 23, 42, 46, 52, 54, 88, 95, 97
Maglie, Sal 91, 104
Maldonado, Candy 195
Mantle, Mickey 90, 91, 92, *93*, 93-4, *94*, 100-01, 102, 110, 114, 116, 118, 119, 122, 123, 186
Manush, Heinie 37, 57
Marberry, Firpo 41
Maris, Roger *116*, 116-17, *118*, 118, 119, 123
Martin, Billy *93*, 94, 132, *136*, 146, 155, 156, 158, 161, *172*, 172, 176, 183, 186
Masi, Phil 83
Mathewson, Christy 15, 21, 22
Mattingly, Don *183*, 183-85, 188, 190, 193
May, Rudi 167
Mays, Carl 37
Mays, Willie 91, 97, 186
Mazeroski, Bill 116
Merkle, Fred 18-19
Messersmith, Andy 150
Meusel, Bob 34, 40, *42*, 42, 43
Mexican League 79
Michael, Gene 174
Miller, Bill 98
Miller, Bing 49
Milwaukee Braves 106, 110
Milwaukee Brewers 143, 167, 172, *174*, 174-75, *175*, 190, 191, 193
Minnesota Twins 118, 119, 123, 129, 132, 141, *171*, 190, 191, 192, 193, 195, *195*, 196, *196*
Minoso, Minnie 101
Miranda, Willie 98
Molitor, Paul 174, 193, *193*
Montreal Expos 131
Moore, Mike 194
Moore, Wilcy 45, 49
Morgan, Joe 152, 193
Morgan, Tom 90, 93
Moriarty, George 19
Morris, Jack 185, *195*, 196
Mullin, George 18
Munson, Thurman 141, *142*, 155, 161

Murphy, Dwayne *172*
Murray, Eddie *167*, 173, 180

National Baseball Commission 13, 18, 26; Commissioner 27, 78, 88, 183, authority of 37
National League: franchises 9, 10; monopoly of 8, 9, 12
Nettles, Graig 158, *158-59*, 183
New York Giants 14, 15, 20, 21, 25, 38, 42, 90, 118
New York Highlanders 13, 14
New York Mets 133-35, 189
New York Yankees, 34, 37-40, 43, 44-7, 49, 52-3, 54-5, 57-8, 60-1, 63-7, *66*, 70, 73, 74, 75-6, 80-1, 84, 85, 88, 89, 90, 93, 94, 95-100, 101-02, 106-07, 110, 114-18, 119, 121-23, 125, 155, 156, 158, 160-61, 167, 168, 171, 172, 177-80, 185-86, 189, 190, 192, 193; attendance at games 31, 43, 46, 110; instruction school 90; players bought and traded 34, 98; unrest in 155, 156-58, 173-74, 177, 183
Newcombe, Don 105
Newsom, Bobo 70, 71
Niekro, Phil *183*, 183, 188
Northrup, Jim 130
Nuxhall, Joe 76

Oakland A's 130, 143, 145-47, 148, 152, 155, 156, 172, 190, 193, *193*, 194, *194*, 195, *195*
Oglivie, Ben *167*, 174
Oliva, Tony *120*, 120, 123
Owen, Marv 57, 58

Page, Joe *80*
Paige, Satchel *82*, 82
Palmer, Jim 126, 132, *135*, 138, *139*, 150
Pappas, Milt *100*
Pascual, Camilo *119*
Pearson, Monte 61, 90
pennant races 12, 14, 18, 20, 21, 22, 23, 24, 33, 34, 37, 39, 40, 43, 45, 47, 56, 58, 66, 74, 76, 79, 82, 85, 88-9, 90, 94, 98, 110, 111, 114, 117, 119, 122, 124, 126-28; divisional rules 131; divisional titles 132, 141, 143, 145-46, 150, 152, 155-56, 158, 167, 168, 171, 172, 174, 177, 183-85; playoffs 83, 133, 141, 144, 146, 147-48, 150, 155, 156, 158, 161, 168, 175, 180, 185 (1981: 171-72)
Pennock, Herb 34, *39*, 39, 45, 49, 55
Pepitone, Joe 123
Perry, Gaylord 146, 149, 175-76
Perry, Jim 141
Pesky, Johnny 79, *80*, 80
Petrocelli, Rico 129
Petry, Dan *177*
Philadelphia Athletics 13, 15, 20, 22, 23, 42, 44, 47-9, 52, 53-4; moving 95; rebuilding 46. *See also* Kansas City
Philadelphia Phillies 23-4, 89, 180
Pipgras, George 39, 45, 46, 55
pitching: records 12, 20-1, 22, 34, 41, 47, 49, 52, 62, 63, 79, 122, 144, 149, 173, 176; no hitters 70, 90, 104, 146, 152, 183, 186, and shutouts 15, 82, 114, 117; rules 131; trick pitches 30-1, 32, 128

Pittsburgh Pirates 14, 19, 42, 46, 114-16, 144, 161
Plank, Eddie *13*, 13, 15, 23
Podres, Johnny 98-9
Potter, Nels 76
Powell, John 'Boog' *121*, 121, 132, 141
Puckett, Kirby *190*, 191, 196
Pulliam, Harry 13

Quinn, Jack *30*
Quisenberry, Dan *162*, 183, 183

Radatz, Dick 120
Randolph, Willie *170*
Raschi, Vic *89*
Reach, Albert *10*, 10
Reardon, Jeff 191, 193
reserve clause 138-39, 145, 152, 164
Reynolds, Allie *85, 90*, 90
Rice, Jim *150*, 150, 186, 188
Rice, Sam 37, 41, *45*
Richards, Paul 95
Rickey, Branch 75
Righetti, Dave 183
Ripken, Cal 180, *181, 196*
Risberg 'Swede' 25
Rivera, Jim 101
Rivers, Mickey 155
Rizzuto, Phil *74*, 74, *93*
Robinson, Brooks *114, 124*, 124-5, 126, 141, 143, *145*
Robinson, Frank *124*, 124-5, 126, 132, *149*, 149
Robinson, Jackie 70, 78-9, 190
Rohe, Billy 126
Rohe, George 16
Rolfe, Red *66*
Rosen, Al 97
Rowe, 'Schoolboy' *57*, 56, 58, 71
Rudi, Joe 145, 152
Ruel, 'Muddy' 41, 42
Ruether, Dutch 45
Ruffing, Red 53, 55, 58, 61, *63*, 63, 65, 74, 75
Runnels, Pete 110
Ruppert, Jacob 34, 38
Ruth, 'Babe' 23, *24*, 24, 25, 27, *28*, 31, 33-4, *35*, 38, 40, 42, *44*, 45, 46, *50*, 52, 53, 55, 57-8; influence of 34-6, *35*, 43; as pitcher 34; suspension of 42-3
Ryan, Nolan 146-47, *147*, 149, 152, 156, 161, 196, *196*

Saberhagen, Bret *188*
St Louis Browns 13, 37-8, 63, 76, 77, 90, *91*. *See also* Baltimore Orioles
St Louis Cardinals 75, 79, 129, 130, 189, 193
San Diego Padres 131
Schalk, Ray 25
Schang, Wally 34
Schulte, Fred 56
Score, Herb 98, *106*, 106
Scott, Everett 34, 43
Seattle Mariners 155, 176, 194, *194*
Seattle Pilots 131. *See also* Milwaukee Brewers
Seaver, Tom 133, 134, *182*, 189
Segrist, Kal 98
Selkirk, George 61, 65
Sewell, Joe *43*, and Luke *43, 56*
Shawkey, Bob 23, *38*, 39
Shocker, Urban 37, 45
Shore, Ernie *24*

Sievers, Roy 106, *107*
Simmons, Al 37, 45, 48-9, *49*, 52, 56
Simmons, Ted 174
Singleton, Ken *161*, 167, 180
Sisler, George *32*, 33, 34, 36-7, 38, 45
Skowron, Bill 111, 114, *115*, 117
Slaughter, Enos 80
Smith, Elmer *33*, 33
Smith, Hal 98
Spahn, Warren 106, 107
Speaker, Tris *17*, 17, 20, 21, 23, *32-3*, 33, 47
Spink, Taylor 9
Sportsman Park *91*
Stanley, Mickey 130
Stallings, George 23
Steinbrenner, George 155, 156, 173-74, 195
Stengel, Casey 84-5, *86*, 88, 89-90, 94, 96, 97, 99, 107, 110, 114; firing of 16
Stephens, Vern *76*
Stirnweiss, George *78*
Stone, Steve 167
Stottlemyre, Mel 122, 123
Sullivan, Frank 98
Summers, Ed 18
Sutton, Don 174, 189

Tebbetts, Birdie *71*
television, effect on baseball 70, 110, 155, 164, 176
Tenace, Gene 145, 146, 147
Terry, Ralph *118*, 118
Tesreau, Jeff *22*
Texas Rangers 143, 180, 189, 190, *196*
Thigpen, Bobby 195
Thomas, Gorman 174
Thompson, Henry 70
Thornton, Andre *156-57*
Tiant, Luis 120, 150, *151*
'Tinker to Evers to Chance' 18
Toronto Blue Jays 155, 185-86, 189, 190, 191, 194, 195, *195*
Torrez, Mike 150, *159*
Trammell, Alan *185*, 185, 193
Travis, Cecil *55*
Triandos, Gus 98, *101*
Trosky, Hal *61*, 61
Turley, Bob 98, 110

Ueberroth, Peter 183, 188
Uhle, George 43
umpires, altercations with 12, 38, *149*, 176, 177-80
uniform numbers: introduced 49; retired 65

van der Ahe, Chris 9
Veeck, Bill 90, 94
Vernon, Mickey *93*
Viola, Frank 191, *191*

Waddell, Rube *12*, 13, 15, 79
Wagner, 'Honus' 19
Walsh, Ed *16*, 18
Wambsganss, Bill 33

Washington Senators 17, 22, 40-2, 55-6, *78. See also* Minnesota Twins; Texas Rangers
Weaver, 'Buck' 25, 27
Weaver, Earl 132, 141, 161, 174, 186
Weiss, George 55, 116
Wertz, Vic 97
Western League 9. *See also* American League
Whitaker, Lou *180, 193*
White, Devon 195
White, 'Doc' 16
White, Frank *154*
White, Jo-Jo 57
Whitehill, Earl 55
Whiteman, George 25
Willett, Ed 18
Williams, Claude 25, 26
Williams, Dick 126-27, 144, 148
Williams, Ken 38
Williams, Ted 66, *72*, 72-3, 74, 79, 80, 93, 94, 101, 102, 106, 110, 114, 135
Wilson, Willie *169*
Winfield, Dave *165*, 167, 176, 183
Wood, Smokey Joe 20, 21, *22*
Woodling, Gene 98
World Series 8, 14; importance 19; rules 15, 25, 26; 1903: *14*, 14; 1905: 15; 1906: 16; 1907: 18; 1908: 18; 1909: 19; 1910: 20; 1911: 20; 1912: 21, *22*; 1913: 22, 1914: 22; 1915: 23-4; 1916: 25; 1918: 25; 1920: 33; 1922: 38; 1923: 40; 1924: 42; 1925: 42; 1926: 44; 1927: 46; 1928: 46; 1929: 49; 1930: 52; 1931: 53-4; 1932: 55; 1936: 61; 1937: 63-4; 1939: 66; 1940: 71; 1941: 73; 1942: 75; 1943: 75; 1944: 76; 1946: 79; 1947: 80-1; 1948: 83; 1949: 85; 1950: 89; 1951: 90-1; 1954: 97; 1955: 98-9; 1956: 102-05; 1957: 106-07; 1958: 110-11; 1959: 111; 1960: 114-16; 1962: 118; 1965: 123; 1966: *124*, 125-6; 1967: 129; 1968: 130; 1969: 133-35; 1971: 144; 1972: 146; 1973: 148; 1974: 148; 1975: 150, 152; 1976: 155; 1977: 156; 1979: 161; 1980: 169; 1981: 172-73; 1982: 175; 1984: *185*, 185; 1985: *2-3*, 188-89; 1986: 189; 1988: 193; 1989: 194; 1991: *195*, 195, 196, *196*
World War II, effect on baseball 70, 71, 74, 75-7
Wynn, Early *96*, 96, 118-19

Yankee Stadium *38-9*, 39-40, 121, *140-41*, 174
Yastrzemski, Carl *126*, 126, 127, 128, 129, 130, *138*, 183
York, Rudy *79*
Young, Cy 11, 12, 14, *19*, 19, 62
Young, Nick 10
Yount, Robin *174*, 174, 175

Zernial, Gus *101*
Zimmerman, Heinrich 20, 25

Photo credits

All photographs courtesy of the National Baseball Library, Cooperstown, New York, except for the following:
The Baltimore Sun: 132.
Chicago White Sox: 140-41 (bottom).
The Greer Studios, Inc., Baltimore, MD: 95 (top).
Nancy Hogue: 121 (top), 126 (top), 138, 139, 142, 145 (top), 148 (bottom), 149, 150, 151 (all three), 152, 155 (bottom), 156-57 (all three), 159 (top and bottom right), 161, 165, 166 (inset), 167 (both), 169 (bottom), 170, 172 (bottom), 173 (both), 174-75 (two top), 177, 180 (bottom), 181, 184 (large picture), 185 (top), 186 (both).
Mrs. Al Kaline: 128 (bottom).
Ron Modra: front cover, 1, 2-3, 153, 154, 158-59 (top), 160 (top), 162, 164, 166 (large picture), 168 (bottom), 169 (top), 171, 172 (top), 174 (bottom), 176, 178-79 (both), 182, 183 (right), 185 (bottom), 187, 188, 189, 190 (both), 191 (both), 192, 193 (both).
New York Yankees: 140-41 (top)
Ponzini Photography: 193 (top right), 194 (top left and bottom right), 195 (bottom), 196 (top left).
UPI/Bettmann Newsphotos: 194 (center left), 195 (top left and center), 196 (bottom left).
US Navy: 68, 107 (top).

Acknowledgments

The author and publisher would like to thank the following people who have helped in the preparation of this book: Brooks Robards and Stephen Minkin, who contributed to the history; Design 23, who designed it; Barbara Paulding Thrasher, who edited it; Mary R Raho, who did the picture research; Cynthia Klein, who prepared the index. Special thanks also go to the following personnel at the National Baseball Hall of Fame and Museum, Inc.: Thomas R Heitz, librarian; Donna Cornell, manager, photo collection; Elizabeth Zayat and Paul Cunningham, summer interns.